TIME DOES TRANSFIX

Recollections of a Forres Railwayman

TIME DOES TRANSFIX

Recollections of a Forres Railwayman

Alfred H. Forbes

Time doth transfix the flourish set on youth
And delves the parallels in beauty's brow,
Feeds on the rarities of nature's truth,
And nothing stands but for his scythe to mow.

William Shakespeare, *Sonnets LX*

First published 1997

© Julie Mackenzie, Valerie Dalziel,
Felicity Dalman and Althea Forbes 1997

ISBN 0 906265 23 1

Printed by BPC AUP-ABERDEEN LTD

INTRODUCTION

Time Does Transfix was written by the author in later life as a backward glance at his early days. Its abrupt ending with his leaving the railway service, getting married and entering a very different type of life is best explained by the intense sadness he experienced at the loss of his wife in 1962 from cancer. He was devoted to Jenny and could not bring himself to put on paper the story of his subsequent career as she was central to every aspect of his later life. The pain of remembering was too great.

From his marriage in 1932 until his sudden death in 1977 he led a busy and successful life as a family man (he had four daughters, all associated with the publication of this book), a business man and a servant of his home town of Forres through life long public service. He made the transition from railway employee to bakery worker rapidly and soon became a skilled confectioner. His administrative experience was put to good use in the business where he added "keeping the books" to his activities in the bake house. At first working for his father-in-law, William Deas, he subsequently entered partnership with Mr and Mrs Deas and ultimately became sole proprietor of Deas the Bakers, retiring from business in 1973.

In 1934 his union experience and his interest in public affairs led him to attend a meeting of Forres Town Council as an interested ratepayer. The meeting was concerned with the advent of electricity to the Burgh and with the redevelopment of the Town. To his astonishment he ended the evening by being co-opted onto the Council. Thus began a period of public service interrupted by a brief period when he came out of the Council because he felt he was becoming stale (he soon returned), by his war service and, sadly, by the years he devoted to his wife in her last illness. He served the Town Council in many capacities. Among his many appointments were Convenor of Housing, County Council Representative, Member of the Hospital Board, Member of the Joint Police Board, Baillie of the Town and ultimately he achieved the distinction of being the last Provost of Forres, serving for two terms leading up to reorganisation, and the disappearance of the Town Councils in 1975. Even after that event he took up a seat on the new district council, representing his Town until his death.

As Justice of the Peace he frequently presided in the Burgh Court, where his wide experience of life and his respect for human dignity were apparent in his decision on the fate of those before the Bench.

Always a champion of the underdog he avoided involvement in party politics and yet managed to top the poll in every election he contested. Many are the tangible memorials in Forres to his time in Local Government though few bear his name. He was well ahead of his time in environmental concerns though at times his plans to improve the town met with stiff opposition, even earning him on one occasion a rebuke from the pulpit of the parish kirk! Housing and employment were other major interests and he welcomed the economic benefit to the area of RAF Kinloss, fostering excellent relations between the Town and Service authorities. An able public speaker, he was a brilliant raconteur who could bring laughter to the most dull occasion. His sharp wit and wicked asides made him a formidable opponent in debate.

The outbreak of war in 1939 saw him first in the Home Guard, then called to the Royal Corps of Signals where his early telegraph experience was put to good use. Unfortunately his health broke down and he had to take a medical discharge. His time in the army provided a rich source of anecdote to add to his store of railway stories, council stories, etc.

His range of interests was wide – literature, foreign languages, history (both international and local), travel and above all the welfare of his fellow man. He wrote newspaper articles for both local and national press, short stories for BBC radio and, ultimately, his first book was published in 1975 entitled *Forres a Royal Burgh 1150–1975*. The present volume has lain unpublished for nearly twenty years since his death.

His interest and appreciation of the value of archives led him to cause the Old Toll Booth in Forres to become an archive centre for Moray and with it the appointment of one of the first local authority archivists.

Always conscious of the fact that he had to leave school early because of family circumstances, he never missed an opportunity to improve his education. He attended evening classes in many subjects, read avidly and widely and even attended a University summer school in Uppsala. For him the advent of Open University presented the opportunity circumstances had denied him in early life, and at the age of 64 he enrolled on a course in social sciences.

Travel was another consuming passion and many of the people he met on his travels in America, India, Europe and Asia ended up as guests in his home in Forres. His contacts and friends were worldwide. He was a familiar figure around Forres for most of his life – a character who was never afraid to speak his mind; a doubty opponent and a staunch friend who tried always to follow his father's maxim: "He who does no service to the community is not a whole man."

I gratefully acknowledge the help and support I received from my husband, Sandy Mackenzie, during the uphill struggle to get my father's work published; my thanks also go to Dr John Smith of the Centre for Scottish Studies for agreeing to publish the book, and to Miss Marjorie Leith of Leith Editorial Services for her assistance in the preparation of the text for publication.

The illustrations within the text are by his granddaughter, Trina Dalziel.

J.M.

Family Tree

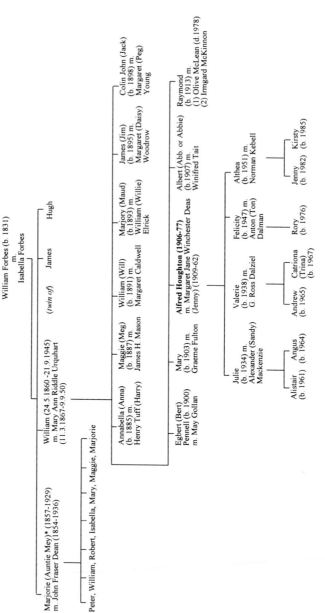

William Forbes (b. 1831)
m.
Isabella Forbes

William (24.5.1860 –21.9.1945)
m. Mary Ann Riddle Urquhart
(11.3.1867-9.9.50)

James   (*twin of*)   Hugh

Marjorie (Auntie Mey)* (1857-1929)
m. John Fraser Dean (1854-1936)

Peter, William, Robert, Isabella, Mary, Maggie, Marjorie

Annabella (Anna)
(b. 1885) m.
Henry Tuff (Harry)

Maggie (Meg)
(b. 1887) m.
James H. Mason

William (Will)
(b. 1891) m.
Margaret Caldwell

Marjory (Maud)
(b. 1893) m.
William (Willie)
Elrick

James (Jim)
(b. 1895) m.
Margaret (Daisy)
Woodrow

Colin John (Jack)
(b. 1898) m.
Margaret (Peg)
Young

Egbert (Bert)
Pennell (b. 1900)
m. May Gollan

Mary
(b. 1903) m.
Graeme Fulton

Alfred Houghton (1906-77)
m. Margaret Jane Winchester Deas
(Jenny) (1909-62)

Albert (Abb. or Abbie)
(b.1907) m.
Winifred Tait

Raymond
(b. 1913) m.
(1) Olive McLean (d.1978)
(2) Irmgard McKinnon

Julie
(b. 1934) m.
Alexander (Sandy)
Mackenzie

Valerie
(b. 1938) m.
G. Ross Dalziel

Felicity
(b. 1947) m.
Anton (Ton)
Dalman

Althea
(b. 1951) m.
Norman Kebell

Alistair
(b. 1961)

Angus
(b. 1964)

Andrew
(b. 1965)

Catriona
(Trina)
(b. 1967)

Rory
(b. 1976)

Jenny
(b. 1982)

Kirsty
(b. 1985)

* 'Mey' in Gaelic 'oldest'

FAMILY LIFE IN FORRES

My arrival in the early hours of Sunday, 4 March 1906 had little impact on anyone but myself. To my parents the event was now commonplace for I was the twelfth child of their twenty-one years of marriage. I was the ninth to be born alive, a girl and two boys being stillborn. To the four boys and four girls I was probably as unexpected as my two younger brothers were to me, for love, sex and pregnancy were subjects never discussed before children. But all the children were welcomed and much later I learned that my mother had long and secretly mourned the loss of her three babies.

But my birth had a great impact on myself as I learned many years later when I was interviewed by an Army psychiatrist. This was after the fall of France in 1941 when Britain began building a network of secret agents in Europe in preparation for their future invasion of Europe.

In my thirty-fifth year I was enlisted at Ossett in Yorkshire into the Royal Corps of Signals at 10s. 8d. a week of which 8d. was deducted, in part to meet "barrack room damage" and the balance towards a potato peeling machine that, we were told, would save an enormous amount of labour on our part. However, the time thus saved, we found, was occupied by work of an even more strenuous nature. The records showed that in my youth I had been a telegraphist and therefore a person now much in demand. I tried desperately to explain that I was experienced only on the earliest type of single needle telegraphy, invented about 1854 and using two notes of the same length, and not the military system of short dots and long dashes, but the message was not received. Recruits for this secret work had to be of the proper mental calibre, as many would eventually be parachuted into enemy territory, so an examination by a psychiatrist was the first test. He was a young lieutenant very keen on dreams and indeed dealt with little else. During the session he dredged from my buried memories much that interested him and embarrassed me. One experience was of special interest to us both, for it recurred many times when I was young, and left me nervous and apprehensive after awakening. I dreamt of a golden glow in which three round colourless objects, each with two dark spots, slowly revolved. This, he claimed, was the moment of my birth, and the three floating objects were the faces of those present. Neonates, as he termed new born babies, saw only the eyes of people, the other features of the face making no impression. The memory of birth was usually buried in the subconscious although some held clear recollections of it, one well known case being that of the poet Goethe who had written fully of his experience. Goethe I have found to be heavy reading and I have not found the relevant passage which would confirm the psychiatrist's statement.

My mother confirmed the theory, however, telling me that I was born early in the morning at home in her bedroom, illuminated by a large paraffin lamp placed high on the chest of drawers. The faces were those of mother, Dr Petrie Hay and the midwife, Mrs Jack, who lived next door and was performing a neighbourly duty. When I was born the doctor held me upside down by the legs and applied a smart slap on my buttocks to make me cry and thus draw air into my lungs, and then handed me to Mrs Jack to be washed. These actions explained the swinging movements of the faces and lamp.

For the rest of the world my birth was overshadowed by the dramatic events taking place in connection with the opening of the new parish church on the same day. The weekly *Forres Gazette* – normally eager to print gratis all local events such as births, marriages and deaths, for it was such items that gave it a world wide circulation to the many hundreds of emigrants – could, for that week and for some time thereafter, find no space for anything but the ecclesiastic sensations.

The newly erected church was the fifth on that site and with its soaring spires dominated the old town as its predecessors had dominated the lives of its adherents. There were another six churches and one mission hall in Forres, catering to the various sects of the Protestant religion; Catholics were almost unknown. All seven had been built in the previous seventy years but some were already abandoned and adapted to other uses. The new edifice was the Parish Church - the Auld Kirk - the national church - the Church of Scotland. It did not wholly please architects and aesthetes for a large but late donation from Lord Strathcona, a local boy who had made good in Canada by building the Trans Canadian Railroad among other things, had allowed a tall spire to be added after work had been started on the main building, thereby preventing the appropriate changes to the design.

The Reverend Buchanan, the minister, was already suspected of unorthodoxy by the more percipient members of his own and other congregations, especially those more strict and puritanical than the "Established Church" catered for. But only at the dedication ceremony on the day of my birth was the full enormity of his departure from the paths of rectitude made evident. Now visible to the righteous were the idolatrous innovations made possible by the thousands of Canadian dollars. There had been much gossip – discounted by the church members as inspired by the envy of those whose church had so little – but nothing as scandalous as now made public had been expected.

On a lectern a brass eagle hovered with outspread wings, in its claws a large Bible. Beyond was a white marble communion table, intricately carved and with large red Greek letters on its panels at the front. It was said later that the "O" of "Omega" was upside down, which was either the work of the Devil or one of the mason's apprentices (either being capable of such action) or perhaps the sculptor's Greek was poor. On the shallow steps leading to the elaborate wooden pulpit was a richly embroidered carpet, obviously Oriental and a clear sign of the luxury and corruption of the Vatican, which seemed to have taken over.

Enough had been known of the likely horror to be seen inside to deter the most devout and apprehensive members from entering the church, and these, together with the idle and curious, blocked the High Street at the entry to the church, awaiting the approaching procession of clergymen, elders, civic dignitaries and county gentry. Leading the procession was the minister walking beside the Moderator of the Church of Scotland, both in the full panoply of their offices. As they turned to mount the steps the crowd surged forward led by an elderly lady of great, and probably untested, virtue who had been the leader of the opposition during the previous years of preparation. Arms thrown high, she declaimed: "See the mighty host advancing – Satan leads them on." It was long and often heatedly debated as to whom this title applied. This was a form of theology in which all could join. Some held it to be the minister, others favoured the Moderator; while the more mystically minded claimed that Satan was there in person, visible only to the elect and pure in spirit. But this was not the worst, for once seated in the pews the worshippers were instructed to sit during prayers and to stand while singing. The more moderate were willing to stand while singing, for hymns only, for this comparatively recent introduction was considered to be only a little less frivolous than the ballads sung at church concerts. But for the zealous it was asking them to fly in the face of the Deity. As one dissident said later, "It was not only blasphemous but disrespectful", a point seized upon by the less theologically minded.

All this passed into history, or rather legend - told and retold with additions and elaborations. Many developed a surprising dramatic talent in their recitals, earning invitations to supper followed or accompanied by a nip of whisky, which for the sake of decorum and propriety was served in a cup instead of the usual glass.

It is difficult to describe the position of the parish minister at that time. They were held in awe, respect, fear and often hatred. The unquestioning deference paid them often lead them to be arrogant and overbearing as they grew older, for the greater part of their congregation were working class. Anyone rising socially preferred to go to one of the "Free" churches, where the ministers were paid by the congregation and not by the State, and thus had a pleasant feeling of having proprietorial rights. Those rising even higher could gravitate finally to the "English" church, the Scots Episcopalians, and so rub shoulders with the gentry, the professional people, and occasionally a real bishop.

It occasioned no surprise when on the morning after my birth, Mr Buchanan came to see my mother and intimated that my christening would take place on the following Sunday, when it would be the first sacrament to be held in the new building. He added that I would be named Benjamin, and that his sermon would be based on a text from the 35th chapter of Genesis. Mother was adamant, after his departure, that the naming of her children was her privilege, which she would not give up. Outwardly respectful she inwardly rebelled, as did many women, against the inferior status given to her sex by the religion preached in the Auld Kirk, in which all except the "elect" who were chosen by the Almighty before their birth, were doomed to an eternity of punishment in a fiery Hell - the worship of the Angry God of John Calvin.

When father returned home in the evening he refused to discuss the matter and retired to his workshop to follow his hobby of woodworking. He would have accepted the name if Meg had not looked up the text which included the words "but his father called him Benjamin". The original Benjamin had been named "Benoni" by his mother at birth, but she had then expired. When his father, Jacob, arrived he changed the name to Benjamin. This reference to him from the pulpit was more than father could endure, for he knew that the parallel between himself and Jacob would be brought up frequently by those of his workmates who were cognoscenti of Biblical texts.

A name had to be chosen for me, one with a good reason for its adoption. Mother's quick wit soon found a solution. Some weeks earlier an old school friend arrived on a visit after a lapse of many years. She was accompanied by her husband, Alfred Houghton, an Englishman but now an officer in the American Merchant Marine, both now residing in California. This was to be my name and Meg and Maude, two older sisters, were quickly rehearsed in the story. This was to the effect that mother and her friend had made a promise that each would name a child after the husband of the other. This promise had been brought out by Mrs Houghton, and at mother's age this would probably be the last opportunity to name a baby. The two girls returned after a time, without accomplishing their mission. They claimed that they had been overtaken by uncontrollable giggling as they approached the manse. Will was now home from work and volunteered to carry the message, and reported with some satisfaction, that the minister did not seem pleased. Will, my eldest brother, disliked the minister, a distaste reinforced by Will's employer, a butcher, who was of another church that carried on a guerrilla warfare against the "parish".

My christening took place, unmentioned from the pulpit, the *Gazette* still ignoring it for lack of space. Normally, if requested, the notice of birth, or other event, would have a rider added saying "Canadian (or American or Australian as the need was) papers please copy". One can conjure up a pleasant picture of a harassed editor in one of these countries scanning the columns of the *Gazette* for these entries.

My Anglo-Saxon name was a great burden to me when young; the commonest form of address was "Alfred the Great" – with various witticisms added. My only consolation was that I was more fortunate than my elder brother, Egbert Pannell, but who refused to answer to anything other than Bert. No one knew the origin of this name except mother and she refused to divulge it. It was unlikely that she invented it and in that crowded little town it could not be that of a secret lover. As Bert himself once remarked, "Anyone coming to Forres with a name like that would become a public figure". I suspect that it came from fiction, probably that of Annie S. Swan. This prolific writer had each week for a half century a romance in the Dundee *Peoples Friend*, price one penny, and the most popular home magazine in the country. It was said to have been read in the best houses, behind discreetly drawn curtains of course. The plot scarcely varied, only the names and settings. A handsome young man of some mystery came to live in a Highland fishing village, or lonely glen, and after many misunderstandings, wrongly delivered letters and other setbacks, married the beautiful and talented daughter of the laird, doctor or minister despite the forebodings of the wiseacres. Unexpectedly news came that he had, equally unexpectedly, fallen heir to a title, an estate, or great wealth and all was well. One of these could have been Egbert Pannell.

The new church did not give Mr Buchanan a happy life and within a year he resigned his charge and "went over" to the Episcopalian church, for which he was more temperamentally suited. Father took this opportunity to resign quietly his eldership, but continued to attend church regularly on Sunday mornings. Until we left school we had to attend church in the morning, followed by Sunday School. In the afternoon the boys went to the Brotherhood, the predecessor of the YMCA and often in the evening went to church again, followed in wintertime by the Bible Class. This was not as restrictive as one might think, for there was little to do on the Sabbath, especially in the winter days. There was no drinking, sport or recreation, not even golf that in the reign of James VI had been allowable. Nor were there any Sunday papers, until the First World War broke out in August 1914.

All fourteen children were born over a period of 28 years so that by the time of my birth my oldest sister Anna was already married and living in York. She had trained as a nurse in York and became one of the two nurses who cared for Lady Geddes, the wife of either Sir Eric or Sir Auckland Geddes. These prominent North of England businessmen were both knighted for their service in the Government during the First World War, and later became peers. Lady Geddes would live only in a tent on the lawn of the house. Anne had married Harry Tuff, who had a good position on the North Eastern Railway which had its headquarters in York. Meg, Will, Maud and Jim were now also employed and as father had two jobs mother received six pay packets each week, which she opened and handed back to each what she thought was sufficient for the coming week; all pays were received on Saturdays at the end of the working week. By this time, the family were comparatively wealthy and only the older members had experienced the poverty obvious all around us, for north of High Street was the working class area. The very poor, the incomers from the rural areas and the casual workers mostly resided in the Pilmuir on the edge of town.

Maude, Jim, Jack and Bert were at school when I was born, and twenty-one months after me came my brother Abb. In 1913 the last member of our family was born – Raymond, who had a niece waiting for him, Will's daughter Maidie. She was properly Mary but was given this diminutive to distinguish her from my sister.

Will had married Margaret Caldwell, a beautiful and talented girl who had come from Stranraer to make her home with an aunt, her only living relative, who lived in our street. Her parents had been fairly well to do but within a short time she lost both parents and her two brothers to the dreaded scourge of the time, tuberculosis or "consumption". The form which had killed them was the variety known as "galloping". Margaret had all the charm and vivacity which was said to be the hallmark of those fated to die young. Her gaiety and wit, as well as her almost English accent, contrasted strongly with the reserve of those among whom she found herself, where a display of affection or emotion was considered almost reprehensible.

She was beloved by mother who still retained similar traits, being herself of Highland birth and descent. Mother favoured her sons above her girls, and this caused some heartburnings and resentment among my sisters.

Not long after their baby was born, Will developed a feverish cold which was recognised as consumption. Because the disease was unknown in our family, the doctor said there was no resistance to its onslaught, and he advised the only course for working people, emigration to a hot, dry climate. The places most favoured were New Mexico or Queensland and within weeks Will was on his way to Brisbane. (There was a possible cure for wealthy people, a long sojourn in the cool, pure air of the Swiss mountains and a diet mainly of grapes, with residence in a sanitarium.) Upon his arrival in Australia, Will got a job with the crews extending the telegraph lines to Darwin. This arduous life cured him and, after fighting in two wars, he was still active in Brisbane at the age of 91 (he died in 1982).

Will's wife was anxious to follow him, and to earn the cost of her passage took a position as manageress of a bookshop in Aberdeen as there were few well paid jobs in Forres. Maidie remained with us. Each week Abbie and I received a packet of children's comics. These had only lately been introduced by Northcliffe of the *Daily Mail*, and soon *Comic Cuts* and *Lot o' Fun* made Abbie and me the most popular and sought out boys in the neighbourhood. We looked forward to Margaret's occasional weekend visits, for she entranced us with her songs, recitations and acting which brought a new dimension into our lives.

While at home, Will, like most young men, had joined the 6th Battalion Seaforth Highlanders, the local Territorial Army unit, and had become sergeant in charge of the sole Maxim gun. When war broke out suddenly in August 1914 his wife knew instinctively that he would join up at once and sent a cablegram asking him not to do so as she would get a passage as soon as possible. But Will had enlisted on the announcement of war. He knew that with his experience he would be sent to Europe quickly. He wrote but ships now took more than the normal six weeks for a voyage between Britain and Australia, and Margaret had already sailed in the *Waipara*, a name which has remained with me for so much went with it.

I was ill in bed when she came to kiss me goodbye. I do not think I had been kissed before and it was a long time before I was kissed again, and the feeling of loss and desolation at her departure was with me for long. It was half a century before I experienced such black misery again.

In due course a letter was received from Margaret; the voyage had not had the good result that was expected, but she was now feeling better in the sunshine of Queensland, and Will was able to see her often.

Not long after the receipt of this letter Meg entered mother's bedroom early, weeping and upset. She had dreamt that Margaret had looked at her with a sad but sweet expression and had then gone. Mother with her Highland background and superstitions believed the worse and a cablegram from Will confirmed her fears. Five days later another cablegram announced that her daughter also was dead. Will's troopship sailed two days after that sad event and he arrived in England before his letter giving the details. The position in France was desperate and his unit was sent almost directly into action at a point where the Germans were pressing forward strongly. When he did arrive on leave it was as a second lieutenant, and a fellow officer who accompanied him told us that he had refused to withdraw when the members of his gun crew were casualties and had held the post. Will explained that bravery was not involved; he just did not care what happened.

Colonial troops, as they were still termed, had much higher pay than the British, where a private received one shilling a day. As his wife and child were dead he changed his "family allowance" to mother as his closest relative. This allowance was £2 each week, more than double what father earned, and this helped to maintain our standard of living. Maude and Meg were now married and away from home, and Jim and Jack were in the army.

These deaths were not the first blow that the family had received for when Abbie was only two and a half years old he was struck down by poliomyelitis, then known as "infantile paralysis". It was some days before the trouble was diagnosed, and mother decided to take him to Edinburgh for advice. His treatment was that he had to be kept in bed with weights tied to his ankle and suspended over the end of the bed. As his muscles strengthened these weights would be increased until such time as he was fully recovered, but of course he did not improve. As he grew older he had to support himself to move, and when he started school he had to be carried there. I was unfit to do this, and a neighbour's boy did this four times daily. We were told that he must not get any stick or crutches as this would weaken his will to recover. In exasperation at this advice, father made him a set of light crutches, and Abbie was soon as active, if not more so, than I.

MY FATHER

My father, William Forbes and his twin brother James were the eldest of four boys and one girl born in a small cottage at Gateside of Alves, at a spot marked by a giant boulder left by some retreating glacier. It was around this boulder that the children, holding hands and singing, danced "widdershins" or anti-clockwise, to raise the ghost of a warrior in armour holding a gleaming sword. Their courage may have failed them for there is no record of his appearance.

About the turn of the century, father heard that a party of Edinburgh antiquarians were working at this site and cycled to see them. In course of conversation he asked what had guided them to this remote site, where they had found a skeleton with the remains of a spear and some beads. The clue was in the children's traditional plays and rhymes, and apparently it is children who carry the memories and not adults.

His home was in the parish of Rafford and father and the other members of the family spent two hours daily, walking to and from the school there. On Mondays, the pupils carried a single peat to be added to the pile reserved for the fires of winter, on Fridays, a penny fee, and every day their lunch. The school was on the south side of the 600 feet high Califer Hill.

Schooling finished at twelve years of age, except for those who could afford to attend Forres Academy, which was only for those who were to enter the professions or go to university. James was apprenticed to a joiner near at hand and, on completion of his apprenticeship, moved to Dundee where eventually he set up in business making bodies for the tramcars of the city service. He retired when the trams had to make way for motor buses, which required almost no woodwork.

Father went to work on the farm of Grangegreen, two miles west of Forres as "orra loon" or odd job boy, at the beck and call of the seven men there - the grieve, the foreman, four horsemen and the cattleman. The Laird of Dalvey was farmer and the grieve occupied the farm house, and was responsible for feeding the staff, for which he charged his employer. The other six lived in an outhouse or bothy, getting their meals in the farm kitchen. Porridge and milk night and morning, and at noon, soup, vegetables and a piece of meat or poultry cooked in the broth. At night the men could brew themselves tea or make a bowl of brose to be supped with milk. Brose was an instant porridge made by pouring boiling water into oatmeal and salt, and stirring it. This could be enriched with some butter and by some was preferred to porridge. Each man had a large wooden chest or trunk which served also as a seat. Everyone had to make a mattress of sacking filled with straw, or if possible, with chaff which was more comfortable but had to be renewed more often.

Occasionally the nest of a straying hen would be found, and eggs were swallowed raw quickly as eggs were the normal perquisite and usually the only source of income of the housewife or housekeeper, in this case, the wife of the grieve. The hours of work were long and exhausting. They rose at five o'clock when the horses were groomed, fed, and prepared for harnessing. The men then breakfasted and returned to harness up and start work. The cattleman attended to his beasts, and with a dairy herd, assisted the milkmaid, in this case the grieve's wife again, while the orra loon did anything he was told to do.

In summer, work finished at six o'clock for the horses but the men might have to do other work, except at harvest time when work stopped when the grieve tired.

In winter, outdoor work stopped earlier but much work was done by lantern light in the barn, mending harness and equipment, sacking grain and such like. The men liked this indoor work, as they were able to talk, tell tales and sing. On Sundays the animals had to be attended to as on weekdays, but one man could get away if the others covered his duties.

After the spring planting the staff was supplemented by a score of women from the town, who walked from Forres to the ferry at the Broom of Moy, paying a penny for the return crossing of the Findhorn. Bringing their mid day meal with them, they picked by hand the weeds among the corn, for there were then no insecticides, for which they were paid a penny an hour. At harvest time they were replaced by gangs of itinerant Irish scythemen and their wives and children, all sleeping in barns or in the open air. These gangs were a sight worth seeing for they worked as a team, six or seven men in echelon swinging the long handled Irish scythe in perfect unison and rhythm. The families followed, gathering the cut stalks under the left arm and grasping some, made a straw rope to bind the bundles into a sheaf. The children gathered the sheaves and built them into stooks of eight or ten sheaves leaning against each other.

The stooks stood until the farm horsemen carted them away to the stackyard. The two wheeled carts had wide wooden extensions fitted to enable the maximum amount of the crop to be taken. Hard as the work was, the Irish brought a gaiety into the evenings, for they seemed inexhaustible and could always produce some whisky to add to the jollity, the singing and the dancing.

Conventional wisdom held that "Moray has forty more fine days than the rest of the country" a belief supported by meteorologists. Crops could be sown and harvested earlier and with greater yields than elsewhere. Farmers were more prosperous also, and many did not themselves work at the "hairst", and could pay a little above the less favoured areas. When the railways arrived in the 1860s they brought an influx of workers from the colder and harsher lands of Banff and Buchan. As one old ploughman said, his reasons for moving west were, "for a kindlier climate and a pound more in the half year".

Those interested in language noted a change in the local dialect from that time, making it more akin to the Doric of the Grampian region, whereas it had in the past the cadences of the Highlands.

The term of employment was for six months, and "feeing" markets were held in May and November, on a Saturday. Most workers were very mobile, always looking for a better place, although married men would stay for a year. At those markets the town was crowded, the square and side streets filled with huckster's stalls, while the public houses had the busiest days of the year. At the end of each month, the workers received a small advance of their wages, and now the balance of the money was handed over, most of it spent swiftly on clothes and other necessities.

The workers stood in little groups on the street waiting to be approached by the employers. Good workers were quickly engaged, and once the wages for the following term were agreed, a shilling was pressed into the new employee's hand, making the agreement binding in law. A man reputed to be a poor worker or difficult might not get a "fee", and would have to wait for the "rascal's market" a fortnight later. Those unable to get employment at this market, where wages were lower, had little choice but to join the army, whose recruiting sergeants were always in attendance at these markets accompanied by pipers from Fort George, all gorgeous in feathered bonnets, red and green coats, hairy sporrans, dirks and white gaiters, or move into town to add to the numbers already there looking for the few casual jobs available, where they were unwelcome as they tended, in desperation, to accept any wage offered.

As the Saturday progressed and most workers had new posts, the atmosphere became that of a holiday. There was now time to look at the cheap watches, clothes and jewellery spread out for sale. Engagement rings costing two shillings were bought and put on fingers with an agreement between the newly betrothed that the male suitor would look for a married man's job before the next term and, if successful, they would be married on the Feeing Market day. Fortunes were told, infallible health cures purchased, snake, bear or goose oil bought, either to improve hair or skin, or as a cure for rheumatism. This was rampant among farm workers, for rain did not stop work, and the only protection a sack around one's shoulders.

The police force, consisting of an inspector and three men, stayed quietly in the background, leaving the occasional fight to fade from exhaustion, and then in the evening went round the side streets to pick up those now unconscious. Few were jailed to be kept until the Tuesday court. The burgh would have to feed them, and there would be no money to pay a fine. So, discreetly, they were laid in the now empty stables and yards, or in any convenient empty building, to find their ways home next morning. After all, they were doing little harm, and it was "the plooman's day off", the only wholly free one in six months.

The Second World War put an end to this system, which was in slow decline in any case. Hours, wages and conditions common to other industries, were now applied to farming, which in wartime became almost the most important of all.

After two years at Grangegreen, father was offered a job at Presley farm, five miles to the south and 900 feet above sea level, and therefore much colder. But the Calders were good masters, and his sleeping quarters were above the kitchen of the farmhouse, and he was fed in the kitchen also. The farms here were smaller in arable ground but the moors spread around for miles and were used for grazing sheep in summer. There were fewer workers but there was a village, a church and friendly people. Here he made friends, learned to make and play the violin, and had some time to read and study, and spent three happy years.

He had the ability and the application to do what he did well, and with a good reputation he was offered the position of post boy at Burgie Lodge. This was only a short distance from his home. His new job was higher in the hierarchy of the working class, his main duty being to ride into Forres for mail, newspapers and purchases required by the household. He helped, and when required, replaced other members of the indoor staff, for at that time mansion houses of no great size could have as many as twenty members of domestic staff. All were paid half yearly, not much above, if as much as, a farm worker, but food was supplied and usually a uniform. A license had to be purchased for most male workers, butlers, footmen, grooms etc. For a gamekeeper it was £3 per annum; for his assistant, only ten shillings (50p). Father recalled the estate blacksmith making a bicycle after seeing one brought home by a son of the family. It had no brakes or rubber tyres, simply many plies of cord bound round the wheels, and was used only on the downward sloping road from the big house to the main road.

The Highland Railway, which ran from Keith to Wick, was expanding and the Goods Manager was moved from Inverness to Elgin to help meet the competition for freight between Aberdeen and the north from the Great North of Scotland Railway. My grandfather took this chance of approaching the manager, Mr Ellis, who knew him, and obtained a job for father as a porter at Forres station.

The railways in the north brought opportunities for employment for intelligent and literate people, as it was the only alternative for those who could not afford long apprenticeships, with little or no pay, in occupations suitable to their abilities. The railways had a wide choice and chose carefully and well. Many men started in the most humble jobs and by sheer ability reached high posts. South African railways were said to have been run almost wholly by men from the Highland, North British and Caledonian Railways. Others went to North America where they were always well received.

This new form of transport made it easier for those who had little or no employment to move away, and in Sutherlandshire in just over a half century the population fell from 28,000 to 14,000 a fall not yet halted. The Highland lines have been compared to the developing railroads of USA and Canada. They opened the country and joined communities long separated by mountains, seas, and lack of roads. Each little station was in communication with the outside world by the telegraph.

Cattle no longer walked to the markets in the south, losing weight and value each day they were on the drove roads. Now they went swiftly by rail, as did the catches of fish so that boats became larger and fishing a worthwhile employment. When father started at Forres station it was the most important one of the whole line, as the track from the south via Perth joined the line from Aberdeen. The staff numbered more than one hundred. There was a locomotive department, a creosoting works to treat all the timber required for the whole system, and a licensed restaurant. An enormous wooden roofed bridge straddled the four tracks at their junction.

Soon father was promoted to marshalman or shunter, and later to a semi-clerical job in a little wooden office at the entrance to the freight yard, checking and weighing all traffic leaving and entering, and recording the arrival and despatch of rail and road vehicles. This brought him in contact with all the business men of the district, and one of these, David Ross, later to become one of the largest builders in the area and provost of the town, asked him to act as his part-time clerk, which involved evening work four times a week. The family was increasing, and this welcome addition to his income was accepted, and held for twenty-seven and a half years.

Despite his two jobs he found time to learn Pitmans shorthand, in which he kept a diary for many years. He improved his violin playing by taking lessons from Scott Skinner, still judged to be the greatest fiddler since the legendary Neil Gow. He had always been adept with his hands, and now was able to erect a workshop in the garden and equip it with odd tools. This also lead to another source of income. Miss Chadwick was the brother of the Laird of Binsness, a small estate nearby, and while in America with her brother, who helped build the National Railway of Mexico and other foreign lines, saw the chance of selling antiques, especially furniture, to the Americans who were already the wealthiest race in the world. When at home she went round the countryside buying articles from people eager to sell, although most of the articles were not as old as she would have liked.

Hearing of father's skill as a woodworker, she employed him to make her goods look more ancient. This was done by boring tiny holes and filling them with a very fine wood powder, which she supplied. Her gambit with a doubtful customer who questioned the antiquity of an article was to examine carefully until she found a hole or two. A slight tap with her finger released some dust which was accepted as a proof of age. Father was doubtful of the morality of the work but he was well paid for the little labour involved.

In addition to these activities he was a rifleman with the Morayshire Volunteers, and became a good marksman. When he had time he fished in the river Findhorn; a brown or sea trout and occasionally a salmon was a welcome addition to the provisions of a large family. Residents in the burgh could angle in this river for one pound a year. He liked a game of billiards on a Saturday evening. His main interest, however, was music. The violin was his favourite instrument but he played the piano and the American harmonium, the latter usually on Sunday as he thought organ music the most suitable on that day. He was a dedicated teetotaller although he never attempted to enforce his views, or criticised those who drank in moderation. He was handsome, neat and erect, and just two inches short of six feet tall. None of his family came within three inches of his height. He died in 1945, aged almost 85, just before the war ended. He had followed its progress daily by radio and newspaper. An operation could possibly have extended his life, but he refused it and said goodbye to all at home, calmly and reasonably as always, and died within three days

He was of a period which produced men and women of a character that the age required. Able, industrious, eager for knowledge; self trained and pioneering in new skills, yet satisfied to remain in the class into which they were born. He was not unique; in 1929 I was in a convalescent home in Dawlish and there met a Mr Goullee from East London. By occupation a coach painter with the Great Western Railway, his hobby was freezing animal and human tissue and then slicing this into wafers in a machine made by himself. He did this for some of the leading surgeons in London, but had no intention of giving up his trade, which was secure if poorly paid. At this time he would have been about sixty years old.

Father had always been interested in local history and it was from him that I learned so much of it, for he speculated on the traditions and the inspirations of those who had preceded us. He had been attracted by Hellenic history and thinking, and quoted what he had read. Among these apothegms some still remain with me: "No one is a whole man who does not give a service to his community". "Time makes a disorder of all things" and "Learn to say I do not know", although I think the last is from the Bible.

EARLY DAYS

I was born in one of a group of recently built cottages known as "Lady Gordon Cumming's". The eponymous builder was the wife of the Laird of Altyre, Sir William Gordon Cumming, one of the most ancient families in Scotland, and the owner of much of the land around the town. If an ancestor had not been murdered in the thirteenth century in the Kirk of Alloway the family might have been the royal family today. His wife was an American heiress living in London when news of the sensational affair known as the "Baccarat Scandal"[1] was made known. She then announced her engagement to Sir William and rallied to his assistance, sharing the publicity of the legal proceedings in the Old Bailey where the Prince of Wales, later King Edward VII, had to appear in the witness box.

Her quixotic action did not result in a happy marriage, and she seemed to have sublimated her unhappiness by indulging in a frenzy of architecture that finally exhausted her wealth. Her chief work was a new Altyre House which, after being used as a wartime hospital and then an extension to Gordonstoun, was demolished as it was too expensive to maintain as a home. The adjoining Blairs farm was built in an Italianate style and would fit admirably into the plains of Tuscany.

Although my family moved from this cottage when I was two years old, I retain some memories of it. The Mosset burn flowed on the other side of the

---

[1] At Doncaster Races during St Leger week (May) in 1891, the Prince of Wales was staying at the house of a wealthy shipowner, Arthur Wilson. A group played baccarat (a card game), the Prince being the banker. During the course of the game Wilson's som accused a good friend of the Prince, Sir William Gordon-Cumming, of cheating, and five of the company supported this charge. Sir William was induced to sign a confession of guilt and promised never to touch cards again. He thought that was the end of it but it became part of London gossip so he sued for slander – and lost. He was expelled from the army and thrown out of all his clubs.

road, and an opening in the fence there allowed cattle to drink when on their way to the station yard or the slaughterhouse, for both were near. At this opening, also, steam traction engines drew a supply of water from the stream by means of a long hose. Motor lorries were still unknown and most vehicles were drawn by horses, larger vehicles often having a pair of giant Clydesdale horses. Occasionally a steam driven Foden or Sentinel lorry passed, swift, silent and dangerous with their solid rubber tyres.

To one side of the cottages was a nursery famous for its roses, and on the other, a busy sawmill, so that the air was redolent of both rose perfume and the tang of resin and fir. Upstream, two weirs held back water, which when opened turn into the mill lade and so to the weaving mills and laundry. The grassed area where the clothes were hung out to dry by the laundry, and the new blankets fixed to hooked frames for stretching, was our only playground. There was a public park across the High Street to the south but it was reserved for the St Lawrence Cricket Club and the occasional ceremony. The proper name was Roysvale but it was always referred to as the Band Park.

It was on the road outside our house that I saw my first motor driven vehicle, the tricycle of our doctor, Dr Petrie Hay. He wore a top hat even when driving, and had long side whiskers and a moustache of the kind known as "Lord Dundreary's". His pince-nez hung from his neck at the end of a long black ribbon. His son, changing his name to Hay Petrie, was one of Britain's first film stars, continuing into the days of talking pictures. Dr Petrie Hay was typical of his time, depending as much on his relationship with his patients as on the provision of medication and treatment. He was apparently omniscient and was known as "a character".

One of our neighbours was a family from the Outer Islands, with very little English and low intelligence. The father was a labourer in the railway creosoting works, where preservative was applied to all the wooden sleepers used by the entire railway system throughout the Highlands. Little personal or domestic hygiene was practised and not only he but the other members of his family reeked with the smell.

One pay day he arrived home, as usual drunk and complaining that he was ill. Throwing himself on the untidy bed which stood in the middle of the living room, he roared and bellowed so much that his son was sent to call the doctor, who arrived rapidly on his noisy tricycle. Little examination was required, and calling for a cup of water to which he added some white powder, the doctor tried to make the patient drink it. Striking away the doctor's arm he roared that he was dying. Dr Petrie Hay seized him by the hair of his head, and holding his face shouted as loudly, "You may die, man, but by God, you'll never rot".

Our cottage was again overcrowded and a room had to be rented from a neighbour, so in 1908 we "flitted" to a larger house in Milne's Wynd. Only the wynd, or lane, separated us from the High Church, now St Leonards, and I was able to watch from my bedroom window when the church went on fire. For safety we moved to High Street with the other residents, and there saw the arrival of the fire brigade – two men pulling a two wheeled handcart with a hand operated pump. Soon other part-time firemen arrived and were successful in extinguishing the blaze which had broken through the slated roof. Charlie Mackerron was a slater and after removing slates to allow the hose to play on the exposed woodwork, he slipped and plummeted to the ground. He survived the fall with broken bones, and was hurried to hospital lying on the floor of a horse cab.

Charlie was noted for the number of times he had fallen from heights, for he was rarely sober after lunch time. His wife had the same failing, and it was not uncommon to see both being wheeled to the police station on one of the hand carts. It was said that Charlie lived under the special providence granted to "fools, drunks and wee bairns".

Two-wheeled handcarts were a common sight on the streets. The chief users were commercial travellers who arrived by train with a multitude of hampers and boxes filled with their samples. The hotel "bootboys" met every train, and pulled the laden barrows to the shops being visited. This trade meant much to the hotels, and each town of any size had its "Commercial Hotel" where the fraternity, as they described themselves, met for dinner. The senior traveller acted as chairman, ladling the soup from a large tureen before him, and calling for songs and toasts. They were a convivial class, and took the place of present day "pop" stars, bringing the latest songs and stories, as well as replenishing the stores held by their customers.

We moved again, this time to a house large enough to hold us all when the family was united, to 14 North Street Place. It still stands, returned to its original shape and size, a three storey square building – a former "laird's" house, that being the title given to the owner of a number of houses. When the population had expanded in the mid nineteenth century, and land inside the town was scarce, additions had been made to the house in a style known as "stake and rice", a form of jerry building. Three bedrooms, a kitchen and a scullery had been added at the north end, while a wooden house was added to the opposite gable. Two families occupied the wooden extension, each having one room belonging to the original house. We had a water closet within our door, also a wooden addition, but those other tenants had to share a WC, as it was termed, with several other families.

Our new home was completely isolated by walls, and wooden fences, and also had the original garden which was of considerable extent with a number of apple and pear trees, and a drying green. Inside, the rooms were well proportioned and there was a landing half way up each stair as well as when the floor was reached. These were large enough to take a "made up" bed when the house was crowded, and the lowest landing had a couch which also served as a bed when necessary.

The kitchen was small and was of an odd shape, with five walls, and the scullery had awkward steps into it. There was no gas supply and electricity was sometime in the future. A range with an oven at one side of the fire and a boiler at the other completed the services. The boiler had long been cracked and could not be used for anything. Below was a very large cellar extending under the whole length of the house. At one time the merchants of Forres had been large importers of claret, the drink of the mid centuries before whisky became known. The claret was imported through the little port of Findhorn, five miles away at the entrance to Findhorn Bay and the harbour. The merchants had lived in Forres in houses on the ridge facing the sea, where with a glass or a keen eye they could see their brigs arrive.

The rent was £14 a year, a considerable sum at a time when father's wage from the railway was 19 shillings (95p) a week.

The street was narrow with pavements for only the first thirty yards, then one had to walk in a cobbled gutter if the street was being used by a vehicle. Although quite a short street there were two distinct communities, the "top" and the "bottom". At the top the gables of a winemerchant's shop faced those of the principal draper's, both having entrances on the High Street. On the west side was a very narrow lane in which two people would have had difficulty passing. This lane led to a narrow court or "close", all that was left of the former gardens of the shop and house on the High Street. There was a huddle of houses, divided and subdivided, with a continually changing number of tenants and lodgers. A wooden lean-to at the back of the Eagle Bar was the WC which served this little community. This area, cramped and so overshadowed by the buildings that the sun made only fitful appearances, was also the favoured playground of the children of the whole street. Here were held shows, circuses, recitations and singing, boasting, quarrelling and all the things with which children fill their days. Sometimes a charge would be made, the usual entry fee being one pin, for money was something that other people had.

The residents were tolerant of the noise, for many were transients, moving on as soon as they fell into arrears of rent of more than one week, when the police would be asked to see them move away. None sought protection of the law knowing that it did not apply to them, for the magistrates were recruited from the house owners and shopkeepers who made up the Town Council, where a working man was unknown.

There was a chip shop opposite the Eagle Bar for a time, the first one in town, where one halfpenny could buy an adequate bag of chipped potatoes fried in dripping or mutton fat. For a further halfpenny the bag could be filled with hot peas.

Evans the tailor worked in a little wooden shop attached to the gable of his thatched cottage. When he had work he sat cross-legged on a table, his frock coat removed but ready to be put on along with his billycock hat if a customer came.

For a working man to obtain a steady job he had to be presentably dressed and thus able to go to church on Sunday. All clothes were made by hand and a new suit was a sign that the wearer was getting married, or had recently been married; the arrival of children put a second new suit out of the question. It was the custom for the widows of business men or the well-to-do to give away the clothes of the deceased. This was usually to the woman who helped in the house, for the smallest shopkeeper could afford a maid or daily help. Evans was always busy altering and cutting down to size these old suits, for he was cheap and quick. The "bespoke" tailors preferred to work with new material only, as handling suits to be altered lowered the tone of the establishment, and each trader was extremely jealous of his standing in the eyes of the other traders of the town.

Then there was the house of the man who drowned himself. He was a blacksmith, and treasurer of the Friendly Society, which met every Monday night in the Town Hall to collect the weekly payments of the members. Having been paid off for a spell during a quiet period, he had spent two pounds of the funds and then, as no employment came, he started drinking with money from the same source. Realising that he could never make up such sums, he threw himself in the river. This created a great sensation for despite the hardships, poverty and ill health prevalent in the town, this was an uncommon thing. Patiently, without complaint, the poverty was endured and only as a last resort was application made to the Poor Law Office, the committee being again recruited from the merchant class who viewed poverty and unemployment as an offence.

Next came our neighbour, Robert Forsyth, tinsmith and bailie of the town. The provost and the three bailies of the Town Council were the magistrates, calling a court on the morning after someone was arrested, and with power to send men to prison: the six cells in the Tolbooth were often occupied, by drunks and tramps mostly.

Bailie Forsyth was almost a professional councillor, and a master of the pompous phrase, for he modelled himself on W G Gladstone, the greatest orator of the nineteenth century. The bailie wore a frock coat and a bowler hat; these, with the trousers, were of a greenish hue through age. He also wore a "dickey", a celluloid shirt front which concealed the rough woollen workingman's shirt below. He was bearded and did not use a tie, as his beard hid most of the dickey, so a tie would be superfluous. He paid little attention to his trade, and his shop window in Tolbooth Street held nothing but a tin milk pail, and a flask of the kind used by workmen to hold their tea when away all day. The dead flies lay in the dust for years.

He had a wispy dwarf-like daughter, and two sons, both alcoholics and addicted to football. I recall the oldest's funeral, and heard mother tell of the "dreadful end", for she was called in as nurse and as midwife in the neighbourhood. John had apparently died from "delirium tremens" a form of madness. The other son had lost an arm in the First World War and never worked again, his pension and the few pence he earned on cattle market day, driving the beasts from the station to the mart and the slaughterhouse, meeting all his needs. After his father's death he lived "rough" at the riverside, and was found dead one January morning. The bailie boasted often of his wealth to father, and told of his will leaving a third to each of his family. Mother attended him also on his death bed, and as soon as he had breathed his last, performed the first rite which was to search through his clothes for a key to the cupboard where his papers and valuables were stored. The search produced exactly twopence in his pockets, and Lizzie, his widow, was homeless and on "parish relief". A Miss Munro had a little shop in Tolbooth Street and started to stock fiction; this was so successful that the shop had books not only on the shelves but also on the floor. The Poor Law Office offered Miss Munro less than the full amount of relief if she would keep Lizzie in her house and feed her, and use her as an unpaid assistant. It seemed like slavery but it was cheap.

Only ten of the thirty houses in North Street still exist [i.e. in 1977]. Among them at the very foot stands the cottage of "Curley Auntie" still neat and whitewashed, the thatched roof replaced by one of corrugated iron. Embedded into the foundation is the large boulder used as a seat by the tenant. Here she sat selling her cockles, ready boiled, for a penny a pint, measured with a battered white mug. The boulder seems too small now to provide a seat, but she was a very tiny old lady, reputed to be a witch who could charm away warts. My family like so many Scots, did not eat shellfish so I had never to approach her. How often had she made the long walk to the Cockle Shore, paying a halfpenny to cross by the ferry, or if the river was low, risking the ford downstream, at all hours to fit the tides, to eke out a living?

It was a hard life for old widows in a town which had so many young ones. For the work among the acid of the Chemical Works or the Bone Mill tore out the lungs of young husbands, their only protection a piece of wet sacking over their mouths.

The house next door, six steps below the level of the street, was the home of the Marshalls. We had arrived in North Street in May, and now in November they were emigrating to Australia. On the evening before their departure there was a roup of all that they could not take with them, and Jockie my friend slept with me, the other seven members of the family sharing beds elsewhere in the street. In bed he promised to see my brother Will in Australia, which to us was simply another street.

When we crossed the street in the morning it was blocked with large wooden cases of belongings, waiting to be picked up by Wordie's horses and taken to the railway station, for each emigrant could have 150 kilos of luggage free on the train and ship. The loading took so long that the milk cart and the coal lorry had to be backed carefully but noisily all the way to the High Street.

Even the residents of the "model lodging" house around the corner were there, some for farewells, others to take anything left behind. But two stood still and silent, the twins "Treacle Dab" and "Knot" (The "k" sounded Scots fashion) thin and neat in their moleskin trousers and rough worn shirts. Clean shaven, their cheeks pink with the consumption that had made them orphans as boys, they were "bonny men" as mother said, hastening their deaths, already speeded by the acid fumes when they got occasional hours of work, by their diet of bread and polony sausage washed down by the methylated spirits as clear and colourless as the water they mixed it with.

They could be seen on the evenings when they had had a day's work hurrying to spend what was left of the two shillings after paying for their night's shelter, and perhaps arrears of the previous night. Mr Marshall was a stonemason who, when he had work, helped less fortunate workmates, usually the twins, the orphaned sons of a workmate.

Gone also is the stable loft where Jeems, the hunchbacked cobbler, lived and worked at the window facing the street, At the other end of the loft was his bed, table and chair and before it was the wooden chest providing a seat for the visitor. Here was our haven on bad days; anyone older than eight years was debarred, for Jeems was afraid of anyone older. Not here did we hear of daring tales or eerie happenings, for he had little to say, a weak smile at some childish remark was all.

Outside the window was the gas lamp, one of the two in the street, which allowed Jeems to go to bed without a candle; it was extinguished at ten o'clock, and in the dark winter days Jeems had to wait until nine o'clock before he could see to rise for the day. Jeems was the poor person of the street, the recipient of a bowl of soup or perhaps some potatoes at the "tattie lifting" time. Perhaps on occasion a shred or two of mutton when some housewife bought a sheep's head for sixpence from the slaughterhouse, the blacksmith in Caroline Street obligingly singeing it in the forge for one halfpenny.

Further up the street was the site of a house of an emigrant returned. Her mother dead, and no longer young, she had gone by emigrant ship to Philadelphia with a £6 ticket, and a promise of a job at her destination. Seasick during the whole voyage from Greenock, she was ushered on deck to go ashore. Viewing the dismal prospect ashore in the grey light of a foreign dawn, she refused to move, saying, in version bowdlerised by a fellow townsman and passenger in a letter, "If that's America, the Red Indians can have it". Having to be taken back home by the shipping company, she returned home to marry the suitor she had rejected as a cowardly weakling a few years earlier for refusing to accompany her to the USA. A cheerful, forthright woman, for the rest of her life she answered to the nickname of "Philadelphia".

In the little pool of light from the street lamp we carried on our games which varied from season to season. A favourite was "cattie", played with a short piece of stick, pointed at each end with the Roman numerals I to IV burned on with a poker and a longer piece of the same stick. A slit was made in the road and the cattie placed across it, this was thrown as far as possible by placing the stick below. The throwing stick was then used as measure, and the winner was the one with the longest throw. Further strokes could be taken by striking the cattie into the air and striking it further.

When cars became common this game fell into disuse as it broke up the road, now tarred for smoothness. The wooden hoops from barrels were used, "girds" as they were called. Many families, like my own, bought a half barrel, or a firkin, of salt herring as a store of food for the winter.

There were many other games for the street, but football and cricket were played in the Burn Green, often with a ball made of newspapers tied with string and the goals marked by jackets or jerseys. Cricket was played with one of the poles supporting the laundry's drying lines as wickets. In the summer we roved in the many woods and along the banks of the river and the Mosset Burn, down to the sea.

ON THE FARM AT RAFFORD

Mother came with me to the top of the street to await the arrival of Charlie Hay who drove the Post Office gig to Dallas. It was February 1916, and a cold wind blew along High Street making me shiver in the coat that had already served four of my brothers and was now getting thin. I clutched a brown paper parcel containing a shirt, a pair of home knitted stockings and a suit of thick woollen combinations, a form of underwear known in America as "long johns".

I had been ailing for some time, the weakest of the family. The doctor had finally diagnosed a "sluggish liver" and prescribed a long stay in mountain air. I have never heard of any other case of this disease, but now know that it had a psychological origin, and with hindsight can recognise the cause. The nearest mountain that was available was at the farm of my uncle John Dean, in Rafford, several hundred feet higher than my home.

Charlie, portly but smart in his uniform, brought his vehicle to a smart stop and leaning down hauled me to the small seat beside him. As instructed I quickly slipped the sixpence for my fare into his hand, for it was illegal to carry an unauthorised person with His Majesty's Mails, but my father was a discreet and responsible person. With a short injunction to be a good boy my mother turned away quickly, for a show of affection or emotion in public was frowned upon as a sign of a weak nature and a lack of confidence in God's will. She was both affectionate and emotional.

Touching his shako with one hand Charlie tugged at the reins with the other, clicking encouragement to his smart brown sheltie at the same time. He was silent until we left the town. "I've nothing today for either Brockloch or Damhead so I'll have to let you off at Miss James's shoppie, and you'll have to make your own way, but I'll be in by tomorrow and be able to tell your folks that you are fine and settled in."

I did not feel fine for I was already homesick and lonely and did not answer. I held firmly to the metal bar of the seat for I had never been so high above the ground in a moving vehicle and feared I would fall off. A cyclist overtook us and I could see men working in the fields ploughing with their great horses. An occasional halt was made to deliver a letter or a parcel, each stop requiring a short exchange of news, much of which seemed to concern me and I was, no doubt, a welcome topic on the daily round. Passing Rafford school I was able to espy through the window the children sitting round a bright fire. Charlie pointed out the Free and Parish churches and other places of interest, dismounting at Rafford Post Office. I was invited to get down and have a cup of tea but silently shook my head in refusal. As Mrs Walker took the mailbag she looked at me and remarked, "So you're Willie Forbes's loon. Tell him I'm asking for him", and another voice added "and your mother too". I nodded politely in acknowledgement, trying to smile with little success.

I tried self encouragement by repeating silently that I would soon be ten years old, and in a year or two could get a job as a message boy, when I would have to call at all sorts of doors and meet all kinds of people. Charlie reappeared wiping his sweeping gray moustache with a large red handkerchief and remounted. After a few minutes he halted at the entrance to a farm road and pointed to an adjacent house gable. "That's the shoppie", he said, "and that's the road to your aunts. You can see Brochlach to your left, but carry on until you come to Starrywells. That's where your grandfather Forbes bides, but don't go in, for he's not well enough to see you so early in the day. Carry on a bit further and you're at your Auntie Mey's." With that he drove away.

I stood terrified and desolate: never had the world seemed so large and strange with unknown terrors behind each grass bank. I was not unused to open spaces for we roamed in little parties through the spacious woods and river banks surrounding the town, sometimes as far as Findhorn five miles away by the sea, or taking our lives, as we thought, in our hands crossed the tubular iron bridge which carried the railway over the River Findhorn. This was done on Sundays when there were no railwaymen in sight, and of course no trains, although we did not appreciate this. Once across the river it was not far to the village of Dyke or Brodie Castle. But here there were no bold companions, only the unknown.

Until Brockloch farm was passed the road was level, but now it climbed and became progressively rougher and with deeper ruts making walking difficult. Each twist and bend held the threat of a galloping horse or a herd of bellowing cattle. I tried to see how quickly I could scramble up the steep banks on either side but the grass was damp and the whins stabbed my hands. There was nothing to do but advance.

Turning a bend I came to a dry stone dyke and beyond a patch of rough grass two cottages, each with a brown barn type door, two windows and a thatched roof. This must be Starrywells and I gazed for a little span of time, hoping that someone would recognise me and come out to greet me. But there was no movement and I walked on. Passing a small wood I came suddenly on the farm court with a cartshed facing me, with a cast iron hand pump in front. On my right the hedge, till I came to its end, concealed the farmhouse. It was small and low with a slated roof and beyond were other low thatched byres, stable and cattlefold.

A large dog chained to its kennel barked furiously and tugged wildly at its chain inspiring a tremor of fear. My aunt came to the door, the signal for a noisy rush of hens and ducks taking her appearance as a sign of feeding time. My heart rose for she was our most welcome visitor at home.

She was tall like father but twisted with the continuous toil of a crofter's wife, for despite its 90 acres it was little more than a croft with its sour, boggy and hungry soil, liable to flooding in its lower reaches. A common saying was that the only life worse than that of a crofter's horse was that of the crofter's wife. Her gray hair was tied tightly out of the way to allow her to press her head against the side of the cow she milked, and her nondescript dress was protected by a potato sack tied round her waist with a piece of the tarred rope used for binding hay ricks. Her face was worn and tired, and when she smiled as she did now, she exposed a few large crooked teeth, which reminded me of the tottering tombstones in a churchyard. But at the same time she looked beautiful to me. She was kind and understanding. I came to love her although I could not verbalise my feelings in that word, which was almost forbidden in our lives of monastic austerity.

She loved books and stole a few minutes every day from her toil, usually when her husband John retired after dinner at eleven o'clock each morning to the little room off the kitchen for an hour's nap, no matter how much had to be done. He was a big man with a heavy spade beard, bluff, cheerful and kind, selfish only in this respect. Aunt Mey, pronounced as in the first syllable of "height", was my father's only sister.

Much of my time was spent in the large kitchen, entered through a wooden porch lined with shelves holding the waterpails out of reach of dogs and poultry. The water was obtained from the pump twenty yards away, and care had to be taken that there was always enough water retained to prime the pump until the water began to flow. The kitchen was sparsely furnished with a well scrubbed table, with a wooden form at each side, and a wooden armchair at the end next the fire for the master. The fireplace was large enough for a man to stand in, with an iron gantry in the chimney to which was fixed a chain and hook to hold the large cast iron pots used for cooking. Iron bars made a firebasket for the large pieces of wood used for fuel, augmented when a quick blaze was required, with dried broom and the needles and twigs of fir. A large unpainted dresser and a few odd chairs completed the furniture, the only decoration a calendar on the wall, and a large brass paraffin lamp. The bare wooden floor was spread with green rushes when these were available, for the supply was drawn from a pile cut for bedding for the beasts to save the straw.

A large pot was always above the fire, for many potatoes had to be boiled each day for the sow and the hens. For these the potatoes were boiled without cleaning away the earth, and at times maize, oats and if these were scarce, chaff or chopped straw was added. The mixture gave off a very disagreeable odour of which only I seemed conscious. This was to be expected for across the yard and only partly concealed by the byre gable was the large farm midden where the animal manure was stored until such time as it could be spread on the fields. After my first few days I was given the task of cleaning the byres where three cows spent milking time and night time. No doubt I was as redolent of the prevailing stench as the others for I had only one change of underwear, and in wet weather had to wait until the clothes dried on the washline before a change could be made.

The midday meal was the principal one, the chief dish being a pot of boiled potatoes, accompanied by oatcakes, scones and pancakes made daily, for the "bakers" bread was reserved for Sunday or for the occasional visitor. If there was an ailing fowl it was quickly killed and eaten, beef or mutton, like bread, were for special occasions, but there were many rabbits, for Uncle always had snares set, and on occasion he took his gun and shot what was edible or troublesome.

My uncle Sandy Forbes lodged with his sister but I saw little of him as he left early in the morning to cycle to his work as a stone breaker for the county council. Each parish had one, to be seen usually beside the neat pile of broken granite ready for the road squad. Roads were of "water bound macadam", these stones laid on the surface and levelled by a steam road roller, sand and water being sprayed on the metal. He had the peculiarities of an old bachelor. Each evening on arrival from work, and after he had washed and shaved, he ate the same meal – stew and potatoes, followed by a freshly made tapioca pudding to which had to be added a raw egg before being poured on to his plate. This had to be stirred only slightly and to me the streaks of raw egg were repellent, and ever since I have been unable to eat tapioca in any form.

He then retired to his bedroom which was well furnished in comparison with the other rooms in the house. On the chest of drawers, well polished, was a gramophone with a large horn and beside it a good stock of records. He favoured Scots music and songs, Sir Harry Lauder coming first as a singer. On a few occasions I was invited to his sanctum but after listening to a few records I would be dismissed.

He held, perhaps with good reason, that the horn should be as near the ceiling as possible, although this meant that he had continually to rise from his chair, turn it round, climb on it, change the record, step down and turn the chair again before listening. He was stout and moved ponderously and much time was taken by these stately manoeuvres.

The other member of the household was my cousin Maggie. She was only twenty-one at that time, but looked older to my young eye, probably because, like her mother, she had so much work to do. Her brother Bob had joined the army at the outbreak of war and much of his work fell on her shoulders. Perhaps also the brain tumour which blinded her and caused her death eight years later was already in being.

I soon fitted into the rhythm of the daily darg, which seemed endless; feeding the cows in their stalls if the weather did not allow them out to graze; searching the likely places for eggs as the hens and ducks ranged freely; pumping and carrying water; chopping firewood and performing any tasks within my physical abilities. The most disagreeable was that of breaking the great oblong slabs of oilcake with a hammer. This was done on the concrete floor of the threshing mill, which was bitterly cold in winter and rarely warm in summer. The pieces had to be of a small size for cows are inclined to choke to death on anything large, which meant that turnips also had to be sliced before they were eaten by the cattle. This was done in a machine, the cutting blades operated by pulling down a weighted handle. To reach this handle I had to stand on a box or, lacking this, pile the slabs to a sufficient height, no easy task because of their weight and size.

The road continued past the farm, alongside the dam holding the water for the waterwheel of the threshing mill, then joined another road. The path to the left led to the farm of Fernielea, and to the right, even more rough and overgrown, led to Wester Brockloch, neither road being used much by these two farms. But right ahead was a stile, the path beyond reaching a group of four tiny cottages each occupied by an old person, three men and one woman. These were the last of the families who had been engaged in winning the rough and inferior slates from nearby Slatehaugh, still marked on the Ordnance Survey maps.

All had retired when the Old Age Pension of five shillings a week was introduced about 1909 by the then Chancellor of the Exchequer, David Lloyd George. Maggie and I went there often, for she collected their pensions from the Post Office and delivered the groceries and bread left for them at Damhead. There I feasted on the most delightful gooseberries for that was all they had to offer. The walls of the houses still survive as do the roses, lilacs and flowers.

On my first morning in Damhead I was awakened at five o'clock to go to the threshing mill where I was stationed on the lower floor. Above, my uncle, aunt and Maggie put through grooved rollers the sheaves of straw stored in the room next to me, while the straw cascaded down a chute to the floor; it was my task to move this with a pitchfork and build it up against the wall behind me. The dam held only enough water to operate the millwheel for less than an hour, by which time I was exhausted. We then returned to the kitchen for breakfast. My fingers had clutched the polished wooden handle of the pitchfork and this combined with the bitter cold froze them, so that Maggie had to place the spoon in my hand. At home I was unable to eat before going to school, but now I was ravenous, as I continued to be during the whole of my stay at Damhead.

Once a week a large wooden oblong box churn was hoisted on to the kitchen table and filled with the cream from the week's milk. To turn the handle which worked the paddles was almost beyond my reach on the upper stroke and I stood on tiptoe most of the time. At first the cream was fluid but when the butter began to form the job became more arduous until my aunt had to help me. In time my muscles strengthened and my height extended and I was able to deal with the butter making alone. Delicious cheese was also made with the surplus milk, flavoured with caraway seeds which were gathered annually by my aunt. The most profitable area was in the surroundings of Pluscarden Abbey a mile or so away. I was informed that this area was rich in herbs that had strayed from the gardens of the monks, now in the last quarter century reinstated in the Abbey.

Other very strenuous work was the sawing of the logs for firewood. Each year the laird's tenants could buy a number of standing trees, which they then felled and took back to the farm, where they were sawed into lengths suitable for building once they were dried out. Then once or twice a week I assisted my uncle at one end of a crosscut saw, he doing most of the work naturally. The farm was almost self supporting and used little money. The baker was paid in eggs and butter, the butcher's van with poultry, and some cheese was taken by the grocer, and also honey when there was a surplus.

In the evening the cattle had to be brought from the fields when it grew cold at night. It was only necessary to open the field gate and give a peculiar cry to bring them home. The nearest approach to this call is "pee-ochie, pee-ochie". Soon I was allowed to handle the two Clydesdale horses; Nell, who was white with age and 27 years old was easily handled, and knew what to do. Taken to the cartshed she backed into the shafts without guidance, and all that had to be done was fix her harness. The other horse was a young gelding named Clyde, but I was unable to handle it as in the morning it was lively and restive. I could place the bridle and the breeching, or "britchen", but the collar was too large and heavy for me to lift over their heads.

I once drove Nell to Forres, behind uncle, with a load of oats to be ground into oatmeal at the Mills of Forres, the miller holding back his "multures" which met the cost. We returned with the year's supply of coal, loose in the carts. On the return I sat on the foreboard, negligently with one foot on the shaft and the other dangling, as I saw other carters do. My legs were short and I was seated precariously, and it was with difficulty that I retained my seat on the rougher parts of the road. All went well until we took the sharp turn near Rafford church where a car, driven by Dr Adam, emerged from the side road and Nell shied. For such an ancient and staid beast the word "shied" may be an exaggeration, but her change of pace was enough to make me lose my balance and I fell on the roadway, fortunately missed by the six foot iron shod wheel. Dr Adam stopped and ran back, but I was uninjured.

As the days lengthened there was time for some leisure and I was allowed to visit Brockloch farm. The tenant there worked with Damhead when necessary and I knew the two men, Jimmy and Alec, who invited me to their bothy. They were pleased to have company as all their time was spent on the farm apart from an occasional Saturday evening.

Jimmy had a melodeon, a simple form of accordion and Alec had a repertoire of bothy ballads, most of them scabrous if not obscene. The

Grampian region is said to lead the world in its breadth and wealth of music, song and poetry of the traditional kind. Many of these songs are still popular, very much bowdlerised, but perversely it is the original version that stays in one's memory.

At the end of that year Jimmy joined the army and was killed in France, while Alec moved away at the same time. Farm workers were a very mobile people.

At Damhead our visitors were infrequent, and mostly from nearby, and it was rare for one to arrive without a present. As few had money for gifts, such things as eggs would be brought with the explanation that they were the eggs "of the wee Rhode Island hennie you admired last time you were over". In return they would receive one of our Khaki Campbell duck eggs or a piece of "carvie cheese".

The harvest was now near at hand, but with adverse weather there was much activity during the dry hours to win as much of the harvest as possible. Work went on as long as the horses could continue, for their patient endurance was not as great as that of the human workers. Brockloch and Damhead worked together, our two horses being a welcome relief for those at Brockloch, for that farm had the binder. I helped to stook the sheaves and carried pails of tea and bundles of scones and oatcakes to the fields to save time. It was during one of the short meal breaks that Jimmy gave me a few draws of his pipe, filled with Bogie Roll tobacco, the cheapest and strongest on the market. It was in the form of a rope well soaked in treacle, and had to be cut into thick shavings before being smoked. The few puffs I had were enough to make me sick, a misery only equalled by a sickness incurred on the infamous "Vomiting Venus" of the Bergen Line during a voyage to Norway.

Before the sheaves could be driven to the stackyard the weather worsened and the ditches and drains broke their banks, sweeping away the crop. Many sheaves were caught in the wire fences crossing the streams and I had to help salvage these, the only protection from the rain being a potato sack wrapped round my shoulders. This disaster was a severe financial blow for the wartime demand for food had driven high the price for grain. No harvest home festivals were held; the slaughter on the battlefields was enough of a deterrent against any jollification, without the loss of so much of the grain.

There was little suitable for me to read, and I tried those books which the minister, the Reverend Ballantyne gave to my aunt. Some of them were very "modern", and such that he would not lend to most of his parishioners, but he talked to her as an equal in this sphere. Rolf Boldrewood and Elinor Glyn are two names I recollect. There was a history of the Japanese-Russian war of 1904, in two illustrated volumes and I read this carefully if painfully slowly because of the foreign names, so that I knew more of that war than I did of the one currently raging all over the world. Kuropatkin, Vladivostok, Yalu and Tsushima Strait came easier to my tongue than Mons, Ypres, Gallipoli or Verdun, and inspired in me a desire to visit those places, whereas I made no attempt to visit the arenas of the greater struggle.

During my stay in Rafford I learned, young as I was, to admire the courage, skill and fortitude of all who work on the land. Good times and bad, the latter the more common, were accepted without question. This almost fatalistic attitude influenced me all my life; although it did not change my natural impatience and impulsive actions, it gave me the philosophy to endure the results of my actions without acrimony.

During my stay I did have one experience of horror and terror. My aunt held in great respect the Reverend Ballantyne, and for his visits the best cream, cheese and cream scones were made. There was a small flower garden at the farm, a most unusual thing to find on crofts and small farms, and this she cared for herself. She had a small plot of strawberries but only the minister got these, although I longed to sample them. All but myself went to church every Sunday morning, and I was in charge of the place apart from Uncle Sandy who never moved out of his room on that day. It was July and there had been a few days of sun, and the berries glowed crimson, and I was tempted and fell. To the west was the sunlit sea backed by the hills of Ross-shire, and clearly visible was the entrance to the Cromarty Firth where much of the Navy lay during the war. Warships and vessels were always to be seen steaming in or out of the estuary, on the lookout for German submarines which were always looking for targets there.

I pulled one strawberry and had scarcely tasted it when there were gun-flashes in the Firth followed by the boom of the heavy guns. I fled ... God was punishing me for stealing the fruits sacred to his servant, the minister of Rafford. It took Maggie some considerable time to trace me to my refuge under the bed in my room. I told her that fear of the guns had driven me there, because I did not dare tell of my sacrilege, and suffered mentally and morally for some time.

Occasionally I had to carry food to my grandfather at Starrywell, when the old lady in the neighbouring cottage who looked after him visited her daughter who lived a mile or two away. My grandfather, William Forbes was now a very frail old man, suffering from heart disease, his dropsy being a symptom of this. Because of this dropsy he could not sleep in a bed and spent his life on a wooden armchair, propped up with cushions, and well wrapped up in a rug or blanket. After my initial shyness we talked a good deal. He was unable to read apart from a Bible with very large type, which always lay at hand on the table. At times it was difficult to hear his voice, so weak was he.

He was of Highland birth, being born near Culloden, the home of the chief of the western branch of the Forbeses, and was employed by him when young. My aunt was able to amplify some of the things he told me, and which I did not fully understand at the time. He had married Isabella Forbes, probably a near relative, who lived with her widowed mother in a cottage belonging to the estate, as did all the houses in the neighbourhood. He had started as a labourer on the estate, and was not entitled to a house, and had to wait until his future wife's mother died before he could get married. She was twelve years older than he, and my aunt thought that the certainty of having a house when her mother died may have encouraged his courtship, for she worked in the Big House and would be left in residence when her mother had been deceased.

While employment on estates was usually for life, and therefore had a security that no other employment then gave, it had its drawbacks. There were no holidays, and no limit to the hours worked, although the work was rarely arduous. He had been responsible for looking after horses which meant rising early every day of the year.

The Laird was one of the promoters of the new Inverness and Nairn Railway, and the estate workers had their first holiday on 5 November 1855 when the first train ran on the line through part of the estate grounds. So attracted was grandfather by this novel form of transport that he gave notice that he was leaving on 11 November, the legal end of the half year. He had to see the laird who advised him not to take this rash step, pointing out hazards of life outside the protection of an estate where he had a job for life. But grandfather persisted, and on his first day of freedom he walked into Inverness but found that there was no vacancy. The laird had given him an excellent character reference and because of that he was offered a job with the contractors who were building an extension of the railway to the east. He had to leave home as the line moved forward, but his wife joined him, moving their home until the line terminated in Keith, where it met the Great North of Scotland Railway from Aberdeen. He then helped to build the branch line from Alves to Burghead, and on its completion was appointed "Ganger" or foreman of the maintenance men on that line. Thus his family were all born in Moray. After I left Damhead at the end of the year I never saw my grandfather again for he died in the following March.

I returned home a few days before Christmas loaded with butter, cheese, eggs and a fowl, as well as the magnificent sum of almost two pounds. Every week my uncle had put aside, in a tiny wooden box, a few pence, and this was presented to me on my departure. Jack was home on leave from France and came for me on a bicycle, and I returned seated precariously on the handlebars, clutching the potato sack as well as my belongings.

Mother, after a brief welcome, and a close scrutiny of the contents of the bag, took the money and gave me back a shilling, with a warning not to dissipate it rashly. My closest friend "Nigger" Jenkins, who lived next door persuaded me to buy one dozen doughnuts from Austin's bakery. It was an easy task for I recalled the sugary covering of this delicious fried treat. Unfortunately sugar was now one of the scarcest commodities and all I had for my money was a lump of dough saturated in fat. I should have learned from a previous experience. On the day I drove the coal cart, my uncle halted at the foot of Tolbooth Street to visit the bootmaker. Next door was Ashers Bakery shop which I entered to spend the two pence uncle had given me. The shelves and trays were bare, but on the counter lay some packets of macaroni, and my money was sufficient to buy one half pound packet. I had never seen macaroni before but it looked edible which it was not for I tried to eat it there and then. My aunt was no wiser and it was added to the pigs food.

Before there was a picture house in the town there was only the occasional concert, organised by local people and with local people performing. During the summer a company of actors would put on a play, and during the winter the main events were the dances. These were very formal with lists of those to whom invitations could be sent, formal dress being necessary. In the summer at the height of the holiday season, a younger set would arrange an informal or "Flannels" dance, but respectable young ladies were not allowed to attend, as many of the women attending were without chaperones.

For ordinary people the principal pastime was gossip; daily after lunch mother put on a clean apron, cleared the kitchen table and put the large cast iron kettle on the fire to boil water. She then waited for callers, her friends from other parts of the town, to exchange reports of all that had happened, no matter how trivial. I was ailing often and absent from school, and on cold days in the winter sat in the kitchen reading, for the warmth there. One had to be really ill before a fire was lit in the bedroom before evening. I usually became engrossed in my book, and pretended always to be so, but when I heard voices drop I would listen carefully, turning over the pages regularly. Much of what I heard I did not understand, but some was so specific that the stories were clear. One lady, whom we had to call Auntie Pheem (from Euphemia), was married to a local gamekeeper, who had an affair with the lady of the house, who was titled. Pheem was fully aware of what was going on, but she lived with her husband in a "tied" house on the estate, and there was little she could do. Much sympathy was shown her, and the matter discussed very fully with many sighs and many expressions such as "The brute" or "What a madam!" When I was much older I was given an unexpurgated copy of *Lady Chatterley's Lover*, and on reading it was surprised at the furore it seemed to have caused, for I had heard it all before.

One of my mother's favourite topics for discussion was the matter of the "Urquhart Millions", for she was certain that a share of these mythical pounds would eventually reach her. She never, however, raised the subject in the presence of father, to whom it was a sensitive matter, for he had been persuaded by the entreaties of his wife to part with the sum of Five Pounds to her cousin Hugh Urquhart.

The Urquharts are a small clan or family, based in the Black Isle of Ross-shire around Cromarty where mother's ancestors came from. Urquhart Castle, on the banks of the Loch Ness, was a powerful and influential focal point of that area. The Urquharts were an intelligent and volatile people who have made their mark in Scottish history. The best known was Sir Thomas Urquhart of Cromarty, the translator of Rabelais, of whom it was said that his work was more exuberant and scabrous than the original, and that he was as colourful and flamboyant as Gargantua or Pantagruel. He was in exile with King Charles at St Germain de Pres when the news came that the king was called back to the throne, and died with laughter at the news.

At that time a number of law firms specialised in getting details from America and the Colonies of estates left by emigrant Scots who had died without making a will, and one such firm had been researching the records of the East India Company with some hopeful results. A sum of money had long been held belonging to an Urquhart, a servant of "John Company" in the eighteenth century, when the company was the virtual owner and ruler of the Indian sub continent. History tells us of the quick accumulation of great fortunes in a short time, and this youth had followed the example of his "betters" but with a lower class of native. Either through inexperience or excessive zeal his "persuasion" had been so persuasive that his victim had died. There was the usual outcry from the Indians, this time with some success. The culprit was a Scot and had no powerful friends or influential family to intercede in London or protect him in India, so an example was made and he was hung.

The lawyers had visited the home of the Urquharts and mother's cousin Hugh took control of the matter, and called on grandfather Urquhart in Forres, as well as others. Old Colin was impecunious and passed Hugh to my mother. Hugh had visited every possible relative and had collected an unknown amount of money to allow him to follow up the matter in Glasgow, and if necessary, in London. To this he added the £5 from father. He left for the south but was never heard from again, although it was rumoured that he had left on an emigrant ship from Greenock bound for Canada. The fare was £6 to Halifax with a promise of work on arrival. William Urquhart, mother's half brother had earlier emigrated to Canada, and mother, obtaining his address, wrote him to ask if he would trace Hugh and get the £5 from him. Willie replied that Canada was a big country and could promise little. When war broke out he joined the army and wrote us from France to say that he would spend his first leave with us. Mother, always optimistic, had hopes that he would by that time have found Hugh, but Willie was killed before he got his leave. My only contact with him was when I looked up his name inscribed in the books at the Menin Gate Memorial in Belgium.

We were never sure whether there actually was an "Indian" Urquhart, but there was another possibility. Donald or "Dan" Urquhart, also of Culbokie in the Black Isle, had been one of the gold miners who had fought against the British Army at the Eureka Stockade in Ballarat, Australia in 1854, when forty men were killed before the miners surrendered. These were tried by the army and all were sentenced to be hanged, but only a few were actually executed before pardons were given. Dan was one of the fortunate ones.

SCHOOL DAYS

I went to school in Forres Academy in August 1911 and was enrolled in a passage where the plasterers were still at work, and was then sent home and told to return in a fortnight when the classrooms of this extension were ready. The school, a two-storeyed Victorian building with a bell tower and stone stairways, was erected in 1877 to meet the requirements of the recent Act making education compulsory for all. It was now showing its age and had become overcrowded the previous year when the "English" school run by the Scottish Episcopalian Church was closed because the church did not have the money to bear the cost of a new school required by the provisions of the same Act.

Across the High Street stood Andersons Institute founded in 1828 but now part of the Academy. It had classrooms only, the upper floor being the residence of the Rector. He had no deputy or assistant, or a secretary although he was responsible for the Infant, Primary, and Secondary school, and in addition had to take certain classes. A fine looking man, he inspired fear in his pupils, and carried in his pocket a leather tawse, or strap, for instant punishment of any offence he observed outside the classrooms but within the school precincts. In the crowded conditions discipline was difficult, and a constant stream of boys called at his office with a note to say that the bearer had refused to put out his or her hand for punishment. One or two pupils in their last year received instruction in Greek in his office and these were often interrupted so that he could strap someone sent to him for punishment.

I could read before I went to school as there was always a brother or sister at homework in the kitchen eager to pass on their new found knowledge and skills. I soon became an insatiable reader, and when I started school read the terms textbooks at once, but I always found it difficult to spend time rereading anything. This brought me trouble sometimes, but I had few problems at school and was often impatient with the slow progress of the class.

Open fires were the only form of heating, one scuttle of coal being supplied each day, and on very cold days this could be consumed before lunch time, but no more was allowed. On such cold afternoons the class had periodically to stand in the space between desks and practise "running on the spot" to generate enough warmth to allow us to continue to write or use our hands. In the war years 1914-18, fuel was even scarcer, but I cannot recall the school ever being dismissed because of the cold. Instead, the whole building would reverberate to the hundreds of feet thumping the floor in pursuit of comfort.

Each room was filled to capacity and for a number of years I shared a room with forty boys, with a class of girls of the same size next door. The women teachers of these two classes were appointed because of their physical strength and severity of their discipline rather than their teaching ability.

There was no outlet for the latent energy of the young; no sports field or open space for their use. Until the outbreak of war some of the senior classes of boys were taken to the nearby Drill Hall where the instructor of the Territorial Army gave them Swedish drill. I never learned whether this was paid for, or was a voluntary service given by the sergeant in charge. The town had its own School Board as had almost every parish and town in Scotland. The chairman was a frequent visitor to the school, often accompanied by another member. They were feared by the staff as they had absolute power, and often abused it. The State had school inspectors but their duties were wholly advisory.

All primary school teachers were women, many of them becoming "pupil teachers" when they became of school leaving age and were suitable. Becoming a teacher was equivalent to taking the veil of a nun, for no married teachers were employed, and getting married meant dismissal. During the war years scarcity resulted in this rule being suspended, but it was put into operation again when hostilities ceased. A few of the "pupil teachers" went for a short time to a Teachers Training College, as this gave them a chance of promotion to a higher post.

In 1913 the Upper Primary boys went on strike, their demands being for "no strap, padded seats and pocket money" with no indication of where the money was to come from for the last demand. The strike started at the morning playtime, when only a fraction of those who had agreed to strike actually ran out of the grounds and fled to the Cluny Hills, to be pursued by the janitor and the Chairman of the School Board, the Reverend Stair

Douglas of the "English" church. The police were called in to pursue the boys, but being more experienced they asked for a list of the absentees and then informed the parents of what had happened. Brother Bert, a born rebel, was a ringleader and returned home as usual for lunch at noon, to be shocked by father seizing him at the door, dragging him into the kitchen, and making him lean over a chair with his trousers down. He was then thrashed with the leather strop which hung on the cupboard door, used by father for sharpening his razor every morning. This was the first time I had seen it put to this use, and never saw it used in that way again.

At the age of twelve those who had passed the Qualifying Examination and intended to stay on beyond the age of fourteen moved to the upper floor. Anyone who had obtained work was able to leave at the age of thirteen, the remainder continuing for another year. In my last year in school my class held four boys and six girls, of whom one boy and two girls eventually went to university. All had to take the same subjects, English, French, Latin, Science, History, Geography and Mathematics. One period a week was given to Art; a teacher travelled from Elgin on one day a week. She was a white haired lady: "Granny" Wallace, and seemed to spend most of the time gossiping in the various classrooms. For weeks we would draw a bottle or a box; linear exactitude and shading was all that was required by her, and anyone failing to reach the necessary standard had to erase the offending part and start over again. Only in the Infants was colour used by the pupils.

In the Higher Grade we had four male and one female teacher, the latter, who taught French, having a delightful sense of humour which made her classes a pleasure. Two of the men had returned from war service, the other two having been over age. For these two, "Sawney" who taught Science and the "Dodo" who taught Maths, I had little respect, and probably did not conceal it. Both were probably bored by teaching and devoted their energies to the Boys Scouts movement, both being scoutmasters. I was not a scout; I did not care for their activities and in any case my family could not afford the costs of uniforms, weekend camps and jamborees. Fortunately my friend Norman refused to join also, and as his father was a prosperous businessman, the accusation of poverty could not be made about him, and the references on this ground to me had to be muted. "Sawney" taught the science of the time of his training, forty years earlier. Just after the war, Harmsworth Press brought out the *New Universal Encyclopedia* in weekly parts, with good paper, print and illustrations, many in colour, and brother Jack bought it regularly. This I found absorbing reading and tried to introduce the things I had read into conversation at science time, to be told abruptly to shut up and learn what was in the text books, which were written long before Rutherford and almost before Darwin, for evolution was never mentioned, the "Garden of Eden" being taught in the classrooms in the lower school.

The other two men were completely different. Mr Buchan, a tiny man, was a graduate of Cambridge and now took us for English; and Mr Marr who taught History and Geography, had served as an officer in France. School for me took on a new aspect. Mr Marr brought matters alive with excursions at the weekend to the woods and moors, the seaside and the historic castles, introducing us to Natural History, Botany and other branches of learning. Mr Buchan did the equivalent in his field – literature and the arts. On a Friday evening in the winter he would have two or three of us to his lodgings, where we talked and drank lemonade and ate small apple tarts heated before his coal fire. Neither was ever referred to by any title but "Mister".

Mr Buchan advised me to buy the *Observer* regularly because of the literary pages, an injunction I have followed for more than half a century, in spite of difficulty when I was in the army or abroad. The editor then was a Mr J L Garvin whose leading articles sometimes required two full pages, and on these occasions on Monday morning Mr Buchan would greet me with a cheerful, "Well! Did you harvest all of the two acres?"

Like all youth, I gave little thought to the future and was happy to stay in school as long as possible, but this was not to be.

In January my father, now the sole wage earner, was brought home from work by horse cab and put to bed immediately. After a few days the doctor said that it was unlikely that he would ever be able to work again. I was now the oldest of the family at home, the four girls being married and in their own homes, none of them in the town. Jack had gone to the mahogany forests of Nigeria, and Bert was already three years in Demerara on the sugar plantations. Will had returned from Australia after demobilisation from the army, and worked for some time. But he was unsettled and followed Bert to British Guiana (now the republic of Guyana), but had then gone on to Canada. Working his way from the east to Vancouver he shipped as a sailor to New Zealand, and after a dozen years there returned to Brisbane. On the outbreak of war in 1939 he joined the army again and was discovered by his former major in New Guinea, and was returned to Australia where he served as an instructor until the end of the war.

Father would be entitled to sickness benefit for some weeks from his Friendly Society, but thereafter there would be no income, for he was still 8 years short of the pensionable age of 70. During his long service he had an excellent record, never having been late for work, and as a lifelong teetotaller, one of the few men to appear for work on New Year's Day, the great Scottish Saturnalia. Because of this he was granted a pension of ten shillings a week by the board of directors of the Highland Railway. Their generosity and consideration may have been influenced by the knowledge that in January of the following year they would lose their positions, and their company would be amalgamated with a dozen or more railways to form the London Midland and Scottish Railway, the largest firm and greatest employer in the country. Even so it was a very generous gesture.

My brothers undertook to help in various ways; one would pay the rent, another the rates, a third the fuel bills but it was urgent that I get some work that could, at least partly if not wholly, reduce the strain on our means.

There were few jobs for boys of my age [16 years old]. Employers liked to start new employees at the age of fourteen at the latest, so that their apprenticeship was completed before they were twenty, the usual marrying age for a working man. In any case, wages were based on years of experience so that I would have had to start work at a wage of 2s. 6d. [12½p.] a week, working with an apprentice of the same age but with two years experience behind him, and therefore getting more than double that figure.

Until the war had changed the pattern, a busy grocer or ironmonger might have a young lady at the cash desk, but the rest of the assistants would be male, except in bakers' shops, for much manual work was involved. Apart from jam, tinned fruit or tobacco, most food came in bulk and had to be made up in smaller quantities for the retail trade. The customers were mostly wives and daughters, and shopping was the main task of the middle and upper classes who attended to this in person and wanted to see what they were buying. Hams, butter, cheese, dried fruit and cereals were all laid out in the window or on marble slabs behind the counters. Cheese was normally delivered once a year, usually in the autumn, and was stored in the cellars for six months at least to allow it to mature. Much time was taken up each week in turning the casks and cases upside down. Sugar came in bags of 224 lbs, flour in sacks of 280 lbs, lard and butter in casks of 11 lbs.

The firms importing food during the war had to pack it in smaller units suitable for quick distribution near the battlefields, and when hostilities ceased they wanted to continue this practice as it gave them a larger element of profit, although it reduced the work of the retail trader and the need for strength in their assistants. This technological change was one additional element in the growth of unemployment. The small firms were conservative, the apprenticeship system encouraged adherence to the old methods of work, and they also began to decrease. Even as late as 1933, I visited a friend's bakery at New Pitsligo in Aberdeenshire, a county noted for the quality of the bakers and their products, and watched while the foreman weighed the ingredients for the special type of biscuit made, and concealed the weights in a paper bag, so that the men would not learn the recipe. When an apprentice in this trade was "time served" he had to move away to obtain a journeyman's job, hence the name. Each had a recipe book and any man with new lines and recipes was more likely to get a new post than one without.

When the millions of men all over the world were demobilised after four years of war, many of them had no experience of civilian work, and were free of the traditions of many occupations, and knew nothing of "craft secrets". They started with new ideas and new machines, and soon the craftsman had difficulty in getting the work he wanted and was trained for and which had made him unwilling to change his ways. Banks only engaged the sons of customers or potential customers, and the more prestigious professions, law, architecture, or estate management required a premium to be paid before taking on a boy at a minimal annual salary. In addition the parent had to bear the costs of examinations and diplomas. All these were closed to me, as were the universities for there were no state grants for students.

There was always the church but this held no appeal for me, although there were ample legacies for the support of divinity students for the six or seven years required to qualify for a "call". The supply of students was falling although the clergy were amongst the best paid people, especially in the rural areas. The manses were large and free, with incomes that could pay the staffs necessary to run them. These buildings can still be seen in the countryside with their fourteen rooms, large gardens and glebe lands. The rents of the latter substantially augmented the stipends.

Their power and influence was also waning, and the Empire and colonies, which formerly took many missionaries, were showing signs that they might in future prefer to have priests more akin in colour, temperament and religion. Many had observed during the war, but perhaps did not remark on it – except perhaps discreetly – that the "Nations Day of Prayer" was closely followed by a major offensive with the most appalling slaughter, as on the first day of the battle of the Somme when 80,000 thousand young men died, many of them from the North of Scotland, where the famous 51st (Highland) Division was recruited, and which, because of their courage, were used as the "storm troopers" of an attack.

My problem was solved when my father's former chief called to say that there was a vacancy for a railway clerk at Burghead and would, if desired, put my name forward. He said it might be some time before a vacancy arose anywhere nearer, and my name went forward. I travelled to Inverness to be interviewed and to sit a written examination. This was passed successfully and I returned for a medical examination. I left home on the morning train for Burghead, nine miles east as the crow flies but eleven miles by rail, necessitating a change at Alves Junction to the little branch train.

At the time my father took ill, my maternal grandfather Colin had to come and live with us, as he was no longer able to care for himself. Mother now had three invalids to look after, father, grandfather and Abbie who was also in poor health. When home at the weekend I spent some time with grandfather, as he was now bedfast. Like most old people he spoke much of the remote past, and I was able to tell mother much that she had never known.

His father and uncle were partners in a joinery and carpentry business of some size in Dingwall. Both also had a tavern or inn, and I later lived in the house in Hill Street, Dingwall which had been my grandfather's tavern. Colin Urquhart, for that was his name, had attended Dingwall Academy and at the age of fourteen had entered the family business, eventually being in charge of supplies and materials. This meant that he was responsible for unloading the cargoes of timber brought to Dingwall's little harbour, now silted up and a mile from the sea.

When around the age of twenty he was at the unloading of a half cargo of Baltic timber from a Swedish schooner, and had spent much time with the captain, drinking. When his father and uncle arrived at the end of the working day they found the work had fallen behind the time allocated, and a quarrel arose between Colin and his two seniors. These two left saying that they would return in two hours when they expected to see the ship cleared, but at the end of that time there were still some slings to be landed. The quarrel became more bitter and eventually Colin struck his uncle, and as the ship moved out he impulsively jumped aboard, to arrive next morning at

Nairn across the Moray Firth, with only a few pence. He never returned home nor made peace with his father who had married again after the death of Colin's mother, and Colin did not care for his stepmother. In the Highlands family disputes can run long and fierce and deep.

He settled in Nairn and lived by doing odd jobs, until he was employed by a Mr Loudon, who owned a hotel in Nairn and also farmed the land of Kildrummy Farm two miles west of Nairn. When necessary he acted as groom, and drove Ann Loudon, his employer's daughter to and from the farm and hotel, and to school. A faded photograph which he still possessed and gave me before his death, shows her as a very pretty girl, dressed in the fashionably military type of dress of the time, that of the Crimean War. He persuaded Ann to marry him, to the great displeasure of her father. He was not a good husband, and always acted like an irresponsible man of means, although he had none. Relations between Colin and his father-in-law became very bitter, so much so that Loudon sold his hotel and farm and left for the south, trying to persuade Ann to go with him, without avail. She died after four years of married life, her death certificate, which I was able to obtain, shows the cause as "pthisis", consumption of the lungs. Mother was three at the time, with a brother only a few months old.

Mother had always feared that she had been conceived out of wedlock, her mother seduced by her father's glib tongue and charm, and was delighted to find at the age of 70 that this was not so. To qualify for the Old Age Pension of ten shillings [50p.] she had to produce a birth certificate from the Register House in Edinburgh, and at the same time one of her mother's birth, death and marriage. She had always understood from her father that her grandfather Loudon's Christian name was Albert, and she had given this name to Abb.; now she found that it was properly David. She found also that she had celebrated her birthday two days early. Her father had never been reliable in any field.

At the age of sixteen, she was in Scots law "of age", and left her father, after seeing her brother and a half brother settled as pages, "living in", in mansion houses in the area.

Colin had married shortly after his first wife's death, and this wife had died in childbirth leaving a baby boy. Mother, who had loved her stepmother had now to leave school at the age of eleven to act as housekeeper and mother to the household. Her father's earnings were erratic as was his presence at home, and she recalled with gratitude the generosity of the fisherfolk of Nairn for their kindness and food. They were no more prosperous than her father but shared what they could.

Mother obtained a post with Mr Campbell of the Royal Hotel in Forres as a general maid in the hotel. He later asked her to emigrate to South Africa with him and his family, as children's maid, and this she accepted. His brother had returned from South Africa with the task of enrolling men in Britain for the newly formed South African Mounted Police.

Father had provisionally enrolled in this body, as had a number of other local men, for the pay offered was high by the standards prevailing at home. He had just finished duty at Forres station when mother alighted with her wooden chest, and he offered to carry this to her destination, which was just at hand. It gave them enough time, however, to be interested enough to arrange for a meeting on the following Sunday when she would be free for the afternoon. Within a week or two he withdrew his name from the list of men for South Africa, and later he discovered that his new friend had decided that she did not want to emigrate either. They were married within a few weeks, and mother, always the romantic, claimed, to our jeers and laughter, that they "were intended for each other, and if they had not met in Scotland, they would have met in South Africa".

Among old Colin's memories of Nairn, were that of his friendship with a veteran of the Napoleonic Wars who, having lost a leg at Waterloo, was taken to Nairn by his officer on his retiral after the war. His name was Paddy Brooman and the officer's name was Captain Grant. A Captain Grant, born in Nairn, and whose father had fought at Waterloo, together with Speke discovered and quarrelled over the source of the Nile. They may have been related, but this link is now unlikely to be traced.

Grandfather died before the summer was out, aged ninety.

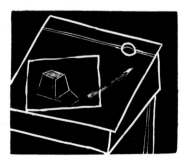

FIRST EMPLOYMENT

Burghead had been a thriving little town and fishing port, with its herring packing yards giving work to the women while the men followed the shoals, but it was now in desperate straits. The herrings, packed in barrels with salt had been shipped to the Baltic ports to feed the peasants of Latvia and Poland. These countries were now in the hands of Russia, with which Britain scarcely had relations, and there were no alternative markets. In any case the herring had changed their breeding grounds as they had done several times since the Hanseatic League had developed this trade. The little wooden steam drifters were tied up in the harbours round the coast, and all the ancillary industries, coaling, repairing, net makers and others were also idle.

Although I did not recall it I had stayed a few weeks there when Abbie had to bathe in salt water twice a day – without effect of course. I found later that our then host "Davity Dey", skipper of the F.V. *Provost*, remembered me and I had an immediate friend. To the west stretched nine miles of the cleanest and most beautiful beach in Scotland. In summer the town became busy with tourists, a welcome addition to the meagre incomes of the shops and landladies. When we had been there ten years earlier the most favoured ornament of the fisherman's mantelpiece was a glass jam jar filled with golden sovereigns, while the bed that graced the same living room was as often as not gold plated.

Always a religious people, the fishers had turned most zealously to the form of religion known as "revivalist". There were prayer meetings daily, and sometimes oftener. Each Saturday I went home and so never saw the gatherings at the harbour in the afternoon, when fervour was whipped up almost to frenzy by visiting preachers. The chief revivalist was a fisherman, Jock Troup, who later emigrated to the Promised Land of all religious zealots, California, where he made a great name for himself and an even greater fortune. At these meetings the listeners would run to their homes, returning laden with the signs of sin, gramophones and records, melodeons, violins, high heeled shoes and one time dance frocks. With these a great bonfire was made to shouts of "Hallelujah" and "Praise the Lord".

On my arrival I reported to Mr Campbell, the stationmaster who escorted me to my new chief, Frank Milne, at the freight station some little distance away on a little spur line ending in the harbour. There he left me, not a word having been said by him except to tell me to accompany him to the office. After a short talk Frank took me to my "digs" which were to be with his mother-in-law, Mrs Anderson. She was a pleasant motherly woman, who showed me my bedroom and asked if it was satisfactory. The thought of a bedroom of my own was very much so. I was then told that this luxury would cost me £1 a week which must have made my face fall, for my salary was to be 13s. 6d. [67p.] a week, and the thought that I would have to receive aid from home of 6s. 6d. [33p.] was a matter of concern. Frank took his mother-in-law aside, and returned with a satisfactory agreement. If I would travel home each weekend, share a bed with her son, and take my meals in the kitchen-living room the cost would be 13 shillings [65p.]. The other two lodgers were a bank teller and the owner of a drapery shop.

I was embarrassed next morning when I went downstairs for breakfast to find a girl still in bed in the living room. She was the daughter, Rose, a rather pretty girl of around twenty, who had left domestic service to return home. Many residents of fishing villages were unwilling to leave home for work, and she and her sister, Frank's wife were among them. Later Frank had to leave the railway as his wife did not want to move with him. Every morning I was there, while I ate my breakfast Rose lay in bed with her head covered by blankets. This meant that I ate hurriedly and left the house as soon as possible. Although I was brought up with four sisters and various nieces, we were very prudish and I had never seen them anything but fully dressed. The girls had a dressing table in their room, marble topped, with flower patterned water ewer and hand basin. The males washed at the kitchen sink, often sharing it with the dishes of the meals that had been eaten by those up earlier for work.

I had little work to do, for the cessation of fishing had been accompanied by the end of the cargo trade. The large chemical works had been closed at the beginning of the war, as the raw material had been imported from enemy countries, and it had never started up again. The line fishermen had better fortune for there was always a demand for good white fish but they had been overtaken by the men at Lossiemouth. There some progressive man had introduced the French seine net, and also modern motor boats with the new diesel engines. These boats were faster and cheaper to run than the motor engined craft of Burghead, which used petrol.

One of the natives of the village had lost a leg in the Navy, and started up as a fish salesman. These salesmen not only sold the fish landed, but also supplied stores, and this one became an agent for "RVO", the trade name for Russian Vaporising Oil. It was cheaper, and apparently just as good as the petrol available. But trade with Russia was a political issue, and the *Daily Express* reporters and photographers swarmed about the harbour. Even I was interviewed but as I knew nothing about it my name did not appear in print.

The fishing community were very close knit, and this was first obvious to me when early in my service the office was filled by men in their thick blue jerseys, many still wearing their sea boots. The table and the floor were occupied when the two chairs were taken. The leader was "Jock Ash", and he took command. I was instructed to take a note of all that he said. First a list of their names, or tee names, for most of the population were Ralphs, Mains or Mackenzies. A few of the tee names were Blucher, Toopah and Blowhard. One stood out – "Annie's Bella's Willie". Nearly all were inter-married and all shared a few boats. The owner might have ten shares, because he would be responsible for repairs, fuel etc. and the shares of the others varied depending on the relationship. Opposite each name I entered the number of shares and announced the total. This was discussed and agreed to. Then the cost of the wagon of mussels from a Fife port was put down, plus the cost of the rail freight. Postages, telegrams and some other items were added. This total was divided by the number of baskets unloaded from the vehicles into each boat, to arrive at the cost of each basket, and finally this was multiplied by the number of shares. It was a long process with much examining of figures and argument. At last agreement was reached, and Jock collected the money from each. I expected some reward for my work, but all left without a word of thanks. The attitude was that this was the work I could do, therefore I did it. If I had needed any help from them, they would have given it on the same terms. But it meant that I was accepted, and could join any group at the harbour or go on board any boat.

I was frequently asked to go fishing, but as the hours of return were uncertain I could not take the risk of landing in the morning at Lossiemouth or Buckie, if they thought the price there might be higher.

I did spend one night at sea fishing but it was an unfortunate experience. I made friends with a boy from South Africa, his father being a native of Burghead and home on holiday. Our mentor was the young fisherman known as "Kruger", who had lost an eye on war service, and who had been one of the men who sailed a number of drifters to Canada after the war. These had been sold and had to be delivered to the buyers in Canada. It was quite a daring voyage for few of the skippers had been much out of sight of land, and had little knowledge of navigation. It was said that several only used a school atlas. I had said something along that line to one of the skippers, but his reply was that "If you kept straight on west it was a difficult place to miss".

Paul, Kruger and myself set out in the little row boat in the evening, and at a reasonable distance from shore cast our lines baited with mussels. We found we were in a shoal of mackerel, and caught so many that our bait was finished. Kruger drew pieces of blue wool from his seaman's jersey, and the fish took this as willingly as the bait. In the excitement we forgot both the time and the rising wind, and it was darkening as we prepared to row back to harbour. One of the oars was lost in trying to fit them in their rowlocks, and our captain tried to scull us home. It was a difficult operation, and anyone more intelligent than our oarsman would have been anxious. But he was cheerful while I was very sick and sorry. It was long after midnight when we made the harbour, where a small crowd was waiting for us. In Scotland there was no sale for mackerel as it was not eaten there, and the few fish that we had managed to keep from being washed overboard were contemptuously thrown into the harbour for the seagulls.

I found that I had no fixed hours of work, as Frank ran a little card playing school in the office at night, and I was expected to keep watch for the local policeman, who was new to the place and had a reputation as a law enforcer. I found that he rarely left his home after his evening mealtime. The game played was Nap, the maximum stake being a halfpenny. Rarely more than half a dozen men attended at a time, none being fishermen, half, however, being "drivers" as the single-handed engineers of drifters were called. All except Frank had been deep water sailors with a fund of stories and jokes, most of them of a bawdy nature. There seems to be some truth in the saying that a sailor has a wife or equivalent in every port.

It had been more than a year since a cargo vessel had called, but now word came that a German ship was due with timber. With disuse the harbour had silted at the entrance, and the harbourmaster, Captain Taylor, decided to give clearance to this ship in order to clear the shoal. He said that he had no scruples about his action, as his ship had been torpedoed by the Germans during the war.

It was a most interesting operation to an ignoramus in nautical matters like myself. The ship was held up until conditions were right, then signalled to enter, when it immediately went aground. By hauling and warping and other means it was turned at a right angle, then with the grinding of windlasses, the threshing of the propeller and much shouting and running about it was brought to its berth.

Unloading proceeded night and day, with work for a great many men. All the timber had to go forward by rail and we also were very busy. My job was to weigh the trucks empty and then full, and make out the invoices.

There was much of interest in Burghead besides the people; it had been a fort used by the Romans, and centuries later the Vikings had occupied it, being finally driven out in 1014 AD their last foothold on the mainland of Scotland. On the Doorie Hill, which overlooked the harbour, stood the Doorie Pot where the clavie was deposited after being carried round the street on the shoulder of the hereditary captain. The "Burning of the Clavie" took place on 12 January each year, its origin in some pagan festival having been lost. It was a barrel filled with Archangel tar and set on fire, parts of the burning barrel had to be thrown in to doors left open, to bring good luck to the occupier.

Below the Doorie Hill was a steep path leading to the Roman Well, a manmade cavern with a pool of water. Around the hill are the remains of the wood and stones used as a defence by the earliest inhabitants.

My personal interest, great as it was in these remains, was in the two steam locomotives attached to the station, striking in their green with gold lettering. They were 4.4.0 outside cylinder tank engines of an exotic appearance. Made in Glasgow for the Uruguayan Eastern Railroad in 1888, they had never been paid for by that company and had been bought by the Highland Railway. One left in the morning to haul the branch trains, while the other stayed for shunting duties, which were now minimal. The crews were glad of my company, for they could not leave their engines unmanned, and I was taught to drive them, an experience that is unequalled to my mind by any other form of transportation.

During my stay there was only one entertainment, a church concert to which I went with one or two of the youths of my own age. I did not spend any money apart from a few pence and despite that I was able to keep company with my friends for they had no money at all, nor had their parents.

In addition to two bakeries, a grocer, a draper and a butcher, there were forty-four houses selling groceries from their kitchens to the neighbours in an attempt to survive. An Elgin wholesale firm sent each week one or two large boxes addressed to "The Stationmaster". I had to open these and arrange for the lorry to deliver the packages to the addresses on them. This was the cheapest way of getting the goods delivered as one consignment, while a penny was added by the station for each one delivered. It was my job to collect these accounts at the end of the month. The largest account was for threepence, and the housewife had to ask me to call at the end of the week when she hoped to have payment for the groceries purchased from her. Yet there was no complaining, no banners or demonstrations, just a grave acceptance of their poverty.

I called on a drifter skipper for the freight charge of nearly £1 on some boxes of "kutch" an oriental bark, with which they boiled their nets to preserve them. He examined the bill and handed it back to me. "Bo'r" he said: "You will have to tell Mr Campbell that he will have to trust in God for this money for I have none". It would have been undoubtedly a difficult message for Mr Campbell to pass on to the accountants in the head office. But no matter how long it took it would be paid. During the Second World War the boatbuilders along the coast were being paid for vessels built twenty years earlier, now lost or broken up, and the amounts written off the builders books.

While it was a hard life for the men it must have been harder for their wives, for the line boats still used the "gratlins", or great lines to catch fish. These lines were up to a mile in length, with a hook every few inches, and they had to be baited every time the boat sailed. The wives and daughters could be seen sitting outside their homes on the ground, fixing pieces of mussel to the hooks, carefully winding the lines in loops on bent covered flat baskets. The hour depended on the times of the tides.

The drifters had been part of the Navy in the First World War, the rank of "skipper" being brought in to use. Few of them talked of their experiences, although their work was as dangerous as any. Only one, more talkative than most fishers, was always willing to spin a yarn. One I recollect was of the time he was on a freighter taking munitions and a deck cargo of motor lorries to Murmansk for the Russians, who were still fighting the Germans. The convoy system had not yet been introduced and his ship sailed alone. A day or two out a German U-boat had surfaced and the crew were told to abandon ship as the German was to sink the vessel by gunfire.

This would allow him to preserve his torpedoes for more dangerous approaches.

The crew took to the boats and pulled away to rest on their oars at a safe distance and waited for the sinking. The third shell penetrated the hold with explosives and the ship blew up with terrific force. Some of the lorries were thrown high in the air, and fell on the submarine damaging the hull so that the Germans had to be picked up by the British seamen until a destroyer took them all back to Scapa Flow. I later asked some of his friends if his story was true, but they simply smiled and told me to ask Jock, as it well might be.

The porter at the passenger station was known as "Whizz Bang" because of his volatile nature. He had been in his younger days a yeoman of signals in the Navy, and he told a tale of the war. He was in the habit of watching the many warships in the Firth, and read their flag and Aldis lamp signals with ease. On this occasion the message to the Coastguard station on the Doorie Hill was to get a motor car to come immediately from Elgin and take an officer of high rank to Inverness to catch the night express to London. A pinnace did arrive in harbour and a gentleman entered the car now awaiting him and they drove off. Whizz Bang claimed that something important was afoot, for the officer was the Admiral of the Fleet. His news was received with the usual disbelief that his tales aroused. A few days later the newspapers released the sensational and to many the alarming news, that Count Louis Battenberg, the Admiral of the Fleet and a cousin of the King, had been relieved of his command. He was German by birth and name but was a true and loyal Briton. A press campaign, politically inspired had accused him of treachery. Retiring into private life he changed his name to Mountbatten, and his son became an outstanding admiral in the next world war.

Another freighter arrived from Sweden with timber, giving welcome employment to the ever growing number of unemployed men. Work went on night and day until the cargo was discharged and loaded on the railway wagons. I had scarcely ever met a foreigner before, and these men were very pleasant and hospitable. Within a fortnight a third arrived, a very peculiar vessel called a "Q" ship, designed during the war to deceive enemy submarines. The bow and the stern were identical so if stationary an observer could not know in which direction it would sail. It would float idly as if its engines had failed, and if a submarine emerged to shoot this easy target, the vessel would start quickly and drop its sides to expose an armament of guns manned and ready to fire. It was the *Curlew*. The name remains in my memory for there were three Adeni firemen aboard.

Three tales come to mind, two historical the third personal. Travellers frequently left papers and magazines in trains, and many guards collected these, sometimes getting a copper or two. One magazine I got for a penny was the *American Geographic Magazine*, which I had heard of but never seen. It had a full page advertisement from the Pennsylvania Railroad Company telling of the attractions on its route, with a map of the system. There was a coupon to fill and post, but I added a letter asking train times and fares from New York to its Western terminus at Harrisburg and returning via Washington and Philadelphia to New York.

Some weeks later on my return home for the weekend mother said that a man had called on Wednesday to see me and was returning this Saturday at 3 o'clock. She thought it must be important because he wore a bowler hat and had a brown flat case full of papers.

I did not have to wait long before a knock was heard at the door and I answered. It was the man for he had his brief case open and glanced at it while sorting something out. "Could I see your father?" he enquired. I replied that I thought he wanted to see me. He looked surprised. "Are you A.H. Forbes?" I said I was. "Did you", he said, his face darkening, "write the Pennsylvania Railroad in America?" I said I did and hastened to add that I intended to make the journey but at present I could not afford it. His mood changed and he laughed. "You little devil ... I've come twice from Aberdeen for this. But if you ever go don't forget Munros of Aberdeen." I assured him I would not and with that he left saying that he was only acting for Thomas Cook & Sons and could claim his expenses for the journey.

Burghead Goods station had at one time been a passenger station, the terminus of the branch line until it was extended to Hopeman, and the telegraph instrument had been left in position. I decided to learn to operate this, although it was not necessary to do so in a Goods office. This telegraph was of an early type, the single needle instrument. The needle, like that in a compass was pivoted in the centre and was fixed to the face of the wooden stand. To the left and right of the needle tip was affixed a "sounder", a piece of tin, each sounder being a different note. The left hand was the equivalent of the dot of the Morse code, and the right hand sound the dash. It was slightly faster than the buzzers of the Post Office and military and navy. The chief advantage, when there was more than one instrument in an office was that the operator could distinguish one instrument from another by the notes.

All of the 161 stations on the system were connected to the Central Office in Inverness, and it was noted there that I was becoming a competent operator. There was a shortage of "reliefmen", and one was required at Orton station over Christmas 1922 when the clerk had leave to be married, and I was instructed to report there for the fortnight. This was a stroke of luck in two ways; firstly I was transferred to the operating side which I would have chosen if I could, for I did not like the idea of spending my working life sitting at a desk all day; secondly, while on relief work I would get a lodging allowance of £2. 12s. 6d. each week, if I could not return daily to my home station, which was Burghead. As I had to report at Orton each morning at 8 a.m. this was not possible as the first train on the branch was later than this. With an income of £3. 6s. at the age of sixteen I was indeed wealthy, if only for a fortnight. This was as much as a passenger guard or signalman got. I travelled every morning the 20 miles from my home at Forres to Orton, and back by the last train, taking a flask of tea and sandwiches for there would be no chance of getting food at the station, as there was no village.

It was a "block" station, at the west end of the bridge over the River Spey, and controlled the section to Mulben, three miles of very uphill track. The outlook from the station looking towards the Spey and the Moray Firth was beautiful, although there was little traffic. The stationmaster was also the postmaster, and used a room in his house for the post office. The morning I arrived the newspapers had reports about John Reith being made general manager of the British Broadcasting Company, and the success of the regular BBC broadcasts The stationmaster, Mr Grant, a handsome bearded West Highlander, after I had introduced myself, asked if I had heard the broadcast. I had not of course, but he had and told me fully of it. A friend nearby was an amateur radio operator and had invited Mr Grant to listen to his reception, which had been very good.

Later in the day Mr Grant asked if I knew how the radio signals were sent and I had to admit ignorance. He then told me that he was one of the first to send a wireless signal, if not the first. About 1870 he was posted to the Telegraph Office in Inverness as a telegraphist. At that time the trains in the Highlands were despatched from a station by a telegram from Inverness. A copy was given to the driver who had to sign the original with the time read, and the guard also read it. On the line north from Inverness there was one difficulty. At the Ness Viaduct which carried the track across the Caledonian Canal, there was a swing bridge that had to be raised to let ships enter the canal and each time the telegraph line had to be disconnected. When the railway extended only 22 miles north to Dingwall with only six or seven trains a day, this did not cause much interference with timekeeping, but as the line extended slowly to Wick and Strome Ferry the matter became serious.

The Telegraph Engineer, a Mr Summerfield whose brother held a similar post in Aberdeen for the Post Office, placed a small copper plate on either side of the canal, and when the line was cut sent a signal across the space, having reinforced the Leclanche cells which produced the electricity. This was successful as long as the weather was dry, but when it rained the sails became wet and blocked the electric spark. Eventually a cable had to be laid across the bottom of the canal.

It was learned later that an obscure country schoolmaster in Aberdeenshire had been able to send a signal from one room to another, but at that time no Morse had been invented.

Many years later I was talking after luncheon and mentioned this experiment on the railway and found that it aroused great interest. I had to write a report for the Scottish office, and made a recorded talk for the BBC, the Canadian Broadcasting Company and also an American company. The weather was very pleasant for winter, and I was able to climb the steep hill above the station to get a most extensive view of the coast as far as Caithness in the clear frosty weather. Mr Grant was a delightful boss; he had been rowed from the Islands to Strome Ferry to join the railway, and his first task had been to learn English, as Gaelic had been his native tongue.

The fortnight passed very pleasantly and for the first time I was able to buy a Christmas present for my parents, and new clothes for myself. I was only back in Burghead for a few weeks when I was transferred to Orbliston Junction, the station to the west of Orton. On the first day of January in that year the Highland Railway was incorporated in the new London Midland and Scottish Railway, which brought great changes.

ORBLISTON JUNCTION

Orbliston Junction was first named Fochabers Station, the village of that name being three miles away, but it was the station for Gordon Castle, the home of the Duke of Richmond and Gordon, one of the greatest landowners in Britain and a leading member of both the Scots and English Peerages. When it was decided to build a branch line to a point opposite the Castle, the new station was named Fochabers, and the original station renamed Orbliston Junction, the name of an adjoining farm of around 1,000 acres – one of the largest in Moray.

The station had three platforms, and the stationmaster's house was above the station proper. There were also three cottages , two for the porter signalmen, and one for the foreman surfaceman, as platelayers were called on the Highland Railway. The station no longer exists.

The stationmaster was a John Shorthouse, referred to always as Shorty because he was tall and slim. He was clever but erratic and temperamentally unreliable. He was also intemperate in his drinking habits, and was spoken of as a difficult boss, but on the whole I got on quite well with him.

There were two men attached to the station, John Mann and Atholl Clark, who worked alternate shifts extending from 6 a.m. to 10 p.m. I found my hours were from 7 a.m. until the last train left, which was normally about nine o'clock. While the hours seemed long there was nowhere to go, and I was free to do what I liked between trains, although apart from reading there was little choice of entertainment or pastime. But my first problem was lodgings; my predecessor had lived at Blackburn Croft within easy walking distance of the station. He had resigned from the service, an action almost unheard of in that time of unemployment. I learned later that he was afflicted by a mild religious mania and was more affected by the supposed immorality of his landlady than by the squalor and dirt in which he had to live.

Mrs Boag was a faded, untidy, grey haired lady of uncertain age, and his suspicions must have been more in his mind than supported by any visible evidence. She had long ceased to cultivate the six acres of ground, and regularly received notices to quit from the Duke's factor, which she regularly put in the fire without reading. She was obviously physically unable to cultivate the ground and with farms going out of cultivation because of an inability to make a profit, she could not pay someone to work the land for her.

Her main income, apart from her lodger, was from payments she received for keeping three boys, who were in the care of the Glasgow Corporation. So great was the problem of children in need of care in that city, that it had a staff continually scouring the country to get homes, especially for the less normal children. One of the "boys" was actually a full grown man about 10 years older than myself, a hulking red head of limited intelligence and an abhorrence of any type of work. His vade-mecum was a Victorian book, *The Locomotive Engineers Handbook*, probably one of the earliest works of its kind. His declared ambition was to be a railway engine driver, but without having to go through the stages of cleaner and then fireman, which could take twenty years.

There was no alternative to living there. If I had had a bicycle I could perhaps have found something within three miles, but it was unlikely to be much better, although it would have a good chance of being cleaner. It was with reluctance that I moved my case into the little room which I had to share with Jock. There was room for a bed and a rickety chair, on which I could place my clothes at night, for the floor was of earth and even in summer cold to the bare feet.

There were two other rooms, one serving as kitchen, living room and bedroom for Mrs Boag and the two younger boys, both of whom were named George, one "Little" and the other "Big" although there was not a notable difference in their heights. The other room was kept locked, for she was always hopeful that a fashionable couple with money would rent it for a considerable sum and thus advance her economic circumstances. This faith was perhaps one of the things that let her bear the unending drudgery of her life. I never knew if there had been a Mr Boag.

Inside a doorway was a bench with a pail of water and an old saucer for soap. I did place my soap in it once, only to find that it had been pecked to the ground by the hens that wandered everywhere, and eaten by one of the young pigs, which seemed to be more often free than constrained. It was a frequent necessity when having a meal, to kick away one or two pigs trying to eat my shoelaces. The water had to be carried from a spring a considerable distance away, requiring the crossing of the Blackburn stream by two planks laid side by side, and which in the frequent winter spates were washed away. There was no other facility of any kind except a number of ramshackle sheds, harbouring poultry, pigs, rats and heaven knows what else, for I never ventured into one of them.

The one saving grace was that it was cheap, 13 shillings [65p.] a week, and within a month my salary increased to 17s. 6d. [87p.] a week, so that now I had a margin over bare subsistence. In January darkness extended over 16 hours a day, and I made my way through the rough fields, guided by the red light of the distant signal, and reaching that, stumbled along the railway track to the station.

On my first day I realised that the station was not run on orthodox lines, for returning from a skimpy meal I was given a very detailed briefing of what to do when the freight train arrived in a short time. I had first to find the destination of any coal trucks on the train, and to note specially if there was one for a certain distillery and if there was, to ignore everything else. I had then to watch from the office window the behaviour of the engine crew and the guard, after the necessary shunting had been done, and the engine recoupled to the train. At this point Shorty and John would engage in conversation with the train crew, which would get animated and noisy. While this was going on I had to stand on the truck buffers and throw as much of the coal as possible on to the track, and then retreat swiftly to the office, and pull off the "Starting" signal. The train should then pull away.

Everything happened as planned; the shouting stopped, the engine whistled and the guard ran towards the approaching guards van to jump in. The foreman surfaceman then appeared with a wheel barrow, the coal was collected and distributed to the four houses.

The train men were zealous trade unionists and supporters of Ramsay Macdonald the Labour leader and later Prime Minister. Shorty and John simply abused the politician in order to rouse the tempers of the train crew. The distillery for which the coal was destined had a private siding, so that the coal did not pass through a station yard to be weighed and the loss of coal discovered.

Within weeks I was involved in an incident which exemplified the power and prestige of the upper class.

The Highland Railway, running as it did, through an area with no industry, would not have been built without the interest of the landowners. In fact the 14 miles from Golspie to Helmsdale was built by the Duke of

Sutherland, and the great curve inland from Helmsdale to Wick, 66 miles long, was built to suit the Duke through whose land it ran, and for most of its route served only the shooting lodges of his estate, which comprised more than a million acres of moors and lochs. The Duke had his own engine, stationed at Golspie near his castle of Dunrobin, and used to drive it himself. It was last used to take King Alfonso of Spain to the castle, the king himself being at the controls for a period. This was shortly before he lost his throne.

For this reason the landed gentry were very influential, paying great attention to those engaged by the company. One well known director, Fletcher of Rosehaugh, in the Black Isle, insisted that anyone considered for a job in the operating section had to visit him for an interview before he was employed. As a result the lairds and their families and indeed their workers were fawned upon, for a complaint would earn a warning from headquarters, not only aimed at the offended but also the stationmaster. The gamekeepers, already high in the hierarchy, were known to require very great attention. The opinion among the railwaymen was that "the factor is worse than the lord".

The Navy had built a little village north of Invergordon, mostly for officers and their wives. It stood a mile or so from the railway, and on one occasion an officer with good local connections arrived at the little station halt as the train drew away. The porter had no control of the train, and could do nothing to delay it. The officer was furious and demanded to know why the station was so far away from his home. The porter, a simple local youth was puzzled by the question, and answered that he thought it was because the company wanted it to be beside the railway track. It was an innocent answer, but passing through Inverness on the following train, several hours later, the offended officer called on the Traffic Manager, insisting that he had been treated "insolently", and the offending youth was dismissed. Like many of the staff in isolated places he was not a member of a union.

At Orbliston the local patrician was the Duke of Richmond and Gordon, who had never acted in such a way, but the same deference was given to anyone connected with him. Two of his daughters, the Duchess of Northumberland and Lady Violet Brassey, whose husbands were considered to be among the wealthiest men in Britain, were staying at Lochindorb Castle with Lord Joucey, and decided to spend a day visiting their old father at Fochabers, and chose to travel by train. They were driven to Nairn station, the stationmaster, Mr Sim being advised of their intentions. He and a porter met the car at the entrance, with two first class single tickets ready for them, and stood with them until the train arrived and they were seated in a suitable compartment. One of the ladies had a small Pekinese dog tucked under her arm, but it was thought diplomatic not to mention that it would also require a ticket, costing sevenpence. When the train left, Mr Sim sent to telegraph Brodie station, where all tickets were checked, to inform them of the two distinguished passengers so that they would not be disturbed.

Mr Sim and his booking clerk had a long standing private war, which got more vicious and petty as the months passed, and the clerk pointed out that he had received no money for the tickets and that a dog ticket had to be issued. His boss paid the personal fares, although the practice was to send an account to the Estate Office, which was against the rules.

But the "Dodger" was still dissatisfied and insisted that a telegram be sent to Brodie, eight miles ahead, and the first checking station. For stereotyped messages there was a code book which reduced the message to two or three words. To assure the travellers of proper treatment their names were given. All messages could be heard on every instrument on the circuit, and Brodie took the wiser course of writing across the telegram form when received "Train delay if acted upon" and passed the message to Mosstowie, twelve miles ahead, who repeated the process and telegraphed Orbliston. The ladies had to alight there to join the branch train, and there was no escape for us. Mr Shorthouse informed me that he was feeling unwell, and was withdrawing to his house to rest, and was not to be disturbed for anything less than the explosion of the locomotive's boiler, a most unlikely occurrence. He then left, pointing to the telegram in my hand.

Collecting "excess" fares was everyday work at a junction, and I carefully wrote out the necessary paper ticket in anticipation and waited until the train arrived. It was easy to identify the two ladies, as such were rare on the platforms of wayside stations, but were glimpsed with awe within the first class compartments of trains. Both wore long fur coats which almost swept the ground, had tweed skirts, and fine upper garments with a string of pearls around their necks, and were bare headed. At home in North Street a lady was recognised by the fact that she wore a hat, and not a shawl, but the smooth delicate skins, the faint blush of the cheeks and the ripe red lips were something I had never seen at such close quarters. I was seventeen, a very susceptible age, and walking in close contact with such visions affected me deeply. I thought of the words, "exotic, esoteric, ethereal" and probably would have thought of "erotic" if I had known what it meant.

I knew instinctively that I did not address them as we did ordinary people, "wifie" for the local women, or "missus" for strangers. Trotting beside them, I repeated "Please ma'am! Sevenpence for the dog" but they ignored me completely. I had never heard before "the accents of the ascendancy" as John later described it, and only comprehended the word "papa"; radio, television, and theatre were still in the future for me. Entranced as I was, my duty was clear, the money must be obtained. We were now approaching the little branch train, with its one coach, only one compartment of which was marked "First Class". I threw myself before the door, and extended my arms to full width, and demanded in clear tones: "Please ma'am, sevenpence for the dog – or I can't let you go in the train".

There was an astonished pause, and then a stare of Medusa-like intensity, and a hand was drawn across my face, not a blow and certainly not a caress, and then a voice compounded of shock and wrath, such as I have never since heard. "Get out of my way, you little bastard".

I am not certain whether I staggered aside or not, but they entered the train and left. Dismayed but undefeated I informed Fochabers that the money had to be collected by them as it was refused at Orbliston. We learned later from Angus, the branch train guard, that the stationmaster, Mr George Fyffe, had paid the sevenpence himself.

It may be of some interest to say more of the peerage and aristocracy for they were important then. The Duke of Richmond and Gordon had been, I think, married three times, all his wives predeceasing him, and he developed a belief that all three had been poisoned. Thenceforth he cooked his own food on a portable paraffin burning stove which accompanied him everywhere. It may have been a year or two later when he decided to go south by train, and we were advised of this. I was told to keep a sharp lookout for him, and see that he was properly seated, as the express was a long train and could not be covered adequately by Shorty alone. When the branch train arrived I saw a tall, portly gentleman in black with a bowler hat, and went towards him. He did not walk towards the main line platform but went to help an old gentleman who had emerged and was trying to take a large odd shaped package out of the compartment. The packet was wrapped in old newspapers tied with an assortment of pieces of string. I was impressed by the Duke's consideration for this frail person, probably a former employee. He wore a very long coat, and also a bowler hat, very old and dusty, below which his long white hair emerged. I helped the "duke" to carry the package, which I still did not recognise as a cooking stove, for I had not yet learned of his idiosyncrasy. The express drew in, and I opened the door of the nearest first class compartment politely, but was surprised to see the tall gentleman climb in and draw the package inside, then descend and help the old gentleman to mount and seated him in the corner. I closed the door, but had to open it again to let the valet, for it was he, dismount and go to the nearest third class coach.

More important, and more demanding than the Duke was the factor, the estate manager. Friday morning was the busiest day of the week, for this was Market Day in Elgin, and almost all travel was still by train. The factor was a regular traveller and, as one of the privileged, took a seat in the office awaiting the main line train; there was usually a fifteen minutes wait. He was very affable and talkative, pot-bellied and walrus moustached, in heavy tweed plus-fours; he looked like a stage squire or retired colonel. His talk was always of the peerage and the class of society he enjoyed on his trips to London.

It was all beyond my ken, but I recall him telling of one of the earliest Labour MPs, a Will Cook, who had been a docker and active in some famous strike of the past. According to the factor, Mr C. was now the darling of society, every duchess hastening to have him to dinner as a new variety of human being, which no hostess could afford to miss. He was famed as a wit, but it appeared that one joke was sufficient to carry him through the "season" – a different period from the "grouse season" of which we heard and knew so much.

He told of the father whose son had been "sent down" from Cambridge, and who was now ready to be introduced to society, the first necessary step or qualification being the art of drinking port, at that time apparently the only suitable beverage. On his first night at home the boy had to remain with his father at the dining table, while the lady withdrew, and a fair amount of port was drunk by father and son. Finally the father said, "Now, my boy at this stage you must watch the candles carefully, and when you see those two candles on the sideboard become four, it is time to stop". "Papa," replied the son, "there *is* only one candle". It took me some time to see the joke, and it is one of the few I have not repeated, until now.

Orbliston was a difficult station to operate efficiently; it was a junction, with a branch train to complicate movements. The section from the west was six miles long, with the manned halt at Lhanbryde in the middle. We had no information as to how long a freight train might have to halt there, or if the passenger train stood for more than the regulation two minutes. From the east the gradient fell very steeply with fast running. The Keith drivers prided themselves on keeping punctually to the "running timetable" and one in particular, Mackintosh, the "Madman" liked to do the three miles in three minutes start to stop. This meant a very fast arrival at Orbliston and hard braking. In addition the view of the line was obscured by a road overbridge, where the line curved. It was thus necessary if a freight was too long at Lhanbryde, for it to be shunted out of the way to allow two passenger trains "crossing".

There were no telephones on the railway and all communication was by telegraph, a much slower means of communication. Theoretically we could get instructions from Inverness, but writing the messages, calling for attention, and waiting for a reply could take several minutes, making the delays worse. While the "tablet" (instruments which controlled the entry of trains in to a section) were my responsibility in the office, the points and signals were controlled by two signal boxes, one porter signalman operating both when it was necessary. These were a considerable distance apart. The whole nine miles we controlled were on a steadily increasing gradient, which slowed heavy freight down trains, and accelerated, up trains, of all kinds.

I soon learned that Shorty was an alcoholic although he was able to conceal this to a great extent. He had been able to prevent his wife learning of this until he had been married some time. He had been appointed company representative in Glasgow, and moved among the business people there and eventually married the only daughter of one of the leading warehousemen in that city. On her marriage her father had settled on her £365 a year, paid quarterly, a very large sum, almost twice her husband's salary of £200 per annum plus a ten percent "aggregation" which covered any emergency calls. Although I had to work long hours, Shorty stuck religiously to his forty-eight hours a week, except when "called out", which I did rarely.

Because of the influence of his father-in-law, he got the post of stationmaster earlier than was normal, and had been in Orbliston some years. At the end of the first quarter year of her marriage, his wife received a cheque for £93 and asked her husband to cash it at the nearest bank, which was at Fochabers. He left on his bicycle hurriedly, removing only his uniform coat and hat but wearing the bottle green trousers of the company. He did not return overnight, and next morning John cycled to the police station to try and trace him. The police found him in a public house in

Cullen, and returned him in a taxi, which had to wait for payment as no money was found on the occupant, and his wife was so distraught and concerned that she could not find her purse.

It was unfortunate that John Mann was also an alcoholic, but a seasoned one, whose wife kept control much better than young Mrs Shorthouse could. John was well educated and was reputed to have acted as a teacher in his native Brora. He knew Latin, and more Greek than I did, but he was now ageing and that along with his years of addiction to alcohol were taking their toll. Pay day was every second Thursday. John's home was only yards away from the office, and when he was on early shift his wife waited outside until he got his pay packet, which came off the train in the morning, and took it from him. It amounted to £4. 16s. [£4.80], although there was occasionally a few pence more from overtime when the last train was very late. Of this John got 2s. 6d. [12½p.], and immediately after his lunch he mounted his bicycle and cycled to Fochabers, where he spent it in a bar immediately he arrived. He boasted occasionally of what he did: his order was a large glass of rum, a pint of beer, a large whisky and a tumbler of port wine. This used all his money. He drunk everything very quickly and then after a short chat with anyone present set off for home, which was mostly uphill. He claimed that he would have fallen off his cycle at least four times before he reached home.

For the rest of the fortnight he depended on what drinks he could get from anyone or on the few tips that came his way. Two miles away on the road to Rothes there was a little cottage which had a "Beer and Ale licence", but these could not be drunk on the premises, so that there was always one or two men sitting on the grass at the roadside drinking from the bottle. John was a frequent visitor there. I believe that there was also the possibility of getting a quantity of whisky illegally, and this he obtained for Shorty, getting a share for his trouble.

The other porter signalman, Atholl Clark was a pleasant quiet man, who seemed very old and slow in his movements. His wife also looked old, and they had a son living with them. He had worked in Glasgow as an engine fitter until a few months before I was appointed. He did not register in Elgin as unemployed, but yet seemed to have an income. Atholl said that he would soon have to retire at the age of 70 when all three would remove to Inverness, his birth place. He was so slow that I often ran to the signal box to change the signals for him. It was many years later when I came across a copy of an early paperback book, *The Iron Track through the Highlands*, published by the *Inverness Courier*, but undated. On page 45 I discovered Atholl's name, and learned that he was one of the first signalmen at Inverness station, but had been dismissed because of some accident for which he was responsible. It said also that he had gone to Edinburgh and joined the North British Railway. Atholl had said once or twice that he had been with that company. He had later returned to the Highland Railway and been given a lower wage. At the time I knew him he had then worked for at least 58 years, and must have been over eighty years of age.

It was inevitable that my boss would be caught out sometime, for so great was his need for money that he began to interfere with the cash receipts. Each morning the previous day's traffic in tickets and parcel stamps had to be recorded, the money put in a leather bag with a lock, and then placed in the safe which travelled on the first passenger train, in charge of the guard. This was my work, and I usually did this as the last thing at night. In the morning on opening the office safe I always checked this, as Atholl had suggested that would be wise. It was only a few weeks before I found that the money had been tampered with. Shorty did not appear at the earlier trains, and I had hurriedly to tear up my return and make a new one to agree with the money in the bag. I raised the matter on his appearance and he promised to make up the shortage before evening. In the end I had to take the money home with me every night, something that was very risky for me, for if it was stolen, which was unlikely, or I was unable to get to the station in the morning in time to put it on the train, I would have to bear the full responsibility. This would inevitably mean dismissal for I should have reported the matter, but this would probably have meant dismissal for my boss, which would have been worse. I was not a member of a union for the simple reason that I could not spare the weekly dues of sixpence. It was a difficult position for a seventeen year old boy to be in, but always of an optimistic nature I hoped that the matter would come to a satisfactory conclusion one way or another. The climax did come earlier than I expected, and I was glad that I was not directly involved in the denouement.

Prior to the First World War, the beautiful grounds at Gordon Castle had been the venue of a most successful Highland Gathering and Games, and this was to be re-introduced the coming August, the peak time of the tourist traffic.

On the Saturday the small branch engine was put into the shed and replaced with a large engine and a complete train of carriages from Keith, to cope with the many hundreds of passengers from the main line, where there were also special trains for the Bank holiday traffic. Atholl was early shift, and Shorty appeared early, as did Mann. Many of the men alighting from the trains were distillery workers, for we were on the fringe of the "Whisky Trail" of Speyside. Mann was not on duty until 2 p.m. but by that time he had had many drinks of undiluted distillery whisky and was almost incapable at times, although he had a wonderful ability to act responsibly when necessary. He was not alone, for Shorty also knew many of the workers, but he did not hold up the work or the trains.

Every Saturday I caught the last train to Forres for the weekend, for I could not contemplate the thought of a Sunday in my digs, with no possibility of escape to the station which was closed on that day. My train left just after seven, and by that time most travellers had returned home, and only the relief train had to come up the branch, and then divide into two portions, the greater part with the engine at the front would go on to Keith. The branch followed it "light" and at the junction coupled on to the rear of this train and, taking off its own coach, had to move to its dock platform for the arrival of the up train from Keith, which I was to join at the last minute. With John and Shorty both drunk, I had great difficulty in getting everything in order before leaving, but Keith had told me that a guard was on the train which I was going to join. This train from Keith was the last to arrive, and therefore was the first to leave. I saw the guard arrive, one whom I had never seen before, but Keith was a joint station, the majority of the staff being those of the Great North of Scotland Railway. Unfortunately Keith did not have a guard available because it was one of the busiest days in the year and they were required on the GNS so sent a porter who had no experience whatsoever. But I relaxed in my train confident that everything would now be all right, and that it did not matter that the two men I had left behind were drunk and almost incapable of making any decisions, for both would be more sober when the last train of the day arrived and left two hours later.

When I returned on Monday morning at 7 a.m. John was on duty, still showing some signs of his Saturday indulgence. He did tell me that there had been some trouble getting the train away to Keith, as the passengers alighting at the station could not get out as the carriage doors were locked, and Shorty objected to some men who had climbed on to the track from the doors on the other side of the carriages. This was the fault of Mr Fyffe at Fochabers, who was a nervous man and adhered strictly to regulations. These said that the doors on the "non working" side of a train had to be locked always. As Fochabers and Orbliston had each only one platform for the branch train with the same "non-working" side, this worked well. John's memory was not clear about what had happened, and when I looked at the "Train Journal" I found no entries had been made at the times of the Keith special. An hour later Mr Grant, stationmaster at Orton, spoke to me on the telegraph, saying that there was a letter on the next train which the guard would give me. I guessed that it must be important before he sent it to a junior clerk like myself. The letter was important, startling and alarming.

The special had arrived at Orton with the Orbliston passengers who were unable, because of the locked carriage doors, to alight at their destination. The laird of Orton had climbed on to the track and reached the engine and was then able to climb on to the platform. He found Shorty vastly amused at the predicament of those wanting to alight, and ordered the train to leave. The laird asked to be allowed to join the train but was told that he had committed an offence by his action, and would therefore have to find his own way home. The acting guard was bewildered and uncertain what to do. He did not even have the standard red and green flags. The engine crew sat in the cab, looking at the scene but refusing to make any decisions. There was always rivalry between the "Black Squad" and the operating people, and they took a malicious pleasure in seeing the difficulties.

Shorty then instructed the driver to start away, which he did, despite the shouts of the locked in travellers. On arrival at Orton, Mr Grant heard the story and, trying to protect Mr Shorthouse, asked the driver to propel the train backwards to Orbliston, deposit the passengers for that station and then return. The driver agreed to do this if Mr Grant accepted all responsibility for one of the greatest breaches of the rules, which he did, and eventually the train reached Keith.

Next morning Miss Wharton Duff, the sister of the laird, called on him to tell him her brother had had to walk three miles to his home and had been caught in a sudden thunderstorm, common in August, and was now in bed suffering from a chill. She intended to travel to Inverness next day to see Mr Thomas McEwen, the Traffic Manager, whom she knew and report the whole matter. She thought it right that Mr Grant should know this and do what he thought proper. He wrote me, and then a full report to the Traffic Manager, but did not send it by the first train, thus ensuring that Miss Wharton Duff would have made her report by the time his letter arrived.

I went to see Mr Shorthouse, and persuaded his wife to let me see him as he was still in bed and obviously worried. He would have had some recollection of what had happened. He read the letter but said nothing, and turned his back on me, with his face to the wall. I could not think of anything suitable to say and also left in silence.

On the following morning, Tuesday, Mr McLeod, the Chief Inspector, and an assistant, Mr Dempster, alighted from the midday train and asked me to get Mr Shorthouse to come and see them. This he did and all three entered the Ladies Waiting Room, where some thirty minutes were spent. I sat in the office anxiously wondering what would happen to me, when Shorty entered. The office door had the two upper panels of glass, and when open blocked the way to the large cupboard sunk into the wall. Here was kept the stock of tickets and any confidential papers. Without a glance at me he closed the office door and unlocked the cupboard, then took out a bottle with some whisky in it and a small Colmans mustard tin. This he filled with whisky and swallowed it in one gulp. He started to close the door but had second thoughts and again took the tin and filled it.

I had frequently seen him act like this, but he had always left the door open behind him so that I had never actually seen him drink. He then closed the cupboard door and turning to open the office door to return to his meeting, saw pressed to the glass panel the face of Mr Dempster who had followed him. Shorty turned to me and with a grimace said, "My number's up" and left. Within a few minutes he returned with his two interviewers and all three stood inside. Mr McLeod said, "We know that you can take charge until someone is sent. I am suspending Mr Shorthouse and you will not allow him to enter this office. He will take any personal belongings now". All I could do was sit silent on my stool, but relieved, for obviously they accepted that I was not involved in any wrongdoing. Mr Shorthouse now seemed quite calm and removed some papers and articles from the cupboard and, handing me the keys, left to enter his house. There had been cases of stationmasters being suspended before, but this was the first time that one had been dismissed on the spot without any further enquiry. The next train was not due for more than an hour, and I felt uneasy in the presence of the inspectors, who were feared by the operating staff. I was tested for my knowledge of signalling and train control, something that should have been done before I could operate the machines without supervision, but was rarely done. With so much time on my hands I had read everything in the office, and having an excellent memory rarely made any errors.

Mr McLeod was a big, impressive man, who because of his firmness and at times, ruthlessness was nicknamed "Von Kluck", after a German general known for his energy and harsh discipline in the late war. I had a good many dealings with him in the next nine years, but always found him fair and straightforward.

He wrote some telegrams which he gave me to transmit; then made arrangement for a van to be sent for Mr Shorthouse's furniture, and for the "Dead Meat" express to be stopped to lift this vehicle when it had been loaded. This train was timed to run non stop to Forres at passenger train speeds. From Forres it ran to London via Perth, between the sleeping car train and the Royal Mail, and arrived at Euston station in time to be delivered at Smithfield Market for sale next morning.

Next day Mr James McIntyre arrived to take charge until a permanent appointment was made. His father was the second-in-command at headquarters in Inverness, and his son had entered the same office on his discharge from the army. When the Peace Treaty was signed in 1919 and troops were demobilised, Mr McIntyre had continued in the army, serving in Russia where the Allies had fought to support the opponents of the Bolsheviks.

He had never worked outside the office and wanted to broaden his experience of railway working, and Orbliston was the first time he had been at a wayside station. He was a keen angler and also shot game, and when he found that his present position gave him the privilege of angling in the Spey, with opportunities for shooting, it did not take long for him to decide to apply for the job at Orbliston, and very soon his young wife and baby arrived. The fact that I could safely be left in charge on his frequent absences was I think, a factor that weighed heavily with him. The period I worked with him was the most pleasant of my ten years of railway work. He was able to enjoy his hobby, while I enjoyed mine, which was railway work.

At the beginning of November I had an accident which affected me greatly in later life, but not in any serious way. The freight train from the east took an unconscionably long time at Lhanbryde on the day in question with the result that the "Dead Meat" Express was held up at Orbliston, and when the freight train arrived I hurried with the tablet for the express to let it leave immediately. To save time I stepped onto the buffers of a truck of the freight train and was going to step on to the other buffer and hand the tablet to the fireman on the engine, when the truck moved. I fell, striking the buffers or the coupling chain, and then toppled to the ground beneath the moving train, fortunately free of the wheels. When the train was clear I had great difficulty in rising and had to be half carried to the office. Mr McIntyre had been in the Royal Army Medical Corps, and was able to say that no bones seemed to be broken, but that I obviously needed treatment in bed.. The thought of being confined to bed in Mrs Boag's care was more than I could face, and I decided to go home to Forres by the first available train, which I did. Dr Bruce diagnosed severe bruising and torn ligaments, and gave his usual treatment, frequent rubbing with olive oil. He was known as the "Olive Oil King" because of his partiality for this oil, which he credited with almost miraculous curative powers. It was reported that he used this oil for cooking, a matter for surprise, for at that time it was not generally known that it was the chief fat used in Mediterranean countries.

There were no facilities for X-ray examination, so it was many years later that the trouble was found to be pressure of some vertebrae on some nerves or muscles. The result was that I could not properly co-ordinate the fingers of my left hand, and the problem also affected the hearing in my right ear. The immediate handicap was that I was unable to use my left hand in operating the telegraph. This was a drawback as most of my colleagues were ambidextrous in this respect, of use when two instruments were in contact with a station, as that station could be called for on two lines.

It was some weeks before I returned to work, where I found that Mrs Boag had at last left Blackburn Croft. The November term day was the legal date and the police had called to warn her to accept the quittal notice. The new tenants were willing to have me as a lodger, more for the company than the money; in fact they said to pay the same sum as I had previously, which was 13 shillings [65p.]. Peter and Mary Leslie came from the Buchan area where they had had a small farm. The people from that part of Scotland are undoubtedly the hardest working in Scotland, and they had soon tired of a life of retirement so had taken this small croft. These lodgings were the best I ever lived in, so that now I was fortunate in every respect. The two cows provided ample milk, butter and cheese, the hens and ducks - more eggs than could be consumed - and I lived with the kindest of people, both full of pawky Aberdeenshire humour. Their two sons and two daughters were frequent visitors, and I was treated as one of the family.

Only once did I nearly offend them. The animals were like pets, each having its name; the cows were "Jinse" and "Elspet" and the sow was "Kitty". The latter was soon to have a brood of young pigs, and the sow was greatly troubled by a rat visiting its sty and eating the food. The house had a single barrelled shotgun, with an interesting history. After the Franco-Russian War of 1871 the victorious Germans sold off many thousands of the Schneider rifle, which had been replaced during the war by a more advanced weapon. An enterprising Glasgow man had brought over many hundreds of these weapons, and had ground out the rifling of the muzzle, making it possible to take the standard cartridge used for rabbit and bird shooting. Peter had paid £1 for his at Wartle Fair, and had used it ever since.

I occasionally used it to shoot a rabbit for the pot, and I was now asked to shoot the rat that troubled Kitty. The evening was fine and there was still an hour or two of sunshine and light, so I took the gun and a book, and found a seat on a fence strainer pole near at hand, and sat there reading until the rat appeared. Soon Kitty began to make strange noises, and looking up I saw the rat at the feeding trough. Aiming quickly, I fired; the rat never appeared again so that I had probably killed it, but my trouble was now from Kitty. I had peppered her with some of the shot, and she acted quickly and alarmingly. Unless one had seen it, no one could credit that such a gross animal could be so athletic, almost gymnastic. Squealing with the intensity of an express whistling for a signal at danger, she gyrated, twisted and almost turned somersaults. Aghast at what I had done I fled to the station, to be welcomed with laughter instead of the sympathy I needed. I waited until late, and returned with forebodings of having to pack and leave, but I found that I was forgiven. Kitty had given birth to fifteen, and of these twelve had survived, apparently as much as she could easily cope with.

The married daughter came for holiday about that time with her husband, who was a railwayman in the south. Before her marriage she had been lady's maid to a society beauty of title in London, and she regaled us with her tales of life in that sphere. The information was startling, although now everyday news in some sections of the Press. At the age of 20 I found this very disturbing, and in my innocence asked if they never went to church. There was no young man of my age to meet or talk to. The nearest farm was over 1000 acres, the crofts had no young people, and neither had the few smaller farms. The majority of the residents were farmworkers, whose sons left at the age of 14 to work in Elgin or elsewhere, later to join the army in large numbers. The wage of an adult farmworker was not much over a pound a week, with a free house, milk, coal, potatoes in addition. The daughters left to go into service as resident maids. The millions of unemployed in Britain had pressed wages so low that there was a bare existence in the rural areas, where crops could sometimes scarcely be sold at any price.

The few houses that I saw were no more comfortable than the bothy life at Brockloch ten years earlier, despite the political promises of a country "fit for heroes to live in" with houses to match. After one term day, a woman apologised for entering the Ladies Waiting Room, afraid that she would be accused of trespassing as she was not travelling by train. I explained that this was no offence and gave the two little girls with her two penny pieces of Reeves chocolate from the automatic vending machines, then to be found in all stations. Her gratitude was embarrassing, for they had rarely tasted sweets; she went on to say that the reason for their presence was that she wanted them to see and use a toilet with flushing water. The mean little thatched cottages shared a "dry closet", and their water supply was drawn by a hand pump placed conveniently for the cattle court, but some distance from the homes. I had never given much thought to such things, but now began to be socially conscious of the hardships and unfairness of much of our society.

In 1924 I had been able to spend a day in London visiting the famous British Empire Exhibition. My travel was of course free, and I spent two nights in the train. I visited Wembley, then pretty much still a village, and after a few hours went into the city proper, I reached in some way, either Aldersgate or Aldgate Pump. I recall seeing an Indian file of lascars making their way back to their ship, the leader with a live hen under his arm, all dressed in jeans, which I saw for the first time. An onlooker, seeing my interest, volunteered the information that the hen was part of their religious exercise, and would then be eaten.

I visited an ABC teashop, the cheapest catering establishment in Britain was its claim, and here had a ham pie and tea with the knife and fork chained to the galvanised table top. Retelling this much later I was greeted with some incredulity by the rest of the company, and was glad when an elderly man stated that he had been in a teashop where the solitary tea spoon hung from the ceiling by a chain convenient for several tables.

In March of 1926 my friend Jim, who worked at Forres Goods station, thought that I should join the trade union, the Railway Clerks Association as there was talk of a strike in support of the miners, whose pay was being reduced. I was now comparatively affluent and could afford the weekly dues, 6d. [2½p.] for Category "C" which would give me strike pay of £1 a week if we were ever called out on strike. My salary was now £2 a week, and I was able to give some money every weekend I spent at home.

I was home in Forres at the end of April and Jim told me that he had transferred me to Category "A". I paid the due of one shilling a week. No-one was sure whether there was to be a strike or not. There had never been one north of Perth before, which meant that no one in the Highland Railway had ever been on strike. I did not go home on the following Saturday, and on Monday morning, 4 May, I found that all the lines and instruments were silent. I awakened Mr McIntyre, but there was nothing he could do. John and the other wages staff were on strike, but I had had no instructions. While at lunch, David Grant, who was clerk at Orton, arrived on his bicycle with the news that the country was at a standstill, and that he was cycling to his home in Nairn, for he could not stay in his lodgings with no pay. Orton, being a sub-post office had a public telephone and was able to get information. I decided I also would go home, and we both set off; on reaching my home David and I had lunch; thereafter I cycled to Nairn with him and then returned home.

All the railwaymen were out on strike, as well as the printers and some other occupations. There was one exception among the railway people, my friend Hamish Deas. His home was in Forres and we had been friends since schooldays, but he remained at work. His father held a high position in the railway at Inverness, where the highest ranking officials remained at work, although there was little to do. My mother was very angry, but mollified when I told her that actually I was a few pence better paid by the union than by my employers, for I did not have the small deduction for the company's Superannuation Fund. Father understood the position, and told me that many years earlier a branch of the association of Railway Servants had been formed in the area, and he had been asked to act as secretary, which he did, although this knowledge was to be kept secret. But the company learned of it, and he was visited by an official from Inverness who told him that if he continued to hold that office he would be dismissed. With several small children, and with a label of "trouble maker", there was little chance of obtaining another position as secure, and he had to resign.

As the strike dragged on, the Government, spurred on by Winston Churchill, enacted harsher measures, and the troops were called out. Tempers grew short, and there were acts of violence, including the derailing of a passenger train in a tunnel in Edinburgh. One afternoon while my friends, Ian MacBean and Jim Paterson and I were walking, Hamish approached us and urged us to go back to work, and "save our skins". A violent argument took place, in which I had perhaps more than my share. The eggs I laid that day were later to hatch into birds that came back to bother me.

Hamish was upset and told his mother what had happened. She told her husband, who reported back to his colleagues. Then the strike collapsed, and there was a rush to get back to work. But traffic was at a standstill and not everyone was re-engaged immediately. Those who did return found that they were not all to receive full work, but to be taken on when needed. I did not get restarted until August. The summer was one of the hottest on record, and with my strike pay I enjoyed my enforced holiday. Jack was home from Nigeria, and Bert was on six months furlough from Demerara, while other members of the family came on holiday as in other years.

In mid July I was informed that I had not had my annual leave for the previous year, which ended in May, and that I would get a free rail pass to any point in Britain, as I was entitled to, and on 1 August could start work at Orbliston.

I spent my holiday in St Andrews where I had an uncle, Jock Urquhart. He owned a large house, Cliff House, and also the open air swimming pool among the rocks. He had been butler, and his wife cook, with a Mr Norman Macleod, and had inherited the property on the death of his employer as a reward for long and faithful service.

He and his wife let this house for long periods to members of the ICS, the Indian Civil Service, and acted as cook and butler during the time of the let. During the mornings of my holiday I was on duty at the swimming pool, taking the entrance money and handing out the bathing suits to the girls of St Margarets and St Leonards schools, who had special terms. Uncle Jock was very generous and offered me the use of his Clyno car, but I could not drive a car and had no licence. His son, John, had a "Wolf" motor cycle, and I was offered this which I accepted, for I had exhausted the attractions of the town and would like to see some of the surrounding area. I claimed that I could ride the cycle, although I had only been on one for about two minutes. This one had to be pushed as fast as possible until the engine fired, and then the driver had to leap in the saddle before the machine dragged him away. He asked if I had a driving licence, and when I gave a negative answer he handed me a ten shilling note, and told me to ride to Cupar, where I could purchase one for five shillings, the balance would purchase enough petrol to last during my holidays.

It took me some considerable running before the engine spluttered into life, but I succeeded in gaining the saddle and went wobbling along the road, rather slowly I thought, until I passed the little village of Guard Bridge, whereupon the engine failed and I came to a halt. I was nonplussed, lacking any knowledge, and indeed interest, in machines of any kind apart from railway locomotives. I sat on the grass for some time speculating on a course of action, while hoping that someone would come to my rescue. But the traffic moved past without a glance. Finally a cyclist did stop; he was in a khaki uniform, brown leggings, peaked cap, and had a leather case at his waist supported by a belt from his shoulders. He asked sympathetically if anything was wrong and I told him of my difficulty. After a brief examination he said that the engine had become overheated, and asked what gear I had been using. No one had spoken to me about gears, and I was still in low gear, the one I had started with. He gave me other valuable information also. I asked what I had to pay for this service, and he replied that he could not state a fee as actually he should have ignored my plight, since he was only supposed to aid the members of his organisation, the Automobile Association. With one of those rash impulsive actions to which I am prone, I produced the ten shilling note my uncle had given me, and pressed it into his grateful hand, and he departed thanking me profusely. It was not long before I realised that the money was all that I possessed, for I had little when I left home. I could not continue to Cupar so turned in the direction of St Andrews until I reached a small copse, where I sat for some time. Fortunately I always carried a book or magazine. When I returned home to Cliff House, I did not report my adventures, as I felt very foolish, and it was taken for granted that I had been at Cupar, and that I had a driving licence.

Daily my uncle suggested a suitable run, Crail, Leven, or somewhere else on the south coast, and dutifully I started the machine and drove to what I think was the Boar Wood where I sat and read until it was time to return. My uncle and aunt were always busy in the evening with the formal dinner served, and no questions were asked about my activities. I did have a narrow shave on my last excursion. I had been told to visit Leven, and passing my uncle in the passage to the kitchen he asked what I thought of the statue, and innocently I answered, "What statue?" He answered rather sharply, "Robinson Crusoe's of course". I answered weakly, "Oh! That statue!"

When I restarted at Orbliston I found that Mr McIntyre had gone, promoted to Carr Bridge station on the Perth line, and found also that I had to carry on alone. I had neither status nor the salary for the job, and nothing in writing giving my duties. To save costs the porter signalmen were not allowed to work overtime, so that I was on duty for the two last trains of the day. Both were down, so that the signals and points did not require to be altered and they remained that way until the following morning. I was not alone in suspecting that headquarters anticipated some errors being made, when I could be brought to book. I determined to do everything to avoid this, and worked very carefully.

Unfortunately something did happen, and quite soon. Each Friday the morning train brought from Fochabers a number of trucks of cattle for the market in Elgin. These were attached to the passenger train which arrived fifteen minutes after the branch train, and quick action was required to get these vehicles detached from the branch train and put into the siding at the West Cabin, to be speedily drawn out by the main line engine, and attached to the train it was hauling. This operation required the action normally of the porter signalman and the stationmaster, while I remained in the office issuing tickets and operating the train tablet machines, and then hurrying over to the platform with the tablet. Now there was only John and myself.

Orton as usual asked for a tablet to be released early so that it could be handed over when the train arrived there from Mulben. This I released by pressing a knob on our machine, and it was only later that I saw that there was a delay, and the trucks were not yet ready to move. I returned to the office and gave the "Obstruction Danger" signal, ten rapid rings on the bell. This was repeated, and I stood by to watch when the branch engine was clear, when I would give the "Line Clear" signal. The branch engine had now passed the office on its way to the East Cabin, with John hanging to the steps, and jumping off when he reached the East cabin which he entered and when the engine and cattletrucks were clear, changed the points and cleared the "Home Signal" and went down the cabin steps, expecting the engine to halt and pick him up to go to the West Cabin, where he had to move the levers again to put the trucks into the siding, to be collected by the main line engine. I stood in horror as I saw the branch engine at maximum speed pass me followed by the main line train applying its brakes furiously. The usual delay was increased by the time it took John to run to the cabin, and finish the operation.

Returning to the office I asked Orton what they meant by letting the train leave, and the reply was that the porter signalman had never heard this signal before, but had repeated it as the regulations required to show that it had been heard, and then had to look up the code to see what it meant. By that time the train had left and he tried to contact us, but I had left the office by this time. I was concerned at the nearness of an accident, but there were always dangers in running trains, and clearly we were not at fault.

This morning train carried a large number of season ticket holders, many of them business men travelling to Elgin, as well as a number of pupils for Elgin Academy. All had a good knowledge of train working, and the incident was the subject, I am certain, of the conversation on that day. It would be mentioned to some of the station staff at Elgin and by late afternoon it would be known in Inverness, whence a telegram later arrived instructing me to report there next day at the superintendent's office.

When I presented myself there I was faced by the superintendent, two of the inspectors I knew, and others, including a shorthand writer. My statement was taken, followed by thrusting questions which I answered with a confidence I did not feel. Gradually the tone became menacing, and I went over to the offensive, claiming that I was doing duties for which I was not paid, and which had never been laid down for me. The reply was that I was salaried and therefore responsible for the correct working of the station. I seized this point, claiming that I was not yet 21 years of age, and could not be responsible in law, despite what my superiors claimed.

The superintendent, after conferring with his chief assistant, pointed out that the age of 16 was majority in Scotland, after which a male was legally responsible. I countered by arguing that the relevant Act was passed on the introduction of railways in the middle of last century by a Parliament in England, and applied to the whole of Britain. I was told to leave and wait outside until called for. This wait lasted nearly an hour, during which I have no doubt enquiries were made to some legal authority. I was not called back but told to return to work, and that a stationmaster would arrive next day to take charge.

I was glad that I had read everything that I could find about railways, and was grateful for my retentive memory. I knew that I had not in any way improved my image at headquarters, and would have to be very careful in the future. Within a few days a Mr David Dewar arrived to take up the stationmaster's post, with his newly wed wife. I had met him before and knew that he was a difficult person to work with, being at times very moody and often over anxious.

On that railway few stationmasters fraternised with their staff, a tradition begun, I believe, by the first stationmaster appointed at Inverness by the

Inverness and Nairn Railway in 1854, who was a sea captain, said to be a Mr Mimms. In a small station as in a ship, familiarity with the crew could rapidly weaken or erode discipline. Of the many stationmasters I worked under, I was invited into the home of only one, and that was in England, at Tewkesbury.

The competition from buses now affected the railways severely, and when a service was started which passed through Fochabers, the regular customers we saw travelling to Elgin now disappeared, for the bus had only six miles to cover in twelve minutes or so, whereas the train journey was nine miles long, with a considerable wait at the junction. All staff were urged to encourage in every way a return to rail travel by the people we had lost, but defeat was inevitable. We now saw few passengers, for the rural area around us did not generate many travellers even before the buses took over. There was rarely a passenger on the last train at night, but Mr Dewar now attended all trains arriving, whereas he had previously rarely appeared after 5 p.m. One dark and stormy night the wind was so strong that two of the oil lamps that dimly illuminated the platform were extinguished, but no door opened in the brightly lit train. When it left I heard his voice, strained and anxious, "Did anyone come off?" I answered that one man had; it was not true, but I thought there was no harm in the lie, if it made him any happier. A day or two later he again asked me if anyone came off, and as the light was quite good, I answered truthfully that none had. He flew into a passion, claiming that I had been discouraging the public from travelling by train, and was concealing from him the number of people alighting. He continued in this strain spasmodically. At last I said that I could tolerate this no longer, that from now on I would work only my eight hours daily, and as I started at 7 a.m. I would finish at 5 p.m.

Old Atholl Clark was retired by this time and had been replaced by a young man, Dan McLeod. He told me that Dewar was now very frequently emerging from his house, ignoring the office, and was heard speaking, then he would enter the office, and pull the "Starting Signal" lever, which was situated in the office. He would then look at the train journal, mutter something and leave without a word to the occupant.

Our attitude could be summed up in a jocular remark I made to John and Dan, when discussing Dewar's behaviour, "All power corrupts, absolute power corrupts absolutely". Most people who are isolated develop idiosyncrasies, and Dewar was self isolated. Some time later, the Chief Inspector, Mr McLeod, alighted from the morning train, and approaching me asked me to come with him to the Ladies Waiting Room, where he had earlier interviewed Mr Shorthouse. We sat down opposite each other at the table, and I waited for what he had to say, wondering what trouble I was now in. He asked how I got on with Mr Dewar, and I replied that I had no complaints; that I did my work and he did his, neither of us having had much to do. What did I think of his behaviour? It was at times odd, but a number of people I had worked with had odd habits, adding that I had been described as mad myself. He dryly said that he would not deal with that remark at present. Had I gone on to the platform with him when there was no train? I had obeyed his order to don my ticket collector's hat, but only once. He seemed satisfied with my answers and then told of letters being received by a member of the public, stating that the residents of the area were afraid to go to the station as the stationmaster and clerk were mad, and believed that "ghost trains" were in the station. I do not know if the famous play "The Ghost Train" had been produced at that time.

Another sign that something was wrong was Mr Dewar's handwriting. The company encouraged a good standard, and normally his was clear and rounded. But it began to degenerate, the first few lines being legible but the end and the signature a scrawl. The medical advisor had given this as a symptom of some mental disease, while my handwriting was unaffected. Mr McLeod then visited Mr Dewar in his house, and emerged to hand me the keys, saying "It's strange, Forbes, that you have twice had to do what has rarely happened on this railway." In the afternoon a reliefman came to take over and I was instructed to go to Dingwall next day. I was never in Orbliston again, and the station no longer exists, the building being converted to a dwelling house.

ACHNASHEEN

I was instructed to go to Achnasheen, on the Dingwall and Skye line. I had never been north of Inverness before, and my informant commiserated with me, saying that it rained every day at Achnasheen and that the name meant "Place of Rain". On arriving there I found both statements to be false, for four inches of snow lay on the ground, although this was unusual, and the name meant "The field or holding of Jean". I learned that the clerk had been absent for a fortnight, but that the stationmaster had not informed the head office, or asked for relief. He had not been contacted by the absent clerk nor had he made any enquiry as to a reason for his absence. The expectation was that the missing person would probably turn up next day. This was typical of the attitude adopted, and only now when the audit and other offices were demanding the weekly traffic returns, was the matter considered worth dealing with.

Achnasheen consisted of the station building which incorporated a hotel, a cottage for the porter signalman, and some distance away a wooden shed which I found to be the Post Office. The station square held a number of buses of a special design. They were not large having a dozen seats for passengers, and the rear part was separated by a strong partition. This part was reserved for the carriage of mails, which had to be kept under lock and key, and also of general merchandise. These were the famous McIvor Coaches, the only means of personal transport to a large part of the west coast of Ross.

Shieldaig, Gairloch, Aultbea, Poolewe and Kinlochewe were names known to the tourist trade, and all were served from Achnasheen. The stationmaster, "Murdo Mor' – big Murdo, was a well known character in the west, and was also the coal merchant for much of that large but thinly populated area. I saw him enter and emerge from the bar of the hotel, which had access from the platform, busily greeting many people, but I did not get a chance to speak to him until the train and finally the buses left, leaving the station quiet and almost deserted apart from myself. Kenny, the porter signalman, as soon as I had made myself known, lead me to the loading of the buses, and handed me the forms for recording the addresses on the packages, bicycles and assorted goods. The forms were strange to me, and I found that they were those of the bus owner, Mr McIvor, and that I had to do this work as well as deal with the railway traffic as a whole. This was a private arrangement between Murdo and McIvor.

McIvor, an old man at the time of writing, had for half a century been accepted as the virtual dictator of the area. The tale is now legend of his treatment of Queen Victoria when she visited and stayed in his hotel. She had expressed a wish to attend church on Sunday, and he provided a coach and driver. Her Majesty had to sit through a ninety minute service in Gaelic, before she heard the service in English. She had not been amused, but the coachman said that he had his orders from Mr McIvor and would not budge from them. This was a tale heard more than once; I cannot vouch for the truth of it, but it is credible.

As soon as the traffic had cleared I looked for Murdo but, failing to find him, asked Kenny to return and give me some indication of what had to be done. Eventually he turned up; he was off duty, working four hours in the morning, and again in the evening, for there were only two trains a day in each direction. My first enquiry was if I could lodge with him, but found that this was not possible because his furniture was packed for removal as he had applied for a vacancy near Stirling. Some months earlier the company had started to circulate all station vacancies in the wages grade, and Kenny had written about this one. I said that it had probably been long filled, but only the successful applicant would know. He was very disappointed to hear this, but added that his wife was determined to move away from this alien environment, for she was a south girl and could tolerate the loneliness no more. I thought it was time to find Murdo, for I was getting hungry and I had been unable to find anyone in the hotel when I ventured there.

Kenny advised me to try in the flat upstairs, which Murdo occupied. After mounting a very dirty and untidy stairway I knocked at the door from which I heard voices. Murdo partly opened the door, through which I could see a table with a bottle and glasses on it, and a lady sitting on a couch. He said abruptly that he would see me later and slammed the door. I returned to the office and surveyed the position there, and decided to deal with the papers and letters which had accumulated for some time. An examination of the working timetable showed that no trains were due for some hours, so I left the office and visited the Post Office in the hope that it stocked groceries or at least some kind of nourishment. The young girl regretted that nothing was stocked, but she gave me an orange which she had included in her lunch basket, all else being consumed. She could not help in any way as she cycled several miles to and from her work.

At last Murdo appeared, and in reply to my request for some guidance as to where I was to stay, said impatiently that he was seeing to it. He then left again and I saw him through the window, wheel out a motorcycle, mount it and drive away. He returned some time before the late afternoon train was due, and again said that he was looking into the question of shelter for me. The buses only attended the station in the morning, and part from mails, a few parcels and some boxes of salmon to be sent by this train, there was only one person alighting, who left after waiting some time for a car to appear.

The final train of the day went on to Kyle of Lochalsh. Again Murdo appeared, and this time he could spare a few minutes. He blandly suggested that I stay in the hotel, as there was nowhere else for many miles where I could stay. I suggested that I was willing to share his quarters and look after my own catering, but this was instantly rejected. Murdo was unmarried and according to Kenny was found irresistible by ladies. This surprised me for he was untidy and ungainly, with a very red face spotted with what was called in my native area, "whisky tackets". He was a native of the district, and undoubtedly had the charm of the Gael. I argued that my 13 shillings a day lodging allowance would not meet the cost of my board and food in the hotel, but I had no choice but to re-enter it and ask for food and lodgings for the night. The aged crone, the only resident other than Mr McIvor, said that there was no food available, and no staff on duty, as the introduction of a dining car on the trains had taken away all the trade which had previously been enjoyed.

Driven to desperation I threatened to return to the office and send telegrams to the Chief Constable and the Sheriff of Ross and Cromarty, the latter being a relative by marriage, which was quite untrue, but hunger makes one reckless. After some hesitation she went upstairs, and returned to say that Mr McIvor had said that I could stay for one night only. That was my intention, and after a plate of cold meat, tea and oatcakes and scones, I returned to the office and on the telegraph asked the clerk on duty at Dingwall if he could find me lodgings there, where I would arrive by the last train from the West. He assured me that this would be arranged.

There was a fair amount of arrears to clear, and I started to do this until it was time to go to bed. After a drink in the bar where one or two men had gathered, and who obviously did not want me to join them, I got a key for my bedroom and received instructions where to find it. It was a tiny room, obviously the staff bedroom of Victorian times, but it was somewhere I could lie down, for I was by this time tired. Next evening I arrived in Dingwall to excellent lodgings in Hill Street, where I found a dozen young fellows of my own age, bank clerks, ironmongers, and others. Mrs McLean liked her lodgers and it was an excellent place where I stayed on more than one occasion in the future. It was pleasant to have the company that I had lacked for the previous five years or so.

Each morning I left with a Thermos flask of tea and a large parcel of food, to travel by a "mixed train" to Achnasheen. This was composed of three carriages and could take a maximum of ten freight wagons, although normally it rarely had as many. The "wintering" sheep were returning to the moors and glens, and there were a number of trucks of sheep on the train. The engine was a "Skye Bogie", specially designed with very small driving wheels and short enough to negotiate the very severe and continuous curves on the route. At times the engine seemed to be travelling in the opposite direction to the guards van at the rear. After leaving Auchterneed, the station for Strathpeffer, the very steep gradient at Ravens Rock had to be climbed, and this the locomotive could not manage it, so the train came to a halt.

The guard had seen me on the previous day and now asked me to leave my seat and take charge of the rear portion, while he uncoupled the engine and carriages which then proceeded to Garve station. This was not an uncommon happening during the busy summer season, when both passenger and freight traffic was heavier. I had to sit in the brake van, to make sure that the brakes held, and that we did not start slipping downhill to the rear, for this could lead to a derailment when a high speed was reached, which would not be long on the steep slope. The shepherd in charge of the sheep was travelling in the brake van and after examining his charges to see that they were all right, he returned and chatted until the engine returned from Garve, and was coupled up to our vehicles, then set out again for Garve, where we rejoined the coach section. Our arrival at Achnasheen was nearly an hour later than the timetable figures, but a good margin was always given to allow lost time to be made up. For four weeks I travelled this route, and rarely did we arrive on time.

Most stations in rural areas were social centres, the only meeting place for long distances, but this was not so in Achnasheen, the proximity of the bar in the hotel militating against this. The days were long, for after mastering the work, including that in relation to the buses, there was little to do. One day an unusual passenger alighted – a young Asian carrying two large suitcases, and wearing a turban but European clothing. His English was adequate, and he was dismayed that he could make not make his calls and return to Inverness the same day. This had been the instructions he had received in Inverness where a band of salesmen had just arrived.

He sat in the waiting room disconsolately, for the many miles of moorland must have appeared intimidating to him, coming from populated India, and at last I asked him into the office and found him to be a very intelligent and interesting young man from the Lahore District. His English was good, for which I was glad. This was unusual, for they had often been made figures of fun by writers and tourists. Always interested in foreign languages I picked up a number of words in his language, including the numbers up to ten, and used some of the words I already knew, most of them from Rudyard Kipling's poems, especially "Gunga Din", a favourite recitation at concerts, and which I knew fairly well. Knowledge is something that takes no space in one's luggage and is always of some value. I thought the language used was Hindustani and that my friend was an Indian, which he was at that time. Many years later I found that his native tongue was Urdu, and that his country later became Pakistan.

My Asian friend was a precursor of that invasion that so affected much of Britain, and which provided Stornoway with a high incidence of people of his race, many of whom are fluent in Gaelic and on occasions don the tartan kilt.

The reader will have realised by this time that life in the Highlands is not as elsewhere, for the inhabitants have a distinctive attitude to such things as timetables, clocks and hours of work. They have been considered lazy but this is untrue, for they are, when necessary, the hardest of workers, being an agricultural and pastoral people, wresting a meagre living from an uncooperative soil and climate, where there is no certainty that the crop sown in the spring will give a harvest in the autumn or at all. Nothing can be hurried. Their disregard of time make them the most delightful companions, who see little sense in abandoning a gathering where everyone is enjoying themselves just because the law says that licensed premises close at eleven o'clock.

I began to envy them, for despite an apparent dilatory approach to the necessary action, trains did run and work was done, and my exasperation was soon replaced by a warm affection, for they remained calm and unruffled where elsewhere there might be anger and confusion. For the following three years much of my time was spent north of Inverness, and most of my memories are pleasant and light-hearted.

There was a blurring of the past and the present, a lack of definition and distinction that was confusing, for there is no Gaelic for a positive "yes" nor a truly negative "no". My old landlady in Helmsdale, when speaking of the past, dated happenings as before or after "Bliadhna na caoirich", the "Year of the sheep", leaving me in doubt not only of the year but of the century. And the not very sober porter at Achnashellach declaiming in the manner of an ancient bard of "the scar on my mother's brow, from the ember that fell from the burning roof, set alight by the sheriff and his men, and her mother too weak to crawl out with her two hour old daughter. It was there till her dying day for all to see. There by the side of Little Loch Broom".

I recall the crofter who grieved for Flowerdale on the road to Gairloch, which had gained its name from the proliferation of flowering plants that once grew there, to be destroyed by the machine-like devastation of the grazing sheep, leaving only heather and dark earth.

With them talk was loved for itself and for its manner, and I was a good listener; but they liked a good tale also. By this time I had travelled much over England and Scotland, for my travel by rail was free, and by asking for a pass to a distant point like Penzance I could cover a great deal of country in my annual fortnightly leave.

But many of the inhabitants of Achnasheen also knew the world, having gone to sea or having emigrated to Canada or Australia only to find the thrall of home to much for them. To be met also were high ranking police officers who had served in the cities, but now working on their crofts with a secure pension behind them, younger than most of the other men, but quickly reverting to the almost primitive way of life without regrets, who had tales of crime and murder alien to their native area. Few took holidays, the only break a visit to the Highland Games, the sheep sales at Rogart, or the Wool Fair at Brora.

From Strathnaver and Strathhalladale the Seceders came annually, or perhaps twice a year, with their little two wheeled carts and small horses to Helmsdale, to celebrate a week long Communion in the stark little church, lacking any decoration apart from white paint, and without music to aid their singing of psalms and paraphrases only. During that week they spoke to no unbeliever if they could avoid doing so, but spoke quietly and civilly when there was some business to transact. So great was their fear of Rome that they approved of Stalin who had suppressed the Catholic and Orthodox religions.

The tinker clans from Caithness met in Helmsdale also, their Sutherland friends, camping on waste ground near the goods yard. Macphees and Whites predominated, and the night was full of their fighting and untuneful bagpipe playing, made more hideous by the atrocious playing of fiddles. None could read music and the music, traditional or otherwise, was corrupted and difficult to recognise. They were talkative and plausible, the younger ones especially; the women bold and forward, but the older ones fawning and ingratiating. Marriages were arranged, it was said mostly by an exchange of partners, with little ceremony.

A few families had ancient motor lorries, kept on the road by the inherited skills of tinkers. These people were said to be the descendants of the least successful and energetic of those dispossessed of their lands during the clearances, and who had lived always on the edge of starvation and want. The tinkers were the favourites of the gentry who allowed them a great deal of familiarity in their speech and approach, and thought of them as the true Highlanders, subservient, or "phrasing" as it was described, with their expressions of gratitude and appreciation, whereas they were never quite certain of the crofters, who showed always their innate courtesy to the lairds, but who could speak mordantly of them when required.

The attitudes were different from those of my native Grampian region, where the landowner had his place and the tenant his, the status of both fixed by many generations of joint and equal participation in the development of a land, basically as inhospitable and difficult to cultivate, but with the saving grace of a much lower rainfall. But the greatest difference between the two races was in their humour. That of the North East was serious faced and mocking, but rarely bordering on the near farce of the extrovert West, where the humour was tinctured with sensuality, and little sexuality.

DINGWALL

I worked several times at Dingwall, which was the junction with the Skye line and the terminus of the Strathpeffer branch line.

One September day in either 1927 or 1928 I received a telegram from Train Control, instructing us to detach from the rear of the train from Wick, the travelling Post Office, and attach it to the Skye Boat train which arrived ten minutes after the mail had left for Inverness, 22 miles away. A local train from Tain followed the first two, but it was unaffected. I walked to the locomotive shed to make sure that the shunting engine driver was fully informed and then returned to the office to instruct the signal cabins and the passenger shunter, but I met on the platform a girl I had met when working at Kildary some weeks earlier. We had a lot to say, and I was startled to see the sixteen coach train arrive. It was now too late for me to do anything, and returning to the office I stuck the form on the metal spike, and said nothing. It was possible that the change would not cause much trouble at Inverness, for it would arrive as normal.

When the three trains had gone I went for lunch, and put the matter out of my mind before I returned. On entering the office I knew by the faces of those present that all was not well, and Willie Sim indicated with his thumbs the door of the stationmaster's office which was closed. I knocked and entered, to find the occupant seated at his desk, wearing his uniform gold braided cap, an ominous sign. He handed me a telegram form, and I quickly read the message. It demanded by return the name of the person responsible for the delay of 40 minutes to the London train, and the reason for the failure to carry out the instructions sent. I could think of nothing to say and stood irresolutely with the paper in my hand. "Black Sandy" stabbed with his forefinger towards the door, and as I turned he shouted "You are not on my staff ... you're on your own", and then added, "Shut the door".

I was soon enlightened; the Duke of Athlone, the only surviving son of Queen Victoria was returning to London after having spent the grouse season at Farr House, and the royal coach had been sent north for his use. It was to have been attached at the rear of the long train, so that the noise of the engine would not disturb him, and the Post Office coach attached at the rear, as it would have a stabilising influence and also act as a buffer if the train was rammed in the rear by another, a most unlikely occurrence for most collisions were "head on".

The Duke, who was now very old, was furious at the delay, and heads would have to roll. As soon as Black Sandy had gone home, the duty staff assembled in the office to discuss my plight. Almost everyone was sure that this was the end of my career, and the first suggestion was that I should resign, as this was better than getting the sack. Traffic had continued to fall after the General Strike, and a number of men in my age group had resigned to take posts in the Benguella Railway, now expanding in Angola, knowing that there would be little promotion for them in the future. All had been on strike in 1926.

I rejected this and asked for suggestions, but these were more jocular than useful; fainting fit, temporary loss of memory, attacked by an enraged passenger, still under the influence of alcohol consumed on the previous evening. "Dynamite Dan" Macgillivray, the branch train guard, offered to give evidence that he had once gone to "Bochans" at Muir of Ord, whose whisky was so potent, being made by a local and illegal whisky still, that it had been several days before the influence wore off. It seemed so far the only possible excuse, but I decided to ignore it. "Townie" the foreman porter returned to the "black out" proposal, and this reminded me of the two Indian peddlers I had casually noticed in the station. Dan said that they had been on the branch train, and this was all the information I required for the explanation I was to give. A few minutes discussion and my reply was ready to be transmitted to the Traffic Manager. It said that I had started to make the necessary arrangements for the change over, but on my way to the signal cabin I had been intercepted by two Indian peddlers, with very poor English and so I gave them the information they needed in Hindustani. They became very importunate, both holding me firmly and questioning me on many matters, with the result that the train concerned had arrived.

The telegraphist at the other end of the line acknowledged receipt with the letters "MIM" and "IMI", instead of the procedural "RD". The first group was our informal code for "amazement" and the second for "incredulous laughter". Townie, a Pontefract man, had been a sergeant major in the "Ross-shire Buffs" and had spent much of his service in India;

he had a stock of the words used by the soldiers there, most of them terms of abuse for the native servants which even private soldiers had to serve them. I memorised as many as possible in the next two days, while Townie attended to the details outside the station.

On the third day Mr Dempster, an inspector, arrived and went into Black Sandy's office, without giving any sign of recognition. After a considerable period of time I was summoned to his presence. Mr Mathieson stood respectfully beside the desk, while "Spring Balance" (Mr Dempster) sat in the chair with a file of papers of alarming thickness before him. Without any preamble he asked, "What's this cock and bull story about you speaking this darkie language?"

Summoning all my aplomb I looked at him, and tried to inject a note of indignation into my voice. I replied, "I beg pardon, sir! I have some knowledge of Hindustani". He seemed nonplussed and fingered the papers before him before turning to the stationmaster to ask. "Have you any knowledge of it, Mr Mathieson?"

It was some seconds before he could reply, so taken aback was he by the query. "No! no! no!... Mr Dempster, just the Gaelic ... nothing more ... nothing more".

Dempster stared at me, while I shuffled uneasily, then he abruptly told me to leave, which I did hurriedly.

I stood outside the closed door, straining to catch what was being said inside, without success, until I was called in again. Did I know anyone in Dingwall fluent in the language. I regretted that I did not, but so many of the men in the area had served abroad that there was certain to be a good number. I suggested "Townie", but Mr Dempster said sharply that he did not want any railwaymen, and then, changing his mind, said that he would like to see the foreman porter. I was again dismissed, and Townie was sent for.

He had given the names of several people, who, he knew had a knowledge of Indian languages but all were rejected. He then added that he had heard that the manager of the Conservative Club had been employed for many years in India, and would perhaps be able to assist. The title of the club obviously impressed Mr Dempster, who told me to accompany him to this establishment. The club was two rooms above a greengrocer's shop, and the manager was Duncan Durward, a friend of Townie's. The area from Dingwall to Invergordon formed the "State Control Area" where all the licensed premises were owned by the Government, a relic of the First World War, when the area was flooded with soldiers, sailors and dockyard workers.

Drunkenness was so rife that the State had to take over all places where it was sold. The State's policy was to reduce drinking, and the only place where a bottle of spirits could be purchased in Dingwall was in the "Liquor Store" a former shop on the High Street with large clear glass windows. Most members of the club were the farmers, and only in this way could they obtain a drink between 3 o'clock and opening time in the evening. No food was made available, and Duncan's job was to see that a stock of drink was always on hand, and to keep the rooms tidy. He had served in the army and had tried many jobs, and claimed that he had been with a troup of actors for a number of years, and had often played the leading part. He was a plausible rogue and was willing to do almost anything for a reward. Townie and he had assiduously rehearsed the part he was now to play.

He met us at the top of the stairs and I introduced myself and Mr Dempster, who outlined what he wanted. Duncan nodded understandingly. "I am most willing to help in any way. I spent many years in India, and in addition to Hindustani I had to pick up many of the varied tongues spoken in that vast and fascinating country. Hindustani I know best, that being the *lingua franca* of the rajahs and princes, and most of my dealings were with these. All speak excellent English but naturally like us to speak their language."

Dempster listened with little interest. "Right then", he said, "let us have a trial".

Duncan turned to me, "Could you say a few sentences?" he asked. Holding my hands behind my back, and gripping them firmly, I drew a deep breath and repeated some of the words and phrases I had learned, starting with the numbers from one to ten. "Eki, do, chin, panj, sat, ath, naw, das" and continued with words like "panee lao, juldee, budmash". I tried to make them sound like sentences.

Duncan responded with a stream of words, and I said "Hang, hang" at intervals, the word I believed meant, yes. Duncan turned to Dempster, "That's quite good", he said. "Naturally his accent is bad, but he can be understood, which is required in everyday life". I interjected that I did not understand all that he had said, in case Dempster asked me what it did mean. But he stood for a minute, undecided as to what he would now do. Then he turned on his heel, and left, saying over his shoulder, "Get back to work". I ventured to stay a few seconds to promise Durward that I would be in the National bar that night.

I got a letter of warning from the Traffic Manager, reminding me that my first duty was to work in the interest of the company, and that the public should be directed to the station office if I was engaged on other duties.

My success in evading any penalty gave me a reputation as an expert in this field, and I was often asked to write letters of explanation for falls from grace. Many of my actions were motivated by vanity, not the only deadly sin I committed.

DORNOCH AND INVERGORDON

My experience at Dingwall was not my last encounter with the peerage by any means. Viscount Rothermere was a brother of the famous Alfred Harmsworth, later Lord Northcliffe and founder of the *Daily Mail*, and inherited the vast Press empire on the death of its founder. He had a residence in Dornoch where he spent much of his time. After the First World War he had spent much time in Paris during the negotiations that later became the Treaty of Versailles: he was attracted by the Hungarians, and became friendly with Admiral Horthy, the Regent of that country, which had now no navy and no king. The Hungarians assiduously cultivated Lord Rothermere, flattering him by hinting that he might someday be the king of their country.

Lord Rothermere began to show traces of the madness which had killed his brother, and his belief in his destiny became an obsession. While on holiday he had played golf at Dornoch Links with Provost Murray and had stayed the night in the provost's home, Burghfield House. The exercise, the air and the peacefulness of the attractive little village induced sound sleep, and in the morning he announced that he had slept for the first time for many weeks, and wished to buy the house, offering a figure that could not be refused. Daily he expected some secret emissary to arrive from Hungary with the news he desired, and he instructed the editor of the *Daily Mail* to send to Dornoch any unknown person who was written about for some unusual reason. This meant, of course, adventurers, cranks, exhibitionists and confidence men.

A constant stream of such people as the Vicar of Stiffkey, who later was killed by a lion in its cage at a seaside resort in England, arrived off the train of the Dornoch Light Railway, having travelled by first class sleeper from Euston to Inverness overnight. So great was the increase in traffic that a clerk was sent to assist the one at Dornoch. With the approach of summer the trickle grew to a flood, and I was despatched to Dornoch to give further assistance. By this time many had already arrived and left. The Viscount's

Rolls-Royce met the train, and on arrival at Burghfield House, the new arrivals were lined up, after partaking a cup of coffee on the lawn. His lordship then walked slowly past them watching their eyes, and looking for any meaningful sign. Those obviously not connected with anything much were indicated by his walking cane making a hole in the turf in front of their right shoe. A secretary noted the name, and after lunch an envelope was presented to them. This contained a third class ticket to London, but no sleeping berth, for at that time these were only first class.

There was much angry disputation, and the little police force of four men, including the chief constable, in uniform like his men, were frequently in attendance at the house and station. The more accomplished, by various means such as the excuse of waiting for further instructions from Budapest were able to spin out their sojourn to a week or more. But all brought no news and the Viscount reconsidered his strategy, concluding that the Hungarian Republicans would naturally watch the departures at Euston, and switched his attention to those who arrived by the more usual local services. I, of course, was one of these and after a few days my stationmaster, John Campbell, "Silent John" intimated that my presence would be appreciated at Burghfield that afternoon.

Everyone knew of the happenings but were not yet aware of the change in procedure, and I puzzled as to what I was wanted for but attended at the time stated. There were several others waiting on the steps of the house, all equally at a loss. A secretary took our names, and we were called when the Viscount was ready to see us. When my turn came I was ushered into a large study, and the door was closed behind me. Behind a large desk slumped in a chair was a gross man, with a heavy unhandsome face. He stared at me unblinkingly while I looked at him with interest. I glanced round the room which was hung with paintings, each one with a small guarded light shining upwards on the picture.

Suddenly he said, "What do you know of Hungary?" I told him what I knew. It was a central European country, formerly part of the Austro-Hungarian Empire, predominantly Catholic and had a strange language called Magyar. This word I pronounced as "Mojjar". Here I was interrupted by "Stop!" He came alive, pulling himself upwards and thrusting his head forward towards me asked "How did you pronounce it that way?"

I explained; as a boy I had attended a class held by the minister of Castlehill church on Sunday evenings. This was not the family church but he showed slides and gave us lemonade and chocolate biscuits. One of his lantern lectures was about Hungary, as he had for a number of years been the incumbent of the Scots Presbyterian Church in Budapest, and even at the age of eight I was interested in languages and had retained this in my memory. He was patently disappointed and rung the bell for the secretary who guided me out.

This period in Dornoch was one of the most pleasant, for it is a delightful place, and one which I frequently visit. Burghfield House is now a hotel, a feature of the tiny town with its baronial tower and high position. My room companion, John, was the son of the stationmaster at Delny, whom I had met before, and who was excellent company. His sole interest was in girls, and Dornoch had many, for the Dornoch Hotel, the pride of the former Highland Railway, employed large numbers during the summer season. The social event of the summer was the Sheriff's Ball held in the hotel ballroom, and Jock's current girlfriend was one of the waitresses there. So eager was he to see her that he purchased two tickets at the exorbitant price of £1 each, and extorted this sum from me. I had occasionally attended a village dance, but these were held only in winter time and were friendly informal affairs where the elders sat on forms round the hall and had tea and gossip.

I rarely had more than the suit I wore, leaving my "Sunday" suit at home. Lodgings were not always to be found near my work, and it was advisable to have the minimum of luggage to carry. My supply of changes of shirts was limited so both Jock and I went to the ball in the clothes we worked in, and these were none too clean or smart. We were received with disfavour, and the sheriff in full Highland dress, dirk and sporran did not shake hands as he did with the other attenders, nor did his spouse in a flowing dress, tiara and other ornamentation smile at us. As the hall filled up we became more, rather than less, conspicuous and eventually we gravitated to the kitchen and the company of the waitresses and other staff. I was willing to leave but Jock would not agree to this, but an ultimatum from the man in charge, that we wash dishes or leave, drove me away. Jock arrived in the early hours of the morning disconsolate. His friend, exhausted, had turned angrily on him, and he was to see her no more. I did not grudge the expense for it was a scene that I have remembered forever.

For most of the year Invergordon was a quiet little town, its very wide street, the main road to the north, adding to its apparent quietness. But each year the Navy returned for exercises, and the town was filled with sailors, "slop dealers" who followed the Fleet, wives and smart young women, as well as others whose interests were unknown. The State Liquor Control had the only licensed bar, but there was no liquor store. It was an impossible task to get a drink unless one was big, strong and brave.

I had difficulty in getting lodgings because of the influx of Navy visitors, having finally to share a bed with two others, in a very small bedroom in a house on Hugh Miller Street. At breakfast on my first morning Mrs Mackenzie asked if I would leave a note and money with the newsagent William Willson; the name remains in my memory because of the unusual spelling of the surname. At lunch time she asked if, when returning home at five o'clock, I would call at the same shop and ask for her winnings, if any. On calling I was handed an envelope containing money, and discerning my curiosity she explained that she betted on horses, and was surprised when she learned that not only had I never placed a bet, but did not even know how to do so. I had never known anyone who did.

I ventured to put one shilling each way on the horse she favoured, and won, and each time she gave me the name of a horse I again placed a bet, and there was money for me. I was now enjoying a good income; my lodging allowance alone came to £2. 12s. 6d. while my salary was £2. 6s., or nearly as much as a mainline locomotive driver. I had asked that £4 be deducted from this each fortnight and deposited in my account in the railway savings bank, which paid four per cent interest, a very high figure then. Lodgings were rarely much higher than £1 a week, so that I was now able to buy clothes and the books and magazines that I wanted.

Within a fortnight I was rather blasé about gambling, and determined to win a large sum. My landlady had given me the name of the horse she was to back, but the odds were low, about 4 to 1, so I looked for the highest figure which was 24 to 1 and placed £2 each way on it. During the few idle minutes at work, for we had to work very hard, I speculated what I could do with all my winnings. I was shocked to learn that I had lost, although there was again money for my landlady. I asked Willson what had happened to my horse, and he suggested that I call in next morning as he expected that it would have arrived by that time.

Mrs Mackenzie saw that I was somewhat disconcerted and I had to tell her that I might not be able to pay her if I had to leave on Saturday. This did not upset her, and she then went on to tell me that she never looked at a horse's name, but gambled on the jockey. She backed only one, a newcomer called Gordon Richards. He became the most successful jockey in British racing, and if I had continued gambling I would probably have won considerable sums, but I never gambled again having lost all interest in that pastime; nor have I been any more successful with the myriad raffle and sweepstake tickets I have bought.

Fearn in Ross-shire served a large agricultural area and a number of fishing villages, Shandwick, Balintore, Hill of Fearn and, nine miles away, the little port of Portmahomack. A two horse railway lorry was stationed there, and arrived each morning at Fearn station with goods, and returned in the afternoon with the freight received by rail.

The stationmaster, Collins, had come from Oban, which was served by the former Caledonian Railway, now part of the LMSR. The authorities encouraged men from this line to come to the Highland line, as they felt that it needed some of the discipline and efficiency of the south. The "Caley" was a well run line, serving the most industrial part of Scotland, and based in Glasgow. Few had applied for transfers, however, and Collins was one who had. Unfortunately he was weak and petty, and favoured three of his staff above the other two. His favourites were the first clerk, Gray, and two of the three porter signalmen, Stavely and Gordon. The second clerk, Dougal and the remaining porter signalman, Dean, found themselves out of favour.

By coincidence, Gray and Stavely went on annual leave at the same time, Stavely doing in the wages for one week only, Dougal for a fortnight. I was sent to relieve Dougal, and George Cormack, a relief signalman, was sent to relieve Stavely. On arrival the first task was to find lodgings for both of us, but Collins refused to suggest where we could live. Dougal had lived some distance away with a Miss Mackenzie, cooking his own food, and looking after his room. Having received instructions how to find this house, I set off on my bicycle, and at last reached the house, a typical Scottish "two up, two down" grey stone house, the garden bleak and uncultivated, and with curtainless windows.

My knocks at the front door brought no answer, and I went round to the door at the rear, and had to enter the kitchen. Again I could get no answer. I found Miss Mackenzie sitting before the small fire, adjusting some blocks of wood, used as fuel. She was tall, and very old, and also very deaf. By the time I could make her understand what I wanted, I was quite hoarse. Finally we came to an agreement after she had first shown me Dougal's room. This was untidy, with piles of dirty cups and plates on the floor, and empty tins in the fender. George and I would have to sleep here, but she would give us food. I said that we would arrive for "dinner" in a couple of hours and returned to the station where Collins complained at the time I had taken. I found that he could not read the telegraph, as that instrument had long been replaced by the telephone on his former line, nor could Gray, who had always been in goods offices, and handled that department.

George and I cycled for our lunch, which comprised boiled eggs, oatcakes and tea. The first mouthful of that liquid almost made me choke, so horrible was the taste, but I did not complain, as this might mean that I would be asked to find other accommodation. I glanced at George, who was trying to talk to Miss Mackenzie, but as she had removed her artificial dentures, we had difficulty in understanding what she said. I gradually swallowed my cup of tea, on which George shouted that I would like another, which she insisted in pouring from a large silver plated teapot of the Georgian type. This second supply tasted even worse than the first and I was unable to take more than the one sip.

On our way back to work I said that something poisonous must have been in my cup previously, to be surprised by George's reply that his had tasted the same, and that he had enjoyed my obvious discomfort, while putting the cup to his own lips without drinking the contents. He was an incorrigible joker, and I had always been glad to work with him. He had to stay on duty longer than I, and at my evening meal, again eggs and oatcakes, Miss Mackenzie asked if I had noticed anything strange about my tea at lunch time. I admitted that I had, so she told me that she had used her best teapot, the first time for many years, and had forgotten to remove her purse, which was usually kept in the teapot on the mantelpiece for safety and convenience. She produced the little black receptacle, still with the coins, copper and silver, and some pound notes. These she was drying out carefully in a pot beside the fire.

In the morning I rose, my stomach greatly upset, probably as a result of the tea of the day before, and wrapping myself in my overcoat, for dressing robes were not used in our circles, asked for the toilet. Miss Mackenzie, or "Eebie", as she was known, looked at me without comprehension and still without her teeth, so I used a more colloquial term. With considerable urgency I used several more euphemisms, and still failing to get a response, used the final and universally understood name, was advised that this facility did not exist, and that I would have to recourse to the whins and bushes behind the house. It was March, bitterly cold and a steely wind was shooting snowflakes which felt like arrows of ice.

George and I were able to augment our monotonous diet with food from the little sub-post office some distance away in the opposite direction. Biscuits, cheese and other comestibles were available. Collins objected to us eating in the office, or boiling a kettle, but Mrs Dean provided us with hot tea, and we ate in the goods shed. Neither George nor I could do anything right, but when we demanded to know how he wanted things done, the answer was "The proper way", which gave his coterie great pleasure. After a noisier argument than usual he would write out a telegram to the Traffic Manager asking replacements for either George or myself. These I would pretend to send, but signalled only pieces of nonsense, as a learner does when practising, and ignored by all the stations on the circuit.

On the Friday, Dean and George got their revenge. A wagon loaded with hogshead of molasses had arrived for Cadboll farm, where prize cattle were kept, and where the molasses was added to the other food to give a fine gloss to the skin of the animals and to add weight. Collins insisted on checking all goods I had already done. The waterproof sheet was removed from the wagon, and I climbed on to the buffers to count the barrels, but Collins preferred to stand on top of the barrels, a practice naturally known to Dean. Either he or Cormack – neither of whom would admit to doing it – had loosed the lid of a barrel, and when Collins stepped onto this lid it gave way, and he sank into the sticky material. No one rushed to help him, knowing that the material was so dense that he would not be immersed, but would be unable to pull himself out without help. Without too much hurry the two men moved the wagon by means of a crowbar used as a lever to the tyre of the vehicle, towards the hand crane. It was placed under the crane, and a rope slipped under the victim's armpits, and then, also unhurriedly, the crane rope was tightened to pull him free. The wagon was then pushed clear of the crane and he was lowered to the ground. It would have been easier to swing the jib round without moving the truck, but that would have been quicker.

Collins was now almost incoherent with shouting, but was guided towards his house, each man holding one hand to assist his slow progress, but keeping as far away as possible. The straw, which littered much of the yard, adhered to the bottom of his trousers, and when he entered his kitchen this extended several feet behind. It was a cruel and savage practical joke, but it was so well managed and staged that it had to be considered an accident. Nor would the authorities have approved of the stationmaster's actions. They would have held that anyone incapable of checking the number of barrels correctly was incompetent and should not have been in the company's employ. Collins had therefore to remain silent. He did not appear again that day.

George was finished next day, Saturday, and I determined to go away for the weekend, as I could not face a Sunday alone. Collins refused to let me go, so I waited until the telegraph was busy ticking away, and then acted as if there was a message for Fearn and wrote it down. This was addressed to myself and instructed me to return home for the weekend to reduce expenses. This I showed to him, saying that I would have to leave by the midday train, since the later one would mean that I would be able to claim overtime, which would be objected to. He asked for a copy, but I claimed that I did not need to give anyone a copy of my correspondence. He was now to be left without a telegraphist but he could ask either Tain or Nigg to intercept any messages for Fearn. As he had bad relations with his neighbours also, this he would be unwilling to do, except in an emergency. I found that he had reported me, and this was raised with me some time later, but I said that I was instructed to save expenses whenever possible, and that there was another clerk in the station in addition to the stationmaster.

The following week was no more pleasant, but I endured it in silence as I could not count on the support of George as I had in the previous week. This was probably the worst time I spent at any station. A relief clerk was often in difficulty as anything that went wrong during his presence was made his responsibility, but this was accepted as one of the hazards of life, and head office also made allowances.

Tain later gave me a problem, but of a different kind. I was unfortunate in my lodgings, and after a week found that I was infested with lice, something that I had never experienced, and which I found embarrassing. The stationmaster was a nice old man, and I explained my quandary. He advised me to buy new underclothes and burn those I had, then buy a large bottle of embrocation, of the powerful kind used on horses, and then stripping, cover myself, including my hair with this liquid, and after a few minutes remove it, using as many old newspapers as I could obtain. He suggested that I could use the ladies waiting room which had a fire and a key to the door.

Waiting until the station closed for the night I followed his advice. Spreading newspaper, of which I had an ample supply from the bookstall, I poured the strong smelling stuff over my head and closing my eyes tightly let it pour over me. It poured into every hollow and interstice, and was so painful that I was tempted to run into the night to the nearest horse trough, which was not far away. Parts of my body burned and stung for days.

HELMSDALE

Helmsdale, approximately 60 miles south of Wick, was an important station, having a loco depot with six engines and the necessary staff to operate them, and was open night and day. A mixed train left Wick every night at midnight and arrived in Helmsdale early in the morning, where it discarded the wagons and became the morning passenger train. This was the only main line mixed train in Britain, all others being on branch lines. My duties started at 5.30 a.m. as the train left at 6.10 a.m. This meant that I finished work daily at 3 p.m. leaving ample time for golf. While the train had to cover the 60 miles to Wick, a bus ran between the two points, serving also Lybster and other fishing villages before reaching Wick, covering only 20 miles or so. Many passengers for Wick alighted therefore at Helmsdale and continued by bus to their destination.

The town of Wick had earlier been voted "dry" under the Local Veto system which controlled the number of bars and licensed hotels in an area. Each day the bus driver had a list of purchases of whisky and beer for customers in Wick, and it is doubtful if much less liquor was drunk in the "dry" town. This Act of Parliament was only rescinded in 1977.

From Helmsdale the railway turned inland to serve the various shooting lodges. As mentioned earlier, it had been built by the Duke of Sutherland at his own cost; he had his own engine, at Golspie just outside his main residence, Dunrobin Castle, which was last used to convey King Alphonso of Spain, who was on holiday with the duke: he returned to Spain to be deposed and driven from his country. The engine is now in British Columbia. The approach from the south is hidden by an overhead road bridge where the line curves. The heavy passenger train usually needed two of the most powerful locomotives in Britain and as the gradient was steep, made an impressive entry to the station, at full power and then braking very sharply and noisily.

Our stationmaster, known as "Holy Smoke", this being the only expletive he used, had had no previous experience on a main line and was always very nervous of this alarming arrival and tried to control it. The two "mail" trains, north and south-bound, met, or "crossed" here, and Smoke stood on the iron footbridge with red and green flags, which he waved furiously as the trains approached, unconscious of the fact that the drivers looked ahead and not up at the bridge. No one had the temerity to tell him that all his efforts were a waste of energy, for he was happy in the thought that he daily assured the safety of the passengers. In any case he was usually hidden by the smoke and steam.

He was nervous also of having to speak to any of the higher officials who happened to be travelling, and as their movements were usually known ahead, he was absent "on important business" in the village when one of the chiefs put his head out of the window to survey the station.

The LMS Railway had the American system of a President and four Vice Presidents, and one of these, Vice President A V C Lemon, wrote to each stationmaster stating that he wished them to be on the platform when he passed through. This concerned Smoke greatly until he struck on a solution, gleefully pointing out that the letter did not state which platform. The mail picked up the dining car at Helmsdale, and to do this the whole train had to be pushed rearwards through the goods shed to the little siding holding the diner. There was not room for an engine and a coach, hence this performance. The gradient was steep here also, and the two engines on this train had to exert their full force, thus blasting red hot cinders into the air as well as massive clouds of smoke and steam. On this day I had to act in Smoke's place, and when Mr Lemon asked if I was the stationmaster I had to say that I was "acting". After a few enquiries about traffic and staff he concentrated on the shunting movements taking place, which were rather unorthodox. When the northbound train had gone, Smoke joined us on the platform as we stood in a line to lift our caps when Mr Lemon passed. The train was now ready to leave, it whistled and started off. The gradient fell steeply and in the short distance before the first carriage passed the speed was considerable. When the vice president passed us Smoke expressed relief that all had gone so well, and then paused in horror. Attached to the dining car were two short wheel based workmen's trucks, heaped with weeds and rubbish collected in an effort to tidy the station, and as a final stroke, the surfacemen's forks sticking up like pennons from the pile of greenery.

While Smoke was helped into his house, we acted quickly. Five miles south was the tiny halt of Loth, fortunately manned although the train which had left did not pause there except by arrangement with the guard, and this happened very rarely. We hurriedly called him on the telegraph, and forewarned of the important official travelling, he was attentive and answered immediately. Instructions were given and he put his signal to "Danger". The guard acted as we anticipated he would, and when the train stopped he dropped to the ground and uncoupled the two trucks, and gave the driver the "right away". Fortunately Mr Lemon did not look out, as Loth was not a scheduled stop on his programme.

An engine had already been sent from Helmsdale to pick up the two trucks, and soon had them back in the yard. It was such opportunities to use one's initiative that made the Highland section unique; control was remote and in the absence of telephones, slow and uncertain. Having two separate engines and vehicles in the same section was a very serious offence, and if discovered would involve very harsh penalties on the offenders.

During the summer the village and the golf course were busy, many visitors coming year after year, and there was always a partner for a game of golf. The course was made more exciting than most by the fact of having a croft in the middle, the tenant of which, made full use of his protected rights under the Crofters Act. Under the terms of this act a Land Court was set up for the purpose of arbitration. The crofter protested when any ball landed within his piece of ground, and if it landed near a cow or a sheep would pursue the player demanding compensation for "disturbance and alarm". Like most crofters, he was well versed in the law relating to his occupation, and it was best to pay a penny or two for the recovery of the erring ball. The Land Court dealt annually with hundreds of cases, mostly disputes among the crofters themselves, for they seemed to enjoy the legal arguments and quiddities of the law.

By mid September the course was deserted, as was the village, for the young and old fishermen left for Wick, to join the drifters for the winter fishing. The Duke of Sutherland granted the residents of the village the privilege of fishing in the Helmsdale (or Bunillodh) river which emptied into the harbour. I found that I did not have the patience for this pastime, and looked for some other way of spending my afternoons. Many local men had emigrated and a number of these had been goldminers in western United States and Alaska. Of all emigrants, the crofters are the most likely to return, drawn back by their way of life, and some of these miners on returning had recognised that gold was likely to be found in the river. Within a short period a shanty town had grown up and the "gold rush" was on. The duke, however, took action and the police and estate workers, with the troops in the background, destroyed the many tents and huts and threatened to prosecute any future goldwashers. There were still in the village little phials of dust, and some owners of watch chains made from the occasional tiny nugget found. I was given a lesson in washing the sand in an old frying pan by one of the local men, but after an afternoon's work had nothing to show for my pains.

In a casual conversation with the PSI (permanent staff instructor) of the local company of the Territorial Army Unit, the Argyll and Sutherland Highlanders, I found that he had served with my brother-in-law Tommy Mason at one time. I mentioned that Tommy had let me use a .303 Lee Enfield rifle, the standard weapon of the British Army, and as a result he asked me if I would help him in completing his "Musketry Roll". Most of his recruits were young fishermen, for most of the year absent through the week, returning for the weekend to their homes.

Religion prevented them from any attendance on Sunday, and Saturday was used, especially by the young men, for drinking. Each man had to fire so many rounds each year to qualify for the "bounty" paid annually. So on a good clear day Sergeant Field called for me at my lodgings, with a motor lorry and a few rifles, and we went up the glen to the rifle range and fired as many rounds as we liked. This rifle had a strong recoil, and after a few shots one's shoulder began to ache. It was the only form of sport at which I showed any aptitude, as my left arm and shoulder were only employed to a minor degree in shooting. When the village lorry was not available we would cycle to the firing range, with only one rifle slung over our shoulders.

The country always seemed to be unoccupied and deserted but on each occasion we were halted on our return by a gamekeeper and assistant. By some "bush telegraph" it was soon known, even on such enormous estates, that men were to be seen with a rifle. Our reasons were legitimate and there was no action taken.

My experiences did have a sequel later in the year. I was asked one afternoon after leaving the station which was a short distance from the village that lay on the north side of the river, if I would like to do some shooting that evening. I accepted the offer with alacrity and was told to be near the Drill Hall at seven o'clock. It was already dark when I arrived punctually, and I was told to climb into the truck waiting around the corner, and remain quiet. This I did, to be joined by a number of others;, the last man to climb in had first handed up a number of rifles, each loaded with a clip of three cartridges. It was not difficult to feel them and know that they were the Army issue, "SMLE" – "shorter model: Lee Enfield", and that they came from the Drill Hall.

We started off towards the north, on the Ord road, with only side lights shining, but there were few cars on the road at that time of year. After a time we left the main road, and progressed slowly over one that was narrow, rough and steep, the side lights now extinguished. There was a full moon with an occasional cloud, and if I had been able to relax the trip would have been enjoyable. Coming to a halt we climbed out and I was led by the elbow to a position on a slope. I was told to lie there until deer appeared on the summit of the ridge, silhouetted against the sky; I had to aim at the animal directly in front of me, but must not fire until I heard the explosion of another gun. If it fell but was not killed, I must try with another bullet to finish it off; if I was unsuccessful in doing this I must take no action.

The time seemed to be interminably long, but at last a stag appeared followed by a herd, all in single file. There was a single shot and then a ragged volley. I was uncertain if I had hit my target, but did not try to distinguish what was going on. A shout told us that we had to return to the lorry at once, and I stumbled towards where it lay, guided by the noise of those more certain than I. My rifle was taken from me as I was pushed up to the tailgate, and within minutes we were driven along the rough track, so fast that we were thrown about on the floor. Then we stopped again, and a number of carcasses were thrown in beside us before we set off for the main road. There a van was waiting, its lights extinguished and the deer were transferred to it. A car then appeared and stopped, the rifles were loaded into it and it left going north, as we turned south this time with all the lights blazing. As we approached Helmsdale, the men dropped off at different points in pairs, to walk to the village.

It was now too late to go to bed, so I walked to the station and kept company with the night shift signalman. No one ever mentioned shooting deer, and I did not venture to raise the subject at any time. Pay day was every alternate Thursday and on that night almost everyone, even those on duty, met at the Bridge Bar for a drink, and some time later when I went to order a round, the barman said that it had been paid for. I did not ask who was my benefactor.

A year or so earlier I had been at Beauly station, in the area owned by Lord Lovat, with large deer forests and fishings, and had to deal with a large number of parcels of venison being despatched. It had been for many years the custom to send a haunch of venison to those people who had been invited by the Lovat family to visit them at Beaufort Castle. A Visitor's Book was kept, and it was the duty of the head gamekeeper to arrange for each visitor to receive a present annually. In the course of time, many of these had died, or were no longer living at the addresses entered in this book. Each season, after the despatch of the meat, telegrams would be received at the station at Beauly informing it that the parcel addressed to so and so could not be delivered as "Not known", and asking for instructions about the disposal of the package. A telegram was sent in reply instructing that the goods be sold, and the money retained by the railway company.

Probably at one time the castle people would have been advised, but this was not now done. Instead a note was made of those names, and when the package arrived for despatch, a fresh label was attached and the original one destroyed. The new address could be that of a friend but mostly it was addressed to butchers and dealers, with whom previous arrangements had been made. I was not involved in this, and the loyalty of members of staff to each other, prevented anyone reporting this violation. Railwaymen were almost to a man radical in politics and this action was felt to be fair, a step to the egalitarianism then thought of as the chief aim.

SIX DAYS AT KILDONAN

On a Monday morning in early September the southbound train from Wick arrived very late, which was unusual, as three hours were allowed for the 66 mile journey. From it alighted a passenger in a towering rage, Mr J B Cairns, the Chief Operating Manager for the whole Scottish Division, an almost legendary figure in the north, none of us having ever seen him. He burst into the office to announce that he had suspended the stationmaster at Kildonan from duty, and ordered that someone be sent immediately to take charge of that station, which was not now manned. The only other member of staff there was a "nightman" on duty from midnight until 8 a.m., to allow the midnight mixed train to travel from Wick to Helmsdale. Cairns had sent the guard of the train to call this man out, but he was in bed and refused to come back on duty.

David Elder, the stationmaster had been "on the bash", drinking steadily for a period, and had refused to let the train leave. Cairns had come to the station to investigate the delay and had intervened, to be told that whatever his post was in Glasgow, he Elder, was in charge at Kildonan. Eventually Mrs Elder had taken her husband into the station house, and the guard obtained a tablet from Helmsdale, opened the level crossing gates and set the "Starter" signal properly.

Smoke was so excited by the presence of this imposing and authoritative man that he could make no decisions, and it was left to Willie and me to make them. It was decided that I should get to Kildonan and take over until a reliefman was sent. Cairns insisted that I leave immediately, but there would not be a train for several hours, and no other form of transport was available, the nearest taxi being at Wick more than twenty miles away. He suggested that I go by bicycle, but I refused to cycle ten miles with my luggage. He was impatient to get to Glasgow, and ordered that I travel by an engine, and signed a permit for me to go on the footplate with the driver and fireman. Mr Cairns had spent a week at Kinbrace fishing, a guest of the laird there.

The only engine available was a goods inside cylinder, 0-6-0 locomotive, which gave a noisy and rough ride. The opposing steam pistons gave it a crab like movement forward, pressed to the rail to one side and then the other with each stroke. I arrived tired with holding on to the handbrake handle, and covered with coal dust and grimed with smoke.

The station was deserted with the doors left open when I arrived. I ventured to knock on the house door, to be answered by Mrs Elder who slammed it in my face when I asked if I could have a word with her husband. She had the reputation of drinking with her husband, and this was now obvious. The Elders would have by now realised that they would have to move away, perhaps to the ranks of the unemployed.

It was not a busy station, for the parish had been depopulated during the "Clearances" of the nineteenth century, and it was not much more than a section "crossing" station, serving a shooting lodge, Suisgill, with the ancillary keepers, household staff, a few crofters, and railway surfacemen. It was also the sub-post office, Elder being postmaster and thus adding £60 a year to his salary from the railway of £220. Everything pertaining to the post office had been taken into his house. One thing left intrigued me, a brass compass-like instrument, with letters instead of points of the compass on its round face, covered by glass. It had only 24 letters, and, as I learned later, required a cable with 48 thin wires, a positive and a negative for each letter. Only three of these instruments were in existence – this one, one at Kinbrace and another in either Arran or Bute. It was the first electric telegraph made, before the invention of the Morse code. During my survey of the office and its contents the needle moved round several times pausing for a fraction of a second at letters, but too swiftly for my untrained eye.

At this point, Polson, the foreman surfaceman came in, and was able to give me the information I needed. He showed me how a current was generated by a small brass dynamo at the side, operated by the left hand, the right hand being used to control the needle. He said also that almost all the telegrams received on it were for the tenant of the Lodge, Brigadier Hicks, who was in residence but who would be leaving soon as the grouse season was nearly past, and he did not lease the deer shooting. The telegraph line led to Helmsdale, with no other office on the circuit. He could not enlighten me, however, on the correct procedure for dealing with messages. Again the needle started to move, as my attempts had shown at the other end that there was now someone present. I spelt out "Send slowly", but the operator's idea of speed differed from mine, and I got only a few letters before the movements ceased. I asked for repetitions, but probably exasperated by the lack of intelligence shown, the sender did not respond. The address had been easy for I knew what it was, but the rest made no sense. The first word I thought could be "holy communion" followed by parts of figures, so I wrote out on the buff telegram form "Holy Communion Sunday twelve noon", and placed it in the regulation orange envelope.

The Lodge was only a mile or so away, and I had ample time on my hands so I set out in the direction of the path from the station to the main North Road, and on to the Lodge, where I presented my envelope to a butler. He invited me inside, and placing the message on a silver tray disappeared. He reappeared to say that the master was not yet ready to deal with it, and offered me a glass of wine and a piece of cake, which I welcomed for I was already hungry. I had never tasted much wine and asked what it was, to be told that it was madeira. I then returned to the station, and was half way there when I heard the sound of horse's hooves and turned to see a smart gig and horse, driven by a young man wearing a sleeved waistcoat of the kind worn by the grooms of the gentry. This was Sam Fay, and he asked me to mount while he turned the vehicle. His master wanted to see me, and was very angry about something. I could guess what it was, but I was not unduly concerned. It was post office work, and I was probably acting illegally in handling private messages, as I was not a post office servant.

This made no difference to the attitude of the Brigadier who told me that if I did not get the message correctly my future was uncertain. He was something important in financial circles in the City of London, his rank being gained during the war when he had something to do with the control of railways, and thus was in touch with my employers. I returned to the office as quickly as possible and got in touch with Willie on the telegraph. He had spent all his life in the neighbourhood and knew exactly what I had to do. This was to contact Seaton, the stationmaster at Kinbrace, who had a post office telegraph of the same kind. He would ask for the original message to be given to him, and he would pass it on to me over our single needle instrument. Kinbrace was the next station to the north, and it took me half an hour of steady calling his sign "KB" before he answered. He was at first unwilling to act as I wanted but at last he relented, and I soon had the correct message. My "holy communion" became, "your communication" and there were many more figures than I had read.

On receiving it I was ready to walk to Suisgill Lodge to deliver it, when again Polson came to my rescue. He pointed to a small telephone mouthpiece fixed to a wall, which lead to the Lodge, and I used this. Sam Fay called every day to collect parcels and packages and had time for a chat. He assured me that the Brigadier would not hold any angry feelings against me, and this was proved when on the Friday morning he announced that I would be welcome at the Lodge that evening where a farewell party was to be held, as the family and staff left for London on Monday morning. During my six days at Kildonan no passenger alighted and none joined a train. The only traffic forwarded was a dog returning to its kennels at Erith, Kent, where the family had its home.

But I must revert to the day of my arrival. Once the business of the telegram was cleared, I had to do something about accommodation, as I was very hungry indeed. Vans called once a week at the homes in the area, and each alternate Friday, after the railway employees were paid, an engine and carriage collected the wives between Georgemas and Kildonan, halting at the isolated cottages of the surfacemen between stations, to convey them to Helmsdale where they bought supplies for the next fortnight, the train taking them home again in the early afternoon. This service had to be provided free of charge, or the line could not be staffed.

I first visited the house of the nightman, but his wife said that her husband slept much of the day, and would be disturbed by a stranger in the house. She said that the only possibility was to persuade Mrs Coghill in the adjoining cottage to accept me as a lodger. She was the widow of a railwayman, but was now very old, with bad eyesight and hard of hearing. She was also very religious, spending much time poring over the large family Bible which lay always on the table.

Mrs Coghill let me enter and sit down and I exerted all the charm and powers of persuasion that I possessed. I had to assure her that I was devout, a regular attender of the church, and culled from the recesses of my memory the phrases used in Burghead: "salvation in faith", "contrite of heart", "the wages of sin are death". I should have felt hypocritical, but I was hungry and tired. I had read the Bible then, as I do now, for the elegance and beauty of the words, but I was not a Christian.

She asked me if I could say a prayer, but I offered to read instead some verses from the Bible, on which she kept her hands all the time, as if for protection. She agreed, and pushed it towards me, and in the dim little room, its window grimy and coated with a thin film of peat smoke and ash, which also covered everything in the room, I read the psalm that began, "I love the Lord, because he hath heard my voice and my supplications".

It was a fortunate if unwitting choice, and I had a home for the time I was there. Before and after each meal I had to read a portion from the scriptures, and before going to bed at night, she would listen until I was hoarse. When I left the station when the nightman came on duty I took over the hand lantern, to add to the poor light of the little paraffin lamp she used, and which she took through to her bedroom. I liked reading and there was little else to read for there were no books in the house apart from the Bible, some "Commentaries" and the Railway Rule Book, which had been her husband's.

I helped to prepare the meals, for her eyesight was so poor that the potatoes and vegetables, which were her staple, would have been put into the pot badly cleaned and prepared. Cooking was a slow process for she used only peat, which smouldered all night and could be awakened to a little flame in the morning with the aid of a bellows, so old and worn, that I found my breath was more efficacious. She was a poor, gentle soul and the pleasure that I gave her by reading eased my conscience.

On Friday evening I presented myself at the kitchen entrance to Suisgill Lodge, and was taken to the Hall. The family with some guests had had an early dinner, and were waiting for the arrival of the indoor and outdoor staff. The Brigadier gave a short speech of thanks, and then signed to the indispensable piper. To the music of that instrument the "Grand March" was formed in rather restricted space, the master and lady walking with linked arms, followed in strict hierarchical order, by the family, guests, butler and the other servants, myself as an outsider being at the rear, with the youngest kitchenmaid. The master of ceremonies, after two circuits, waved the advancing couples left and right alternatively, to return four abreast, and then eight abreast. The piper ceased and each group of eight formed a set to dance the "Eightsome Reel", followed by "The Dashing White Sergeant".

There was a pause while wine, beer and soft drinks were distributed, and a toast drunk to "The Master and His Lady", after which the gentry left. Immediately whisky, brandy, beer and other drinks appeared, filched from the wine cellar almost daily and laid aside for this night, and soon the decorous behaviour was replaced by the rather wild and vigorous dances of the natives. This ceased at midnight and I had to leave. Sam and I were the only single men present, and he and four girls insisted on escorting me back to my lodgings.

It was a beautiful moonlit night, and the rocks and stones of Sutherland reflected the light to look like marble. All were noisy and cheerful, with much bumping and squeezing, and whether accidental or deliberate, all landed in the river which paralleled the road to the station. The party broke up with screams and giggles, the others fleeing back to the big house, while I hurried, wet to my thighs to the office, where the nightman was dozing by a good coal fire. Wrapping myself in his oilskins I dried my trousers before going on tiptoe to bed.

I left by the last train next day, as a reliefman was to arrive in the early hours of Monday from Wick by the "midnight mixed".

Elder was transferred to a goods office near Glasgow, and reduced to the rank of clerk.

The poignant history and melancholy beauty of Kildonan has remained always with me, drawing me back, but I have never dared to return.

It was in Helmsdale that I saw the start of a traditional, or perhaps of what would become a traditional, nursery rhyme. My landlady, Mrs "Sandan Jake" was a very intelligent person, one of the descendants of the crofters cleared from Strathhalladale and full of tales of the past. I heard some children singing at a dancing game on the slabs at the harbour. The words were:

Addie Beela's cow and calf
All in Jeemucks clover
Mrs Lowrie she ran out
And she went tumblin over.

People with these names lived nearby and I asked my hostess if she knew anything about this. It transpired that the subject was actually "Adams Bella" who had a cow and a calf on the little bit of land she had facing the road, and they had trespassed on the ground of a neighbour, James Mackay, the butcher. His neighbour on the other side, Mrs Lowrie had run out to chase back the animals, but the calf had butted her so that she had rolled down the steep slope and fallen on to the road, fortunately with little injury.

It has been said that nothing stands alone, and that everything is inter-related and also that the present is understood by looking at the past.

When Smoke went on holidays Jimmie Walsh came to relieve him. I knew him well and he shared my bed as my room mate had left and no one had come in his place. Walsh was older and senior to me, relieving stationmasters mostly at the larger stations. He had spent most of his time in Inverness where he made his home, but was unmarried. He had one common weakness, a fondness for alcohol. The first week went pleasantly but he found Helmsdale very dull and announced that he was going away on Friday to a big football match in Glasgow. Willie and I covered his duties to allow this.

He returned with the noon train looking tired and rather debauched, but cheerful as always. A train load of sheep was being loaded and he followed me to the loading bank once the station was cleared, and I soon knew that he had been drinking on the train. He admitted that he spent most of the time in the dining car, where he was well known and was able to get a few drinks. He then began to act foolishly, shouting at the sheep, moving the "flakes" which kept them from crushing each other, until I had to ask him to stop acting the fool. He turned his attention to me and seizing my hair gave my head a twist. There was no barber in Helmsdale and it was as long as is now fashionable. I pushed him away, which made him stagger and fall off the bank on to the track. We got him up, fortunately unhurt, but shocked. The work finished, I took him to our digs, and after eating some lunch suggested that he go to bed and that I would return and do his turn.

He was now contrite and apologised for his behaviour, his excuse being that he had not been in bed all weekend, and with a few friends had a "wild time". This I presumed was at the football match and afterwards in Glasgow. On return to the office, where Willie was waiting for me to relieve him for a meal, I found a stranger sitting beside the fire. He asked how his friend Jimmie was and I told him briefly that he was tired and was lying down. He spoke familiarly about various members of the staff at Inverness and I presumed that he was a friend, and spoke fairly frankly. He left with the evening train and I waited for Willie's return, and asked if he knew the stranger. He had not known, but the guard of the train had given him a meaningful look when the stranger had dismounted, and had said little. Willie was not as garrulous as I was.

On finishing work I returned to my room where Walsh was now feeling better. I told him of the few happenings of the day including the stranger. On hearing my description he became alarmed and I now heard a different story. He and his friends had not gone to Glasgow as they intended but had spent all the time in Inverness. Saturday night was like any other Saturday night, but on Sunday the party had become bored. At that time no alcoholic drinks were obtainable except in a hotel, and one had to travel at least a distance of three miles, before becoming a *bona fide* traveller and thus able to get a "refreshment". This was a relic of the days when one either travelled by a horsedrawn vehicle or walked, so that three miles took at least an hour. But the party were all railwaymen and arranged to get bottles of whisky from the Station Hotel staff using their authority as senior, or well known members of staff.

They sat in the various waiting rooms in the station, and had also gone into the only office open on Sunday, the telegraph office. All were now rowdy and skylarking and Walsh had smashed a window with an empty bottle. He said in extenuation that he had not done this intentionally but had simply thrown it through the window to keep the office tidy, all said with the utmost solemnity. The stranger was a sergeant of the railway police, a new introduction to the Highland section, which had depended upon the local police on the rare occasions when there was trouble. But Glasgow, or perhaps the national headquarters at Derby, had decided that the company's property must be better policed.

Walsh felt that there would be repercussions and asked my advice, as I had a reputation for solving such problems. I outlined the only course; he had taken this afternoon off as he was tired; next day Willie would have a half day, and I would also take Wednesday off commencing at 9 a.m. This was because we had covered his duties and this was our reward. Tuesday passed without any development but on Wednesday afternoon one of the men arrived at the golf course where I was playing to say that I was wanted at once by the Chief Inspector. I had my bicycle and soon returned.

There was to be an enquiry on Friday in Inverness to which Walsh and I were called, and the Chief wanted to know the circumstances. I knew that he was a fair man and did not care very much for the men from another, former railway, the Caledonian, coming into his area and telling how things must be done. I told what I intended to say, which was that I did not think Walsh's behaviour was anything but high spirits, that I knew him well, that at times he appeared to act irresponsibly, but that it was superficial, and that I could maintain that I had smelled no whisky. I could say this, for after my accident at Orbliston I had lost my sense of smell. The Chief made it clear that he expected us to adhere to this story. We knew that he would put matters in as favourable a light as possible. But when he left we talked it over and became discouraged.

I had been troubled for some time with severe abdominal pains and suspected that I would have to have my appendix removed, but delayed taking any action. I decided that I would see Dr Macdonald that night and went to his house. He was a bachelor and lived in squalid lodgings with a slatternly maid who was suspected of having a relationship closer than the normal employer-employee. He examined me and agreed that it would be advisable for me to get an operation as soon as possible. I asked if I could go into Golspie Hospital, the nearest. He had had a dispute with the matron there, and stated that he would not agree to this as nobody came out of it alive. I asked if he could arrange it at Leanchoil Hospital at my home in Forres. He telephoned the surgeon, Dr Gibbons, whom I knew, and it was arranged that I go to that hospital the following week. I returned to the station and sent a message to the Superintendent that I could not be in Inverness on Friday as I had to see my doctor on that day. By return I got a command to visit my doctor that day, or on Saturday, but to be in attendance at Inverness at 10.30 a.m. on Friday. I had to leave by the 6.10 a.m. train, too unwell and concerned to eat any breakfast. Walsh travelled to Dingwall to meet me and discussed the case, asking me to be categoric about his sobriety, but I said I was unwilling to go as far as that, and he became unpleasant and abused me.

The enquiry was formal except that no one was put upon an oath, and I stuck to my story, adding that as I had felt unwell I was perhaps more irascible than I would normally have been. I was closely cross examined, but I insisted that I had smelt no alcohol on Walsh's breath, but that he was obviously very tired and irritable also. The Superintendent asked me to wait outside until recalled, but I asked if I could not be released, as I had eaten nothing since the previous day and felt weak. After a few whispered words with his advisor, he dismissed me, but before leaving I asked for an interview before I returned with the 3.10 p.m. to Helmsdale. He said curtly to be at his office five minutes before the train left. He also was irritated but I was in a state that I did not care what happened, and left to have lunch with Hamish. The trouble between us at the time of the General Strike had been forgotten by us, but not by others.

Punctually I presented myself at the office, and asked that I be transferred to Forres, giving my reasons. For seven years I had been in many lodgings of different quality, had worked long and irregular hours, and now needed better conditions and home care. He said shortly that there was no vacancy, and if one arose I could apply for it. It was known that authority wanted to bring staff north from more ordered and disciplined sections, being of the opinion that the Highland people were too clannish and attached to the traditional ways of working and unwilling to change. We felt that our methods suited the our quite different conditions from those operating in the populated industrial south.

Within a week I was in hospital, had an operation and then spent a very pleasant two weeks in a railway convalescent home in Dawlish on the Devon coast. After an absence of five weeks I returned to Helmsdale, to learn that the Superintendent was in a nursing home because of a nervous breakdown. I took this to mean that he would never be able to return to his arduous and difficult job, and wrote a letter claiming that a vacancy had risen in Forres through one of the staff emigrating to Canada. In my younger days little consideration was given to mental health, and a nervous breakdown meant incarceration in a lunatic asylum, if violent, or left at home if quiet. Those in the first category rarely returned home, and the others probably lived lives of quiet misery with occasional noisy and troublesome periods.

Some days later a telegram from Wick instructed me to join the train at Helmsdale, where I would meet the Chief Inspector, who was now in charge, and travel with him as far as Golspie. He was accompanied by the District Engineer, Mr McMurdo, to whom I was introduced. I was asked about my interview, and confident that it would never be checked, altered the facts to suit my case. He asked Mr McMurdo to take note of what I said, and added that I would get my transfer, although Glasgow had intended to send someone north to fill it. I was fortunately unaware that I was making another "mark" against my name.

It was unlikely that the Chief Inspector fully accepted my story, but he was loyal to those with whom he had worked, and perhaps he resented also the attitude taken towards those who had gone on strike. In a few days I received my transfer, and returned to my home town, permanently I thought.

The staff at Forres station was around 100, ten of those being clerical. I had now regular hours, from 6 a.m. to 3 p.m. and 10 a.m. to 8 p.m. on alternate weeks. The work was routine and not very arduous for competition from buses and cars was steadily eroding rail traffic. I had little to do with the operating of the trains, apart from taking my turn in the telegraphic office. At first I missed the exhilaration and stir of train movements, but this gradually faded.

What made me want to return to my native town was that I could now be nearer Jenny, although her parent's opposition was even more determined than ever. They had, by very hard work, built up a prosperous business, and aimed at having a professional man or a farmer as a husband to their only daughter. I was in any case the antithesis of what they wanted; I was a trade unionist, a striker in the General Strike which adversely affected their business, and a rebel against the existing order, while they were pillars of the Conservative party.

Jenny was at school when I first met her, my friend Hamish being her cousin. To enable us to meet I had to join the Sunday Bible class, which she attended chaperoned by a member of her parent's staff. My weekend leaves were infrequent, but we wrote each other, my letters having to be sent to a friend to be delivered.

While the behaviour of the "Bright Young Things" of London filled the sensational press, Victorian standards of behaviour and propriety still predominated in the smaller towns and rural areas, and nowhere as firmly as in Presbyterian Scotland. While not accepted at her home, we could go to the cinema and golf, or join a picnic party. It is not easy to write of this part of my life.

On one occasion I had to be on duty all night in the telegraph office, because of some emergency, and to fill the empty hours I wrote an essay and posted it in the morning. I had read in the newspaper about an essay competition organised by the Economic League, the winners to have a trip to Europe. My four older brothers had all been overseas and I longed to see other lands. The subject of the essay was "The Return of Prosperity" or some similar title, and after scribbling some ideas I sat at the typewriter until I finished my effort.

Some weeks later I was informed that I was one of the prizewinners, and details of the proposed visit to the Continent were enclosed. The League's aim was to forward the case for capitalism, and to use all the publicity possible, so that the local as well as the national press had reports, and my photograph appeared for the first time. I was now a minor public figure, and connected with a most desirable cause. I was therefore now acceptable, and almost welcome at Jenny's home.

The worldwide depression was now at its worst, and only the rich went abroad for holidays, so that on my return I was invited to speak on my experiences abroad at guilds, women's institutes, literary societies, and the other bodies which at that time proliferated, all providing a cheap night's entertainment.

I had had my annual leave and wrote to the Superintendent asking for two weeks leave without salary, and received a curt refusal. I had been sent much literature by the League, amongst which was a list of its supporters, mostly large industrial firms, and company directors. Among the names was that of Sir Josiah Stamp, later Lord Stamp, the president of the London, Midland and Scottish Railway, who was also a well known economist and advisor to the Government. Although I had had little contact with the headquarters of LMS for two years, as most of my work went to the accountant's department, I recalled seeing Sir Josiah Stamp's name in connection with the company. I therefore wrote to him telling of my problem, and within two days received from the Inverness office leave of absence and a free railway pass to London, thus saving, no doubt, the League the sum of £6. 11s. 6d. [£6. 57p.], the cost of a third class return ticket

I joined my party in London where we spent two days visiting various works and having coffee with Colonel Bruce, the editor of the *Daily Telegraph* and a former explorer, and afternoon tea with Sir Earnest Benn of the publishers of that name, who gave me an autographed copy of his book, *The Letters of an Individualist*. Five years later I was in the company of Wedgwood Benn, the politician and later Lord Stansgate, and mentioned that I had met a Benn previously, to learn, with some surprise, that they were brothers. There could scarcely be two such brothers so different in their views.

The leader of our party was the MP for Margate, Mr John Baker White, a writer and journalist. I spoke of this also to Wedgwood Benn, who knew him, saying that he was a good chap "but saw a Red under every bed". In 1975 I had a letter from Mr Baker White, then over 80 and retired. From London we sailed from Tilbury to Dunkirk, by the ALA, *Alsace-Lorraine-Angleterre* steamer, certainly the most convenient way of crossing the Channel. Antwerp, Brussels, Liege and various places of interest filled our time in Belgium, and then on to northern France, and thence to the German Rhineland, staying in Cologne and Dusseldorf. We were entertained by Krupps of Essen and other great industrial firms, and yet had a good deal of free time. I became friendly with Charles Simpson, a councillor of the City of York, and a captain in the "Koylies", the Kings Own Yorkshire Light Infantry, serving in the Army of Occupation in the Rhineland after the First World War, who knew the area well.

Together we went to Bonn, then still a quiet university town, and met with some of the students. Many students still affected the peaked hat with its dangling tassel, and a few had facial scars made by the edged sabres used in duelling. This was now illegal, but indulged in by the more "Prussian" of the students.

Hitler was striving to seize power, and we could sense the tension and nervousness that prevailed. The police, named "Schupos" because of the strange helmets they wore, went about in twos and fours, well armed. Simpson and I had gone shopping in Dusseldorf before joining the party at the station; suddenly realising that we did not have much time to get there, we hastened our steps, and then began to run. We heard shouts but thought nothing of it, and continued, although we saw pedestrians halt and look at us. Then we heard a bang, and turning saw the Schupos running towards us, while arms were raised by those in front of us to halt us. Pistols were drawn, but showing our tickets and passports, we explained our action, we were waved onwards but warned to walk. Not more than four persons could collect in a group and a running figure was accepted as a terrorist, and if he failed to stop at a warning shot, was shot down. Fortunately we were in time for our train.

During our stay in Germany we had with us a Colonel Karl Hans Abshagen, a tall, typically Prussian officer, immaculately dressed, and with a sabre scar on his face. During the Munich crisis I saw him several times on the newsreels, as he was sent as an emissary from Count Von Ribbentrop, Hitler's foreign minister, carrying messages to Prime Minister Neville Chamberlain. He was undoubtedly a high ranking Nazi but he spoke to us only in general terms, but most interestingly.

FULL CIRCLE – RETURN TO FORRES

Not long after my arrival in Forres I was asked to re-organise my trade union branch, which had been weak since the strike of 1926. I took this in hand and soon had the membership up to the maximum of 100 per cent of the possible. For this I was given an award by the Trade Union Congress, and as a result I was nominated as a worker's representative on the Court of Referees, which operated under the various unemployment acts. Anyone disqualified from getting any of the benefits, or an inadequate benefit, could appeal to this body. It sat in Elgin and was composed of a chairman, who had to be a lawyer, one representative for employers and one for the workers. My brother Jack had been invalided out of Nigeria and was now with the Ministry of Labour, as was Abb. I was able to get a great deal of valuable information from these two, and was successful in a very large proportion of the cases dealt with. The chairmen were always very fair, but some of the employers seemed to consider applicants as offenders, trying to get money by false pretences;, others again were as fair as the chairman.

I was later appointed to the North of Scotland National Assistance Appeal Board which met in Inverness. This dealt with cases of people who had exhausted all the benefits from the unemployment offices, and were now on national assistance from taxes. I was called to one session only. This was after I had left railway service, and the date was the day after a Spanish warship had the temerity to fire on a British warship off the coast of Spain. This was in the early days of the Spanish Civil War. When I arrived at the room for the court the other two members were already there. I was introduced and they continued their conversation: one was a colonel and the other a Naval captain, and the latter was indignant at the incident at sea, claiming that he would have fired back. He was "deuced" if he could recall the name of the Spanish vessel, and I provided it. It was the *Jaime Primero*, and I pronounced it in the Spanish style, for I had studied Spanish. In a quarter deck bellow he demanded to know how I knew the language, and was incredulous when I claimed some knowledge of it.

The three cases we dealt with had already been heard in the Court of Referees and perhaps elsewhere, and had now to be decided by this body, the court of last resort. I had won many cases by resorting to the threat of putting in a minority report, which meant that the majority had to put their case in writing. Rather than do that the appeal would be granted. I did this with all three cases, and the appellants won. One case I recall clearly: he was a tailor in Inverness and having been unemployed for a very long time had been sent to unload loose cement at Inverness Harbour. It had started to rain and he refused to work as his clothes would be ruined, and was refused benefit. Cross examined he told that he had now only the one suit which, as a tailor, he kept neat and repaired. Everything saleable in the house had been sold for the sake of his wife and children. If he was sent for an interview wearing a cement stained suit, no tailor would take him on. He was told that soldiers and sailors had to carry on in all weather conditions, while I argued on different lines. Finally the majority decided on rejection, and I then announced my intention to put in a minority report, refuting the captain's statement that we lived in a democracy where the minority had to accept the decisions of the majority. The chairman had to explain that these principles did not apply in this case, the procedure being clear, although the captain could make these statements in his written report. Although my appointment was for three years I was never called again.

So parlous was the economic position, that even the railways, slow and monolithic, began to speak of redundancies and dismissal of staff, as natural wastage was too slow. It was decided to close the telegraph office and transfer the instruments into the general office, and this was done. I was designated as a telegraphist in the report, which I never saw until later. It was with some surprise and resentment that I found I was made redundant, and was told that I would be transferred to London. I protested, pointing out that I was about two months senior to the third member of staff, and found that I had lost the time I was on strike, and was now the junior in service.

I appealed and was told that it would be dealt with at the next conciliation committee, which was some months in the future, but meantime I had to accept the transfer. At many mainline stations the clerks also sold tickets for the London Underground Railway, which was always short of staff, and it was at one of these that I had to report on my arrival in London. This was at Queens Park station on the main west coast route to Scotland. It serviced also the Bakerloo line, and also the LMS electric lines in the city.

I reported to the stationmaster, Mr Beard, who welcomed me with the words "Why can't you Scots bastards stay in your own country?" It was the first time that my nationality had been objected to, although it was, as always, a subject of joking. The work was monotonous, simply standing at a ticket window issuing thousands of slips of paper daily, and then balancing the cash at the end of one's shift. I knew little of the ramifications of the lines, and this gave Mr Beard plenty of scope for criticisms. The other four men in the office were very pleasant and gave every assistance they could, but had enough to do at peak hours to attend to their own windows. I was not surprised that there was a shortage of booking clerks.

My shifts varied, the earliest one starting before six in the morning: I could purchase a "staff" ticket for twopence, which acted as a season ticket during the day of its date. This allowed me to visit a great part of London, and one shift gave me a break from noon to five o'clock, so that I was able to attend matinee performances, which were very cheap. The largest cinema at that time was the Trocadero, and in the afternoons it engaged vaudeville stars and others to appear, so that it was possible to see Gracie Fields, Vesta Tilley, and Norman Evans at a very low cost. The Old Vic also had matinees, but one had to be in the theatre before the curtain rose, and attendance there meant missing lunch and going direct to the venue.

My salary was £150 a year, and the London allowance added £10 to this. I had excellent lodgings in Harvest Road, which ran from Kensal Rise to Kilburn High Street, and my landlady told me that she had come to the house as a bride when the area was all green fields.

Mr Beard took the money to the bank in a taxi each morning, and on one occasion I was at the window nearest the safe. He stood near me preparing the statement and placing the money in the bag, at the same time watching every movement I made and criticising my every action. So engrossed was he in this pursuit that he placed a bundle of notes near the door of the ticket rack and with a touch of my elbow I pushed this towards the wall, out of immediate sight. When he left I pointed the money out to Tom Neighbour who said to leave it there meantime. Mr Beard returned very excited and accompanied by a policeman and asked me to produce the money. Both Tom and I looked surprised, but one glance disclosed its whereabouts to his intense chagrin. There was the normal quiet period in the afternoon and he called me into his office where we shouted at each other in a most undignified way. When I returned to the office Grady, a Yorkshire man despite his name, sympathised with me and advised me to apply for a transfer to some other station. I said that this was a most unusual course to take, and quite unheard of. He explained that on busy lines in the industrial and city areas, men were under great strain at times, and this was dangerous in an industry like the railways, and it was found expedient to act swiftly when such tensions became unbearable.

I considered the matter for a time and then returned to tell Mr Beard of my intention, and he, now also calmed, agreed to a telegram being sent in my name, and added that he would also send one, thus expediting the matter. I was surprised next morning when coming on duty to have a telegram instructing me to proceed to Tewkesbury in Gloucestershire that day. Fortunately I had enough money to pay my landlady for the complete week, and took the first train to Birmingham, where I had to change to the Bristol line, and then change again at Ashchurch for Tewkesbury.

I arrived there in the late afternoon and introduced myself to the stationmaster, Mr John Birch. We talked for a while and I enquired where I could get accommodation, and after taking me to the goods office for a cup of tea he left me. On his return he asked if I would be willing to stay with him, to which I immediately agreed, and I was taken to his home to meet his wife. They had only been a few weeks in Tewkesbury having previously lived in Kings Norton and had found the people at Tewkesbury pleasant but reserved, and they felt very lonely. One son was away at school and the other, Johnny, was at home. Mrs Birch was Jewish, her father being one of the famous organ makers in England; the name I think was Goldberg. I was one of the family, as one was expected to be in most lodgings in the north of Scotland. Tewkesbury was about the same size as Forres, but the habits were different. Few people went by train anywhere, and those that I did meet were not interested in anything outside the little town. A friend of the Birches, a Lancashire man, Mr Clinton was assisting at a nearby station temporarily and he cycled over every evening, so that we were able to play Newmarket and talk before he cycled away again. However, he had to go elsewhere, and I taught them the only card game I knew at all well, or rather, played at all well, "halfpenny Nap".

Suddenly Mr Birch took ill, and was quickly transferred to hospital, where it was decided that an immediate operation was required, followed probably by some time convalescing. Regretfully I recognised that I would have to go somewhere else, for in a small town conventions had to be considered. I decided that I would go home and regretfully said goodbye to my delightful hostess. Despite the many stations I had been at, this was the first time that I had been inside the home of a stationmaster.

I had to change trains at Birmingham New Street, and had a wait of more than an hour. This street was lined with shabby old shops, one of them being a jewellers, so I bought a wedding ring and was married three weeks later.

I had completed ten years and three months service with the railway, my father forty-four years, and my grandfather forty.

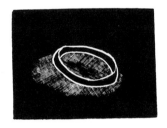

C000242166

The Day
We Won
The Cup

To Jane and Charlie —
hope you enjoy the memories
of England, off as well
as on the field.

Chris

England Then and Now

Chris Arnot

The Day We Won The Cup

England Then and Now

Chris Arnot

The Day We Won The Cup: England then and now

Chris Arnot

First published in Great Britain in 2015 by Step Beach Press Ltd
Brighton

A CIP catalogue record for this title is available from the British
Library.

ISBN 978-1-908779-44-1

Picture credits: ©Empics/PA

Typeset in Brighton, UK by Step Beach Press Ltd

Printed and bound by Spinnaker Print, Southampton

Step Beach Press Ltd, 28 Osborne Villas, Hove, East Sussex BN3 2RE

www.stepbeachpress.co.uk

To my wife Jackie who watched the 1966 Final with her first glass of cider while her Mum saw off her usual schooner of sweet sherry

Acknowledgements

Many thanks to the following, in no particular order, for sparing their time and sharing their anecdotes:

Vince Gledhill, Patrick Collins of the *Mail on Sunday*, James Mossop, Matthew Engel of the *Financial Times*, Frank Bough, Mike Crisp, Jeff Parker, Allister Craddock, John Holmes, David Lowe, David Rosenberg, Rabbi Tony Bayfield, Joanne Rosenthal of the Jewish Museum, Bryan Murphy, John Steel, Eunice Bell, Yvonne Rogerson, John Timewell, John Rubidge, Patrick Freestone, Roger Magraw, Michael Burdis, Malcolm Penny, Mike Berry of *Backpass Magazine*, Michael Jeanes, Betty Lewis, Ros Pedley, Ken Lomas, Brian Mills, Rob Boddie of Sussex CCC, Ian Hands, Jim Cumbes, Sam King, Alan Taylor, Jim Marshall and Bill Walker.

I would also like to thank Chris Parker, Karen Hobden and all at Step Beach Press for their backing and knowhow.

Contents

Foreword

In these days of Premiership football and the tribalism that sadly seems to be the badge to wear when supporting a football team, *The Day We Won the Cup* harks back to more patriotic times – without the tribalism – when the dream of every football supporter was to see their country win the World Cup. We had witnessed the brilliance of the South Americans, and in my particular case, the debut of a teenaged and tearful Pele captivated the world in 1958.

England at last was staging a World cup in 1966 and, although that dream of winning it was still alive, few really believed we could match the skills we had witnessed in previous contests. But that didn't stop the grounds staging matches being full to capacity to see at first-hand foreign players we had only read about. Football was rarely on television, and only then in grainy black and white pictures.

The minimum wage cap had only been removed a few years earlier, and some footballers had seen their wages rocket from £20 a week to the giddy heights of £50 or even £100 a week. What riches! On a personal note, I was just making my way into the first team at Tranmere Rovers at £18 a week, but that was still more than my wages as a professional cricketer: I was making £12-10 shillings a week at Lancashire (this was a full five years before decimalisation).

Chris Arnot, for his sins, was following the fortunes of Aston Villa. Little did we know then that five years later our paths would cross when I moved across Birmingham from West Bromwich Albion to try and help Villa escape from the indignity of the old third division.

For those of us who can remember England's amazing journey to Wembley in 1966, it is still very special – the disappointment of the opening 0–0 draw against Uruguay; the thrill of England's first goal in the competition scored against Mexico by Bobby Charlton with a signature 25 yard thunderbolt; the refusal by Rattin, one of Argentina's 'animals', (Alf Ramsey's words) to leave the field when sent off in the quarter final for a tackle that would get him banned for half a season now. England won 1–0. Then came the Semi Final against Portugal and the great Eusebio, who had single-handedly beaten the North Koreans 4–3 in a group match after being 3–0 down. They were a fine side and I settled down to watch more in hope than expectation. Once again it was that man Bobby Charlton who swept us through and we had to pinch ourselves to realise we really were in the final. Our opponents would later become our penalty shoot-out bogies in world football. But in those days, before the demolition of the Berlin Wall, they were West Germany.

Chris has captured the mood of that never-to-be-forgotten day from an astonishingly varied number of people, from the off-duty policemen, to those on holiday, the dutiful cricketers, and the devastated Scots, not to mention those of little faith who had arranged to get married on that day! For those who weren't in the least bit interested – there were a few – it was a wonderful afternoon. Shops were nearly empty, roads even emptier, and a everywhere there was a general feeling of peace! There were also the dedicated cricket spectators who sat, arms folded, grim-faced, and determined that nothing other than the weather should interrupt their watching.

I was one of those dutiful cricketers, a 'deputy professional' for Chorley in the Northern Cricket League in Lancashire. I've often wondered if the resident professional was really injured, but never found out. My reward was half of the fee, which was £5, the other half going to my employers, Lancashire County Cricket Club. As Chris recounts in Chapter Five, we lost the toss and were therefore fielding. Rain came, but not too heavy, and the umpires said 'it were not 'eavy enough to go off, and t'game must come first'. We had to settle for listening to the 'oohs' and 'ahs' from the distant dressing rooms whilst playing out an unremarkable drawn game.

Even the celebrations couldn't go on long into the night as pubs closed at 10.30 and didn't open again until Sunday lunchtime at 12 noon – and even then only for a couple of hours. Beer, however, was a shilling a pint (5p), although if you wanted to be more civilised and drink in the lounge with the ladies, it was 1/3d (7p).

One day, when there are more English footballers playing Premiership football, Fifa has been reformed, and England stage the world cup again, the dream will come alive once more. If I'm still around, I just hope I won't be anywhere near a cricket field.

Jim Cumbes
(Formerly goalkeeper for Aston Villa and West Bromwich Albion, fast bowler for Worcestershire and chief executive at Lancashire at the other Old Trafford)

Preface

Nostalgia blunts the harder edges of memory and, while this book contains many nostalgic recollections of a memorable day, I hope it also encompasses some sharper observations on life and football then and now. For those of us who fancied ourselves as young bucks in 1966, ours was not the sepia world of our parents; it was black and white. Or, more accurately, a grainy sort of grey. Psychedelia and the hippy culture didn't really become fashionable until the following year, and then it was largely confined to certain parts of London. Greyness was the overwhelming impression given off by the industrial and mining landscapes that covered much of the country, as well as being the shade of many factory overalls, office suits, newspaper front pages, most photographs and the preponderance of macs on the terraces of football grounds.

It was also the 'colour' in which over thirty two million of us saw England win the World Cup. Those who were there were the ones lucky enough to see it in real colour: England's red shirts, Gordon Banks's yellow jumper and the Queen's much brighter yellow coat and matching hat. Not to mention the flags.

In the pages that follow you will find plenty of stories from those who *were* there, including someone who spent the night after the Final sleeping in a graveyard somewhere between Wembley and Cornwall. He was 17 at the time, the same age as me. My own

World Cup memories also include sleeping rough, albeit the night before rather than after the Final. As I've recounted at the beginning of Chapter Four, I also came close to being killed outside Stonehenge on the way to watching the game with two elderly ladies in a remote part of Wiltshire.

At least I didn't have to crawl through a forest of legs to press my nose against the window of a television shop – the fate of a football-mad lad from Liverpool whose parents had been callous enough to drag him away on holiday on the day of the big match. And I wasn't in Germany like the young East Ender trying to focus on Wembley while consuming too much strong lager in a bar in the Black Forest. Nor was I one of the students desperately working out how they were going to see the game instead of performing their summer vacation job of sifting through the pigswill outside the kitchens at Butlin's in Minehead.

There are stories about the police keeping an eye on the match whether they were on duty or not, of those who missed it for one reason or another, and about how a nation celebrated. The football lovers of England who are old enough to remember have never had such a day (or night) before or since. Joy and optimism were by no means confined to Wembley and its immediate environs. Nor was the feeling that life was getting better confined to football.

Admittedly it's not just the blur of nostalgia that casts the past in a deceptively warm glow. The memory simply plays tricks the older you get. That might help to explain why I could tell you the name and position of every one of the England team that won the World Cup in 1966 but would struggle to bring to mind much more than half of the side that played the opening match against Italy in 2014. Or why I can name every FA Cup winner from 1950 to 1980 but can't for the life of me remember who won it the season before last.

Historical facts are easier to pin down. The Beatles split up in 1970, right at the end of the decade they had helped to define. Harold Wilson resigned suddenly in 1976, Mrs Thatcher was elected three years later and the Berlin Wall came down ten years after that, thereby ensuring that in future we'd have to play not just West Germany but what you might call Germany United.

The Hillsborough disaster happened in 1989, by which time the triumph of the 'boys of '66' in front of an un-segregated crowd seemed to belong to much more innocent times. Football hooliganism has gone on since the days when pigs' bladders were being booted about, but the sustained violence and yobbish behaviour that plagued the comparatively modern professional game for so long seems to have begun in earnest in 1967, shortly before the so-called 'summer of love'.

In Chapter Seven you can read author David Rosenberg's memories of cowering in terror as Manchester United supporters invaded a terrace at Upton Park, wielding bottles and lashing about indiscriminately. He was nine at the time and the previous summer he had been dragged away from watching 'West Ham win the World Cup', as he puts it, *before* his beloved Geoff Hurst scored twice in extra time.

At least going to top-flight football is infinitely safer now than it was in 1989, 1979 or even 1969. The players are fitter, the pitches flatter and the facilities better – albeit at a price that would seem unreal to someone who had shelled out just ten bob (50p) to stand behind the goal at Wembley in '66. But for me and, I suspect, many more who don't support the five or six clubs capable of winning the Premier League, the game has lost its soul. No longer can we imagine a Burnley, an Ipswich Town, a Derby County or Nottingham Forest being crowned champions again.

Newcastle United, meanwhile, is now sponsored by a payday loan company. Eleven multi-millionaires turn out in shirts telling supporters where they can borrow money at astronomical interest rates. The players of Aston Villa, another once-great club, have shirts emblazoned with the name of what is described as 'a leading Asian on-line betting syndicate'. Anyone who loses his own shirt betting on-line can, presumably, always get a loan from Wonga.

My Dad, bless him, would be baffled and saddened if I could tell him this about Villa, the club that was once ours. All the more so if he knew that shirt sponsorship is just one way of raising the vast sums needed to lure to these shores players who can earn much more in a week than most of us do in a year and, as a result, a minority of those in the first team squads of English top-flight football clubs are qualified to play for England.

No wonder the *Sun*, with an owner who has put far more into the Premier League than any shirt sponsor, was uncharacteristically downbeat on the day of England's first match in Brazil, 2014. The front page read like this: 'The sun is shining. Friday the 13th is over. BBQ's lit. Pub's open till 1am. Tomorrow's Sunday (lie-in). England play rugby and cricket. And Stevie G's lads are raring to go in the World Cup …

WHAT COULD POSSIBLY GO WRONG?'

CHAPTER ONE

Reflections on the England of 1966 through the cracked mirror of the World Cup, 2014

So far so good. At the time of writing, England look set to qualify for the European Championship Finals to be staged half a century after the country that gave football to the world was crowned champion of the world for the one and only time. But forgive me if I turn down Ray Winstone's charming invitation to 'bet nah' on us becoming so much as champions of Europe in 2016. If, that is, the World Cup Finals of 2014 are anything to go by.

Private Eye was not far wrong. Yes, *Private Eye*, the magazine founded and still run by ex-public schoolboys who spent more of their formative years on the cloistered quadrangles of Oxford colleges than the bleak terraces at football grounds. The front cover for June 13, 2014 had a photograph of the England team arriving in Brazil for the World Cup Finals with a little speech bubble emerging from the pilot's cabin: 'Shall I keep the engines running?' The following night England played their first match.

We'd been at the home of some good friends all evening, enjoying a dinner party. There were 13 around the table (hmmm …) and, as kick-off time approached, the plan was for the football diehards among us to move into the other room. But your intrepid correspondent felt obliged to decline the offer to settle down in a comfortable armchair with a coffee and a brandy. Instead I ventured to a nearby pub that I had been assured would be 'quite lively'. After all it was nearly 11pm, the hour when 'the towels went on' in 1966, if they hadn't gone on already.

Nigh-on 50 years since England's greatest triumph on a football field, there were at least two hours to go before anyone thought about closing time. There was a match to watch and pundits to listen to, if anyone could hear them. Not that the atmosphere was as boisterous as I had expected. Somebody in an England shirt that was bulging over the belt of his jeans was attempting to get us to join in with the national anthem. There were no takers.

Admittedly, I was just about the only person in the flag-bedecked bar not sporting a white plastic hat with a red cross on the top. And that included a blonde in an extremely short skirt who was texting or tweeting furiously until her boyfriend returned from the gents and she felt obliged to at least glance at the screen. Or should I say 'screens' in the plural. There were four altogether. The one on the left was conveying CCTV images of what was going on in the car park. Not much. Showing the match were two screens, both about ten times bigger than the one on which most of us watched the 1966 final. In colour, what's more, with the digital detail that would have been unthinkable even on the most panoramic cinema screen half a century ago. In between was yet another screen offering a rather distracting display of brash adverts on a loop. 'Come with us on a samba holiday,' one suggested, presumably in case any of us felt tempted to set off to Brazil on a hunch that England might go all the way.

Some chance! I dragged my eyes back to one of the main screens in time to see Italy's Claudio Marchisio plant one past Joe Hart from 25 yards. Cue groans of resignation. The relief brought about by Daniel Sturridge's equaliser proved short-lived. Nobody celebrated it more energetically than a black man at the bar who promptly danced around the room, waving his plastic hat with joy. He came originally from Nigeria, it transpired. 'I've lived here over ten years and, if England played Nigeria now, I'd support England,' he told me at half time. By then Mario Balotelli had restored the Italian lead with what turned out to be the last goal of the game. England had lost but had not been disgraced.

Italy are heavyweights in football terms. Four times winners of the Jules Rimet trophy indeed, the fourth time 40 years after England's solitary triumph. No shame there, then. Next up: Uruguay. They'd won it twice before, but the last time was in 1950. Sixteen years earlier than us! Bring 'em on.

They did, and we lost again. At least Wayne Rooney put one in at last. Unfortunately, some bloke called Suarez scored twice and celebrated with almost unseemly relish the fact that the country where he had been earning more in a week than most of his fellow Uruguayans could earn in three lifetimes was hanging on by a thread.

That thread had been snapped before England took the field against Costa Rica for a game that fully lived up to its billing as an anti-climax. A nation yawned. Reluctantly, I dragged myself away from listening to the Headingley Test Match and strolled to the Wetherspoon's pub down the road to meet a mate of similar vintage to myself. It was around 4.50pm.

Had this been 1966 neither of us should have been served. Not legally, anyway. We were both 17, although that never stopped us claiming that we were 18, if challenged. Apart from that, the pub wouldn't have been open. Not until 5pm in London, 5.30 or even 6pm in some parts of the country. Now it's not unusual to see customers sitting outside this place at ten in the morning, tucking into a full English breakfast with a pint of lager and an adjacent packet of filter-tips for the postprandial fag.

Extending licensing hours was meant to make our pubs more like continental café-bars. In that regard it has succeeded only up to a point, Lord Copper, or whoever it was who proposed the toleration of all-day opening in the late 1980s. Those unfortunate souls who have to police our city centres or man our Accident and Emergency departments on Friday nights might also query the view that further extensions in the Noughties have made us drink more responsibly. What's more, the whiff of Gauloises, or even Benson and Hedges, has been absent from our pubs since the passage of the Health Act 40 years after the '66 Final. To my mind that has improved the atmosphere no end, but it may also explain why so many regulars were sitting outside Wetherspoons rather than gathering around the telly as kick-off time arrived. Then again it may just be that the sun was out and so were England of the 2014 World Cup Finals.

'Shall I keep the engines running?' Well, perhaps you'd better switch them off until they've finished this meaningless game against Costa Rica.

There were precisely eight people watching with us as proceedings got underway in Brazil and, despite the abundance of real ales on the bar, the majority were supping lager, widely regarded as a 'ladies' drink' in 1966. A man sporting a duffel coat on a warm June afternoon was clutching a bottle of Budweiser in each hand. 'They're on offer,' he explained. 'Two for four quid.'

Budweiser were one of the major sponsors of the tournament, along with Coca-Cola and McDonald's. Although I didn't say anything, I found myself harrumphing inwardly about the commercial involvement of American multi-national corporations in the game that we gave to the world. What did Americans know about what they call 'soccer'?

More than we might think. Soon after the end of the 2014 Finals, Fifa issued its new world rankings. England, it seems, are now

20th, behind Chile, Greece, Bosnia-Herzegovina and ... er, the United States.

But let's get back to the match between England and Costa Rica on June 24, 2014. Believe it or not, a couple were sitting beneath the screen transmitting the game chatting happily while tucking into what was billed on the menu as 'steak with all the trimmings'. The national obsession with steak is one thing that hasn't changed since 1966 and indeed since 1933 when JB Priestley was embarking on his *English Journey*:

'The reason why English cookery was allowed to lapse into barbarism,' he huffed, 'was that gradually only one item of diet was taken seriously. That is Steak. This is venerated and idealised. When an ordinary English waiter mentions any other dish, he is a realist and his very tone of voice tells you what that dish really is – muck. But when he mentions Steak, his voice is low, hushed and reverent ... it is Steak personal, your Steak. "How will you have *your* Steak, sir?"'

Rare is the pub or restaurant menu that doesn't include steak in some form, even today, although there are more than enough alternatives. The food scene in England has changed beyond measure since Priestley's day and is infinitely better than it was in the '60s when olive oil was a remedy for ear-ache, garlic was for foreigners and Fanny Craddock was telling us how to drain a turkey by prodding it as though it were a particularly disagreeable neighbour. Now there are endless cookery programmes and we're on first-name terms with the likes of Nigella and Jamie, Delia and Rick. London, meanwhile, has become one of the world's great gastronomic cities, partly because it's full of citizens from around the world. It seems a long time since 'Indian' restaurants, decorated with flock wallpaper and piped sitar music, served food rarely seen in the Sub-Continent, and mainly Bangladeshi waiters were routinely addressed as 'Gunga Din' by men trying to prove their virility by shoving down as much vindaloo as possible while cooling their fevered tongues with 'Indian' lager brewed in Northampton.

Apologies if I'm banging on about food rather than football. Perhaps that's because there was very little to report about the game being beamed in from Brazil. We drained our pints at half time and set off for the back room of the pub across the road.

Alas, it was no better over there. Long before the end, the main talking point was coming from the other game between Uruguay and Italy. Mobile phone pictures were circulating of Suarez sinking his teeth into the shoulder of Giorgio Chiellini. The post-match pundits soon moved on from England to the incident that would dominate the following day's front as well as back pages. 'Suarez is looking a bit sheepish,' Danny Murphy observed. Surely 'wolfish' would be a more appropriate term, I found myself reflecting grumpily as I set off home to discover that I'd missed a gripping end to the Headingley Test. England's cricket team had come close, but not close enough, to saving the game and the series.

And England's footballers?

Well, the aeroplane engines had started up again after the briefest of breaks. The players would fly home to see copies of the *Sun* calling Suarez an 'animal' in a strange, perhaps deliberate echo of Alf Ramsey's comments about the Argentina side in '66. At least the otherwise brilliant former Liverpool striker had taken the pressure off them a bit. Yes, there were newspaper inquests to be picked over and apologies to be posted on Twitter. But then they could fly off again, to Caribbean beaches this time, knowing that normal business would soon resume; that business being the Premier League.

The day after Germany – the whole of Germany this time, not just the West – beat Argentina in the Final, Adidas announced a £750 million deal to supply Manchester United with shirts from 2015 onwards. Not to be outdone, chairman Sheikh Mansour unveiled plans to turn Manchester City into a 'global brand' with branches in New York and Melbourne. (Eat your heart out, Franny Lee.) Meanwhile, various transfer deals went through involving astronomical sums for players that few of us had heard of but who would now be gracing what we like to pretend is 'the best league in the world'.

It's not.

And one reason why it's not is that a comparatively small club, Southampton, produces a disproportionate number of future England players and then has to sell them on to one of five or six clubs capable of paying the wages that their agents demand. Those players spend a lot of time sitting on the bench because competition for places is so intense. By the time you read this, FA chairman Greg Dyke's campaign to restrict the number of what he calls 'foreigners' in the Premier League may have set in motion a conveyor belt of Harry Kanes. But as things stand, the majority of those on the field will not be qualified to play for England. And while they'll be very good, they won't be the world's greatest players. The likes of Messi, Robben, Ronaldo and Ibrahomovic play elsewhere – as does the most accomplished living British player, Gareth Bale, who happens to be Welsh.

In a perceptive Final Word on the 2014 finals in the *Observer*, Andrew Anthony reminded readers that 'the Germans have won four World Cups, have been runners-up four times and have reached the last four a total of twelve times since 1954. Compare that with England's solitary World Cup win (on home soil) and a single other semi-final. And to think that we see the Germans as England's greatest football rivals. It's as if we imagine an Austin Allegro can compete with a BMW'.

Anthony began by quoting Gary Neville, England coach and Sky pundit. 'People who write "England should follow the German route" are either oblivious to the obstacle or believe in magic wands!' he tweeted. Neville then used another 140 characters to point out that England needed to 'find our way of doing it because the system we have doesn't allow' what he referred to as Germany's holistic approach.

Our way?

'A dysfunctional marriage of amateur administrators and cut-throat business people, which seems to maximise the incompetence of one and the venality of the other,' Anthony concluded. 'Because, in spite of many decades of debates, promises and announcements, England don't have anything that deserves to be called a "system" and there isn't a way but instead a means of muddling through.'

Come to think of it, the term 'muddling through' could be used to sum up our progress compared to Germany's since 1945 when Berlin and other major cities were reduced to rubble by Allied bombing – and not just on the football field. In retrospect, 1966 seems to have been a false dawn in more ways than one. Yes, there were terrible events in the headlines, notably the Aberfan disaster and what became known as the Moors Murders' trial. But beyond South Wales and Saddleworth Moor, there was a bubble of optimism in the air, and it wasn't just hovering over Wembley on one glorious late-July afternoon.

The so-called 'permissive society' was still in its infancy a few years after the contraceptive pill had liberated so many women from the fear of unwanted pregnancy. As Philip Larkin wryly reminded us, 'Sexual intercourse began in nineteen sixty three .../ Between the end of the Chatterley ban/And the Beatles' first LP'.

There was also full employment. As those who were in work at the time never tire of telling us, you could walk out of one job in the morning and into another one in the afternoon. Comparatively well-paid jobs, too. The gap between rich and poor was narrowing. It was fashionable to be working class, particularly if you had a Liverpool accent. The Beatles may have embarked on their final live performance, but they were busy in the studio recording *Revolver*, Bob Dylan having shown them and many another British 'groups' that pop music didn't have to be vacuous. Silly love songs were *so* last year.

Television, too, was changing fast. Ordinary people could see themselves not as comic parodies but as three-dimensional characters. While *Coronation Street* was pulling in massive audiences for ITV, the BBC, once a bastion for accents rarely heard outside Surrey golf clubs, gave us gritty, often controversial, Wednesday plays such as *Cathy Come Home*.

Satirical comedy continued to boom. Peter Cook, one half of *Not Only ... But Also*, was putting money into *Private Eye*. His Establishment Club had closed two years previously, having been used as another vehicle to lay into those who, like himself, were products of public schools and Oxbridge but just happened to be running the country. By 1966, however, the likes of Harold Macmillan and Sir Alec Douglas-Home, embodiments of the Old Etonian old guard, had been put out to the grouse moors. A brave new world beckoned.

Or did it?

A Rip Van Winkle falling asleep in 1966 and waking up nearly 50 years later would have to rub his eyes in disbelief. Back then tweeting was for the birds, computers were the size of vending machines, bankers were considered pin-striped pillars of probity and Qatar was something we city dwellers lived with in the back of our throats. (Okay, it was spelt differently from the small but immensely wealthy and extremely hot country on the Arabian peninsular that Fifa, in its wisdom, chose as the host nation to stage the 2022 World Cup. Catarrh was a bi-product of all that smoking and all that smoke – from factories, foundries and coal-fired power stations.)

Rip might feel the need for a long lie down on learning that British manufacturing industry had been decimated, coal mining virtually wiped out and trade union power neutered, the process largely overseen by a female prime minister who managed to win three elections. But he might just about recognise another woman whom he last saw taking her seat at Wembley, looking demure and youthful among grey suits and grey hair. Prime ministers come and go but the Queen carries on and the monarchy is, if anything, even more popular now than it was then.

Before sinking back into the arms of Morpheus, Rip might conclude that many poor people are looking fatter while rich people are looking thinner. (For an explanation look no further than all those fried chicken shops and kebab houses on the high street and then check out the annual cost of gym membership.) Politicians, meanwhile, are looking younger while the rock stars capable of filling huge stadia at eye-watering prices are getting older and older. One of them was a Beatle in your day, Rip. Three others were Stones. And they still are. Ancient Stones now, but not yet fossilised. Look at the lines grooved into those weathered faces and compare them to the comparatively cherubic features of the fellow waving from the doorstep of Number 10, Downing Street. His name is David Cameron and he was born just over two months after England won the World Cup. He was educated at Eton and Oxford and is a descendant of King William IV (albeit via William's mistress) and a fifth cousin to the Queen.

Muddling through remains our way, be it football administration or an economy in which recession follows boom-times as certainly as rain clouds eventually eclipse the sun. But never underestimate the capacity for the British, or rather the English, Establishment to adapt to each brave new world and re-invent itself.

CHAPTER TWO

The build-up to the 'Match of the Century' and how it was kept in perspective by the pre-Murdoch media

Alf Ramsey slipped out of the team hotel the night before guiding England's footballers to victory in the World Cup Final. Perhaps he was feeling the strain. Perhaps he felt the need for what passes for fresh air in the vicinity of London's North Circular Road. Perhaps he wanted time alone to think deeply about the challenge ahead. Whatever the reason, he didn't stay on his own for too long.

Half an hour after leaving the Hendon Hall, he knocked on a front door in Finchley. It was opened by one of the sons of Reg Drury, then the football correspondent of the *News of the World*. 'What are you doing up at this time?' the England manager enquired of the child with his customary terseness. Drury senior put the kettle on after bidding the lad goodnight, then the two men sat discussing football over a pot of tea.

They went back a long way, Reg and Alf. One had been a regular in the White Hart Lane press box as the Spurs team in which the other played right-back pushed and ran their way to the title in 1951. Now it was July 29, 1966, and the man who had gone on to win a much more unlikely League championship as manager of Ipswich Town stood on the threshold of his finest hour – or two hours as it turned out.

Ramsey had not been without his newspaper critics in the build-up to that fabled final. He had come under fire for, among other things, calling the Argentinians 'animals', persisting with Nobby Stiles despite his X-certificate tackle on Jacques Simon of France in the final group match, and resisting the clamour to bring back Jimmy Greaves after he had suffered a leg injury in the same game.

The England manager could be prickly with the press – even with those journalists who had backed his judgement throughout. Brian James of the *Daily Mail* and Ken Jones of the *Mirror*, for instance, were somewhat taken aback when they called in at the Royal Garden Hotel, Kensington, on the morning after the celebratory banquet. Instead of some choice quotes for their Monday editions as a reward for their loyalty, they were greeted by two abrupt questions from the man they were supposed to be questioning: 'What are you bothering me for on a Sunday? Don't you know it's my day off?'

Which makes Ramsey's selection of Drury as his pre-match confidant all the more remarkable. He worked for the *News of the World*, for goodness sake! Even in the 1960s it was the nation's most salacious Sunday newspaper, full of stories of de-frocked vicars and scantily-clad tarts from whose seductive clutches reporters somehow extricated themselves. 'I made my excuses and left,' had become a national catchphrase.

More remarkably still, Drury didn't breathe a word of his encounter until many years later. 'Even then he wasn't boasting about it. Somehow it just dropped out in conversation,' says

Patrick Collins, the perceptive columnist and chief sports writer of the *Mail on Sunday*.

Drury, like Ramsey, is no longer with us. Neither is the *News of the World* for that matter. It closed in July, 2011, in the wake of the phone-hacking scandal. But there are still plenty of red-topped tabloids oozing with scandals about 'celebrities', some of whom once appeared on *The X-Factor*. Premier League footballers have long been considered fair game, along with their wives, girlfriends and managers. The idea of England manager Roy Hodgson knocking on the hotel door of, say, the chief football writer of the *Sunday Sun* for a heart-to-heart on the eve of a major match in the World Cup, 2014, would have been as laughable as the notion that England could reach the final.

A journalist of any kind could never have got near the manager or the players without having to negotiate a phalanx of agents and media advisers wielding contracts for copy approval and product-placement. 'These days you can't even catch them at the end of a game as they head for the car park,' says James Mossop, who spent half a century or so as a distinguished sports writer. 'They're attuned to come out talking into mobile phones or with speakers in their ears.'

James, better known as Jim or Jimmy, was 29 in 1966 and working for the *Sunday Express*. 'One of the memories that has always stayed with me was walking up Wembley Way before the game and passing a party of six or seven elderly buskers singing *There'll Always Be an England*', he reflects.

Even the younger men – and they were mainly men – spilling out of Wembley Park tube station were wearing collars and ties for the most part. Three months before the match *Time Magazine* had run its famous cover story on Swinging London. But most of the UK and, indeed, many parts of the capital, did not 'swing'. Those who didn't work nine to five in offices earned their living in factories and foundries, mills or mines. Shipyards, too, in places such as Mossop's home town of Barrow-in-Furnace, Cumbria. On high days and holidays, or even on Sunday lunchtimes in the pub, men who worked all week in overalls liked to put on a suit or blazer over a white shirt and a tie, decorated with a discreet military crest in some cases.

Most of those suits would have been purchased from Burton's, or John Collier's, as the Fifty Shilling Tailors had been re-named by then. There might even have been some de-mob suits among them. The Second World War had ended only just over 20 years previously and the influence of the Sergeant Major still loomed large in many lives. Long hair, colourful shirts, denim jeans and jackets were as rare as recently rolled joints among the abundance of smouldering Woodbines, Park Drives, Player's Weights and Senior Services on Wembley Way.

Memories were still vivid and raw for the many ex-servicemen in the crowd. And some of those too young or too old to fight would have known what it was like to cower in an air-raid shelter and emerge to find their neighbourhoods reduced to rubble by the Luftwaffe. (The wife of Martin Peters, scorer of England's second goal, had lost three aunts during a direct hit on a house in East Ham.) 'Yet I don't remember seeing any overt anti-German sentiment on the day,' Jim Mossop reflects. 'There was no booing and whistling when the band played *Deutschland Uber Alles* after the national anthem. It was all very civilised.'

He's telling me this in a coffee bar near his home in Cheshire where a Christmas card had arrived that morning from Jack Charlton, brother of Bobby and England's centre-back in 1966. Like Alf Ramsey and Reg Drury, Jack and Jim went back a long way. Charlton chose Mossop as his drinking companion for a long night on the town after the celebratory banquet that followed England's victory in the 1966 final (see Chapter Six). Both had endured a hectic afternoon.

Both had experienced bitter disappointment verging on despair when Wolfgang Weber had stabbed home West Germany's equaliser on the stroke of full time. Extra time loomed. Having given his all for 90 minutes, Jack had to summon the energy and concentration for another half hour. Up in the press box, meanwhile, Jim knew that it would be touch and go as to whether he could get a full match report into early editions heading for remote parts of the country such as his native Barrow and the Charltons' home town of Ashington in Northumberland.

'Alan Hoby [the columnist billed as The Man Who Knows] was with me and we scrambled something out around 5.30 when extra time had finally ended,' he recalls. 'Then we had a chance to tickle things up a bit for the second edition.' By then the team coach had made its slow but triumphant progress from Wembley to the Kensington through thronged streets of cheering well-wishers. 'IT'S JUBILATION NIGHT!' was the *Express*'s front page lead in later editions on Sunday morning, over a picture of England captain Bobby Moore raising a glass with his wife Tina. But there were at least five fairly prominent stories around it that had nothing to do with the World Cup, including 'Callaghan may force Cabinet shuffle' and 'Big Yard swoop: 12 held'.

The *Sunday Express* was a broadsheet in those days, along with its daily equivalent. Both considered themselves the most patriotic of papers. So, how had the Saturday edition previewed England's first ever appearance in a World Cup final?

Sparingly, to put it mildly. There was team news on the back page, of course, but the front page lead was about Deputy Prime Minister George Brown turning up two hours late to talk about the Government's wage freeze. The only reference to the forthcoming match was a story about officials insisting that, while footballers' wives were welcome at the Royal Garden Hotel, they would be excluded from the post-match cocktail party and banquet. 'Bunch of Normas and Susans coming down from the

North with their bee-hive hair-dos,' as former *Guardian* columnist Martin Kelner put it in his book *Sit Down and Cheer*. 'Who did they think they were? Fifa officials' wives were fine, by the way.' There was also an advertisement for Vitalis hair oil featuring Bobby Moore's immaculate golden locks. 'The very best of luck to England and Bobby Moore,' read the caption. 'We'll be behind you.'

The BBC, meanwhile, had previewed the match with *World Cup Report*, an opportunity to 'meet the teams and the personalities who play tomorrow'. It had been broadcast at 7pm the previous evening and lasted half an hour. As Kelner points out, that meant 'allocating precisely twenty minutes less screen time to the Match of the Century than to The Hippodrome Circus, Great Yarmouth, which occupied the peak time slot at 8pm'.

ITV didn't preview the game at all, preferring to stick with *Ready Steady Go* on the Friday evening and thereby garnering the vast majority of viewers under 25. It did, however, cover the match itself – live in glorious black and white. Colour television was still a year away in the UK. We had to rely on Hugh Johns on the UK's only commercial station and Kenneth Wolstenholme on the BBC to tell us that England were playing in red shirts.

Mind you, live coverage of any football match was something of a novelty in 1966. Only the FA Cup Final could be guaranteed such a showing at 3pm on a Saturday. *Match of the Day*, which had started two years previously, brought edited highlights into our homes, as it does to this day. And to this day, the 1966 World Cup Final remains the most watched event on British television with 32.3 million viewers, some 200,000 more than tuned in to Princess Diana's funeral in 1997. Worldwide the figure was around 400 million.

Bear in mind, however, that although the BBC began previewing the game well before kick-off on the Saturday, it still devoted less time, in terms of pre and post-match analysis, than Sky would give to a clash between two mid-table Premier League sides on a Monday evening. Bear in mind also that Britain's biggest-selling daily paper, the *Mirror* in those days, led its front page on the Monday after the final with 'A BOUNCING BABY GIRL FOR PRINCESS ALICE'. Perhaps this was a response to Ramsey's Sunday-morning snub to the paper's very own Ken Jones. Or maybe the media simply had more perspective on football's place in the scheme of things back then. Whatever the explanation, the *Mirror* had decided that 'winning the World Cup was not as big as the birth of Maria Ogilvy, the Queen's first cousin once removed', as Tim de Lisle wrote in *Intelligent Life* magazine in 2010 in an article entitled *How Did Sport Get So Big?*

It's a long and thoughtful piece going into the huge growth of commercial sponsorship, multi-channel television, the Internet and fundamental changes in society itself. But one figure stalks what de Lisle calls 'the age of media sport' like a shadowy colossus.

Rupert Murdoch became owner of the *Times* in 1981. One of the first things he did was to summon Harold Evans, an editor of the old school, into his office and tell him: 'Four pages for sport, every day.' That was going too far, Evans replied. Six months later he had resigned, citing differences between himself and Mr Murdoch.

'Four broadsheet pages would now be considered hopelessly meagre,' de Lisle goes on. 'Sports coverage has ballooned to incorporate ghosted columns from players, ghosted columns from ex-players, graphics about tactics, betting columns, gossip columns, sport-on-television reviews, podcasts, vodcasts, and even columns from comedians.'

Imagine what the coverage would have been like had England been remotely good enough to reach the final in the 2014 World

Cup, an event described by Barney Ronay in the *Guardian* as 'a kind of death star hovering above its target nation [Brazil], colonising its infrastructure, suspending its laws, co-opting its leaders'. Now stretch your imagination even further and consider what it would have been like had they won it. There would have been little else in any newspaper, even the serious ones. The American economy could have collapsed and the story would warrant a single column on page six. Television news bulletins would have been extended and the goals and key incidents would have been analysed interminably. There would have been hardly anything else on Sky Sports News for a fortnight.

As it turned out, they weren't good enough to win a single match. Yet, long after England's ignominious departure from Brazil, the *i*, which bills itself as 'Britain's first and only concise quality paper', was still devoting at least eight (admittedly tabloid) pages a day to the World Cup, twice what it devoted to Wimbledon. County cricket and even Test matches struggled to get a look-in at the height of an English summer.

Eight years previously, when the World Cup was held in Germany, the *Times* was running a 16-page tournament supplement every day for three weeks. Yet only once in the intervening four decades had England come close to repeating their triumph of '66. In 1990 they had finished as beaten semi-finalists and come home to a huge airport welcoming party and a ticker-tape parade.

Incidentally, England played Germany at Wembley again in 1996, after 'thirty years of hurt,' as the song put it. Before that celebrated Semi-Final of the European Championship, the *Mirror* ran a splash front-page headline: 'ACHTUNG! SURRENDER! For you, Fritz, ze Euro Championship is over.'

It wasn't. Germany went through to the Final after a penalty shoot-out and the *Mirror* editor, one Piers Morgan, felt obliged to apologise.

And what of the BBC?

Well, England's triumph over lowly Ecuador in the second round of the 2006 World Cup finals was the lead item that evening on the main BBC1 news (as it was, incidentally, on *Telegraph.co.uk* and *Guardian.co.uk*). The Reithian values that had once regulated our public service broadcaster had evidently been infiltrated by what might be termed 'Murdochian' influences. Ten years previously, Mr Murdoch had made a speech in his native Australia proclaiming his intention to use sport as a 'battering ram' for the purpose of expanding his global TV network.

The Premier League had been up and running for four years by that time. It had started in 1992 when Murdoch's Sky TV was paying £38 million for its package of live matches. Today it's around £10 million *per match*. The BBC has to make do with edited highlights when it comes to the Premier League. But it also devotes a national radio channel to football for most of every weekend in the season, starting at noon on a Saturday and continuing until well into Sunday evening with only the briefest of breaks in between. As if that wasn't enough, there are now games on Friday evenings as well. What is now B Sky B has been competing with BT for the rights for a Friday-night package auctioned off by the Football Association.

Somewhere in the midst of all this frenzied commentary and analysis there is, mercifully, space for *Sports Report* to cover those dwindling top-flight matches that still kick off at 3 o'clock on a Saturday.

Most started at 3 back in 1966, give or take a few mid-week or Monday-night games (mostly Cup replays) and never, never on a Sunday. Matches were played in grounds named, for the most part, after districts and streets rather than commercial sponsors. The players' shirts were not embroidered with the names of payday loan companies or on-line betting services. But then, although the maximum wage had been abolished a few years previously, the top players didn't earn much more than the journalists with whom they mingled so freely. Pitches were not encompassed by garish advertisements for junk food and fizzy drinks. Indeed the only advertisement clearly visible at one end of Wembley Stadium on July 30, 1966, was for the *Radio Times*.

It was not only a very different World Cup final from the one staged in Brazil in 2014; it belonged to a very different world.

CHAPTER THREE

Those comparatively few, those happy few who cheered on Bobby, Nobby, England and Sir Alf

Mike Crisp delves into the cardboard box that he has just hoisted onto his dining-room table and plucks out a crumpled packet of Player's Number 6. It's empty. The last cigarette was smoked on the Wembley terraces shortly before full time on July 30, 1966. 'I was 25 and I'd pretty well given up smoking, but I needed something to calm the nerves,' Mike recalls. 'I'd bought this packet at the beginning of the tournament and I had tickets for ten matches. The plan was to have two cigarettes at each game, one in each half. Come the Final, I'd forgotten all about the last one until just before full time. I was still smoking it when the Germans equalised on 90 minutes. My other hand must have been in my jacket pocket because I remember crushing the empty fag packet as Weber finally put the ball into the net.'

And here it is nearly 50 years on, along with umpteen mementos which Mike describes as 'pretty much grot but given a kind of glamour by history'. A bottle of Watney's World Cup Special Pale Ale is probably undrinkable now. Then again, it was probably undrinkable in 1966 if Watney's 'draught' Red Barrel was anything to go by.

And what's this? Ah yes, a beer glass engraved with the cartoon figure of World Cup Willie. He appears in several other manifestations, including a car sticker and what could either be a large handkerchief or an extremely small tea towel. There's also a 45rpm vinyl disc dedicated to Willie by Lonnie Donegan and a couple of other singles as well: *The World Cup March* by Joe Loss and *The Day We Won the Cup* by Roy Hudd. Swinging London indeed!

The only thing that's swing-able in this box is a very 1960s soap-on-a-rope decorated with a small picture of the 1962 winners. (Brazil, as you may recall.) Next to it is a canister of World Cup shaving foam – quite cutting edge, you might say, at a time when most men still used a brush and a stick of Old Spice.

There's more, much more, in this cornucopia of corporate cashing in, bestowed with a kind of innocence by the passage of time. Maybe that's because of a growing awareness of just how insidiously integrated into top-flight football the corporate world of on-line betting, junk food and beer even worse than Watney's has become in the intervening 50 years.

The cardboard 'grot' box will soon be re-located back in the loft. But not before I've had a thumb through Mike's neatly compiled scrapbooks of tournament press cuttings and checked out the tie that he wore on the Big Day. It's entirely maroon apart from a discreet logo marked 'Fifa World Championship, England, 1966'.

He was a civil servant, working for the Department of Transport, and living where he does still: in a semi-detached house in Hornchurch on the outer reaches of the District Line. 'I was with my first wife at the time and I asked if she wanted to go to any of the matches. No, she didn't. Not interested in football. So I went on my own – to all the qualifying matches as well, and to one or two not involving England.'

How did he get the tickets?

'I just wrote to the FA. I thought they'd write back: "Who do you think you are?" But they just sent me a form implying, more or less, "How many do you want?" I bought ten – nine for Wembley and one for the White City on a night when the football clashed with greyhound racing. They were seven and six [37 1/2p in 'new' money] for the qualifiers and ten bob for the Final.' Fifty pence, in other words.

Admittedly, the average weekly wage for a male worker was £23.47 a week and that 'ten bob' bought only the right to stand on a crowded terrace behind one of the goals. 'The view wasn't particularly good,' Mike concedes. 'It was the end where Geoff Hurst volleyed against the underside of the bar. I could see that all right, but I couldn't see it bounce down on to the line.' Or *over* the line, if the so-called 'Russian' linesman was to be believed – in reality an Azerbaijani called Tofik Bakhramov whose funeral Hurst attended 30 years later. 'All eyes switched to the linesman and I could see him quite clearly,' Mike goes on. 'At first I had the impression that he'd ruled out the goal. Then the ref pointed to the centre spot.'

Cue pandemonium, except among the clusters of stunned Germans. 'There was no segregation in those days,' he reminds me. 'Hurst's final goal was at the far end and I didn't know until I got home whether it would stand or not.' All he could see was fans running on the pitch. Like them, he thought it was all over …

It was now.

'For the first time in my life I embraced a total stranger. He was just a bloke standing next to me.' Mike grins at the memory, aware perhaps that so-called 'man hugs' were still some way in the future. Footballers had only recently started throwing their arms around one another to celebrate a goal, much to the disgruntlement of our fathers' generation who felt that such extravagant gestures were for foreigners in general and the French in particular. A manly handshake was quite enough for Englishmen. Upper lips were still stiff among that generation.

But here was a young man of 25 who had just seen his country win the World Cup. He was emotionally drained – 'I felt like a limp rag' – and he hadn't had so much as one Player's Number 6 to sustain him through the eternity of extra time.

* * *

Jeff Parker should have been 'over the moon', as the football fraternity tends to say when they're not 'gutted' or 'sick as a parrot'. As one who turned out regularly on Saturday afternoons for a side in his native Brighton, he had been entered for a draw by the Sussex County FA to win a ticket for the World Cup Final. What's more, he had won. 'I didn't even know about it until the club secretary told me, and even then I wasn't exactly ecstatic,' he admits. 'There was only one ticket. I was 17 and I'd never been on a train on my own before.'

What's more, he had no idea how to get from London Victoria to Wembley Park on the tube. As it turned out, he would see rather a lot of the underground system that day. His parents and sister had already departed for a caravan holiday in Cornwall and he had promised to join them after the match. He would have to go as far south-west as he could on the District Line and hitchhike the rest of the way. What he could never have imagined, as he set off with a packet of cheese and tomato sandwiches in his rucksack, was that he would spend the night of July 30, 1966, sleeping in a cemetery.

First there was the small matter of finding his way to a stadium considerably larger than Brighton and Hove Albion's Goldstone

Ground, the only venue where he had hitherto watched professional football. These days he lives in a wide, tree-lined road near Trent Bridge cricket ground in Nottingham, the city where he trained as a social worker, but, at the time, Wembley seemed like the far North to a youthful Brightonian.

'Although it was quite early when I got to Victoria, there were already plenty of fans, German as well as English, milling about on the concourse,' he recalls. 'I just followed them and arrived in Wembley a couple of hours before the kick-off. I remember sitting down on the kerbside to eat my sandwiches and I wasn't the only one doing that. Most of the people heading towards the ground seemed a lot older than me, and many of them were wearing macs.

'Me? I was a bit of a mod in those days. I had a Ben Sherman shirt under a crew neck with a smart jacked on top and square-toed shoes.'

Having carefully brushed the sandwich crumbs from his Levi jeans, he invested in a scarf, a programme and a rosette from one of many stalls lining Wembley Way. 'I'd been saving up for that. At the time I was working in the Welfare Services Department at the old Brighton Corporation and earning 21 quid. A month, that was, and I had to give my Mum half of it.'

So, shelling out a shilling and sixpence (7½p) for a scarf was quite an investment. 'It was a white knitted job with dark blue ends and ENGLAND written along it.' Still got it? 'No, it's long gone, along with the rosette and the programme. But I treasured it at the time and it felt great to be inside the ground, even when it was half full. I'd only seen it on the telly until the '66 World Cup – black and white telly, of course – and, as I strolled around the terrace, I couldn't get over how green the pitch seemed with those immaculate lines criss-crossing it.

'As the crowd built up, a party of Germans in front kept hoisting a banner and I remember joining the chorus of people around me shouting at them to take it down because it was obscuring our view. And they did lower it. There was no great animosity. We were behind the goal where Geoff Hurst's shot hit the bar and bounced down and, when the ref gave the goal after consulting with the linesman, the Germans were all shouting "Nein, nein, nein!"'.

For them it was evidently an emergency. But what about Hurst's final goal?

'That was at the other end, which seemed a very long way away. I had no idea that he'd scored at first. Everybody was cheering anyway because . . . well, we thought it was all over. Everybody was jumping up and down, hugging one another. I should really have followed the Germans out of the ground. Until then I'd completely forgotten about Cornwall. At the back of my mind was the niggling thought that I had a long way to go. But I didn't want to leave, so I stayed to watch the Cup being presented and the lap of honour. Then it took an eternity to squeeze out of the gates.'

The evening was well advanced by the time he reached the south-western extremity of the underground system and started to walk, thumb outstretched more in hope than expectation until he reached the main road. Hitchhiking was quite common in 1966, even though the risk of coming to harm was considerably higher than it is today. Sexual predators would have been just as common (if not so commonly known about) and attitudes to drink-driving were lax, to put it mildly.

Young Parker's progress was slowed down by the number of passers-by who stopped him and kept asking: 'Have you just come from there? What was it like?' That scarf was a bit of a give-away, as was the rosette.

'When I finally got a lift, the driver wanted to know everything about it as well. "Come on, have a drink," he said after we'd at least covered a few miles. And as soon as we got to into the pub, he shouted out: "Hey, he was there" and pointed to me. Everyone wanted to buy me a drink.'

And so it went on. Another lift, more earnest enquiries, more stops at pubs en route until the 17 year-old could take no more. 'I hadn't got a clue where I was, except that I was in a small town somewhere. All I remember is going into the graveyard, lying next to some marble slab and falling asleep.'

He was awake early the following morning, freezing cold, hungry and hung-over. 'Luckily I got a long lift that Sunday with someone who wasn't remotely interested in football. We were on the edge of Cornwall when he dropped me around lunchtime. Then somebody else pulled up and said: "I'm going St Austell way, but I'm going to have a drink first."'

Another pub, another pint. Hair of the dog, you might say. 'I just about had enough money to afford a packet of crisps.'

That provided enough sustenance, as it turned out, to enable him to walk the last three or four miles. At least there were no more what-was-it-like questions at the caravan. Neither his parents nor his sister were particularly interested in football. 'Only when my older brother Chris turned up some time later did I have the chance to re-live the match. And I don't think I ever saw it repeated on a screen until many years later.'

The idea of watching a football match on a computer any time you wished would have been about as fanciful in 1966 as putting a plastic card in a hole in the wall and a tray full of bank notes emerging that might, just might, be enough to buy you a ticket for the away end at Chelsea.

* * *

It was on the Friday evening before the Final that Ros Pedley picked up the phone at her parents' house in Wolverhampton to hear her good friend Liz asking casually: 'What are you doing tomorrow?'

'I said: "That's the silliest question you've ever asked me. What do you think I'm doing? I'm watching the game of course." And she said: "I know that, but *where* are you watching it." So I said: "I'm coming round to your house, aren't I?" And she said: "Well … erm … actually … do you want to watch it at Wembley instead?"'

Ros was a keen student of football, having stood on the terraces at Molineux with family and friends since 1951 when she was seven. Her beloved Wolverhampton Wanderers had won the FA Cup two years previously and would go on to land the League title three times in the 1950s before lifting the Cup again in 1960. Ros had been at Wembley to witness that great day for the Wolves. Did she want to go again to see England against West Germany in the World Cup Final? Another silly question.

'I remember dancing round the hall when I finally put the phone down,' she recalls. By that time she had established just how her friend had acquired the tickets. 'We'd been to four qualifying matches, two at Goodison Park and two at Villa Park,' she explains. 'And unbeknown to us, our names had been entered into a draw to win tickets for the final. Liz's name had come out and she had two.'

They were young women in their early 20s, Ros a bank clerk who would later train as a primary school teacher, Liz a teacher already. Both earned enough to afford a Mini apiece. A Mini car, that is. And it was in that ultimate '60s mode of transport that they set off at 8 o'clock sharp the following morning to cross a West Midlands that had yet to be blessed by the M6 or Spaghetti

Junction in search of that highway to heaven, or at least Hendon, known as the M1.

'We parked at Stanmore underground station about 3½ hours later, caught the tube to Wembley Park and sat down on the terraces to eat our ham sandwiches about two hours before the kick-off.' As Ros is telling me this, I'm wondering how a woman of not much more than 5ft tall managed to see anything once those terraces started to fill up with tall and burly blokes. 'Well, Wembley was divided into little enclosures, so we didn't feel crushed. What's more, experience at Molineux had taught us how to use our shoulders to manoeuvre our way into good positions. And in those days a lot of guys would say: "Come on, love; you come and stand down the front."'

Not that you could patronise either of these young women when it came to knowledge of football. They knew more about Ray Wilson's defensive abilities and Uwe Seeler's overhead kicks than most of the men around them.

Ros and Liz were still discussing the finer points of the game when they stopped at a motorway service station on the way home to celebrate with egg and chips. Catering standards then were somewhat more primitive than they are now, I reflect, as we sit chatting in a Waitrose café in one of Wolverhampton's more salubrious outer suburbs. Espresso and Americano, cappuccino or latte, were unheard of in the ghastly mass-catering outlets of Watford Gap or Newport Pagnell – or indeed in the Wolverhampton branch of Lyon's Corner House where, as Ros recalls, tea would spurt from the spout of an enormous pot into a line of cups, much of it settling in the saucers. 'I remember walking there from the training ground, chatting to Billy Wright after he'd signed my autograph book.'

At the time, Wright was not only captain of that successful Wolves side; he was also captain of England. He was in the 1950s what Bobby Moore would become in the '60s, although as the *Guardian*'s David Lacey once put it with characteristic perceptiveness, Moore 'managed to embody the spirit of an age without abandoning the values of its predecessor'. He died from cancer in 1993, but Ros assures me that his signature is now worth around £650 at autograph fairs. Being the only English captain to lift the Jules Rimet trophy, having carefully wiped his hands before picking it up, has given him a kind of 'im-Mooretality' as the *Sun* rather than the *Guardian* might put it.

* * *

From Wembley to Harrow and then from Harrow to Watford is not far, and Ian Hands felt as though he could have made both journeys walking on air. 'My Mum couldn't stand football but even she was excited when I came home from the match.'

I don't have to tell you which match. Ian, then 19, emerged from the national stadium as he had gone in: alone. Unlike his friends, he had had the foresight to send off eight pounds ten shillings and sixpence (about a third of his wages at a factory making artists' materials) for a ticket to each match at Wembley and one at the White City. 'As the tournament progressed, you hoped and gradually began believe that England would be at the Final,' he says. 'And they might even win it.' Now they had. As a result, he felt far from alone amid that happy throng jostling back along Wembley Way. He felt part of a huge moment of national celebration. His ears were ringing and his heart was singing as he headed home to Harrow and then prepared to hit the town with one of his mates.

The Top Rank in Watford was the sort of dance hall that teenagers headed for on '60s Saturday nights. There was also Palais de Danses, Meccas, Locarnos and more. Whatever the name, the ritual was much the same. First, you had to get past the doormen, who were old enough to have done National Service and seemed to have inherited the values of the sergeant major. If your hair was short enough, your compulsory tie straight enough and your shoes polished enough, they might do you a favour and allow you to proceed to the box office and part with your money.

Once inside, the potential rewards were all too evident. The dance floor, an island of sprung maple surrounded by a sea of patterned carpet, was full of women dancing around their handbags. Feigning indifference, you walked past them to the bar. After a pint or three of some awful keg beer served in dimpled mugs, you moved closer to the edge of the dance floor to cast an eye over the 'talent'. Tension mounted. You knew that you had to get in first or your mate would beat you to the 'I-don't-like-yours' moment when you spotted a pair of likely lasses and you both made a bee-line for the more attractive one. Sometimes you put down your pint first.

This usually edgy ritual was considerably more relaxed on the night of July 30, 1966 – in the Top Rank, Watford, anyway. 'The whole atmosphere was celebratory,' Ian remembers. 'Everybody was happy, including the women.'

So you 'got off' then?

'Oh, yeah.'

It no doubt helped that he could tell the young lady concerned that he had been at the game – although he knew enough to avoid going on for too long about Roger Hunt's off-the-ball runs and various other images that stick in the memory when you have watched a game live rather than on the telly. 'I was level with the goal line and I could see that Geoff Hurst's volley off the crossbar didn't bounce over it,' says the man who was a goalkeeper at the time. For Ruislip Town FC, since you ask.

He's telling this to me, not her, as we sit in his colourful garden in Crawley, West Sussex, on a beautiful summer's morning nearly

50 years on. Ian has just lit a roll-up and taken a swig of tea from a mug decorated with a rather faded still of Jim Dale peering down Barbara Windsor's cleavage in one of those *Carry On* films that were as popular as saucy seaside postcards in the '60s. 'The other thing that struck me about Wembley that day,' he goes on, 'was the sheer amount of German flags all around the ground. Supporters mixed in back in those days.'

Not for much longer. Ian would see more than enough hooliganism over the next 20 years or so, having left the factory to become a police officer at the very time when behaviour at football grounds went into a steep decline. 'The first thing that went was respect,' he muses. 'When I started going to watch Chelsea with my Dad, you appreciated and applauded the likes of Matthews and Best, even though they were playing against you. But as time went on, anybody planting a 35-yarder past the goalie was greeted by obscene gestures from behind the goal. Dad was brought up round the corner from Stamford Bridge and he'd been going to matches there since the 1920s. But he stopped going in 1974, the year Manchester United were relegated, after their fans started throwing darts at the home supporters. The year after that I became an FA steward for Wembley matches until 1984. I think I can say that I've seen the best and the worst of England.'

At which point he finishes his roll-up and we move to the inner-sanctum of his cluttered back room where there perches a budgie, its cage being just about the only space not crammed or smothered with football memorabilia. Ian has been collecting football programmes from an early age. 'The programme was the only thing I bought on the day of the final in '66,' he confides. 'I got interested in autographs and the other stuff after retiring from the police about 15 years or so ago.'

World Cup Willie features so prominently that I'm surprised the budgie isn't chirruping that wretched tune by Lonnie Donegan.

There's a World Cup Willie puppet, diary, dice set, ashtray, stopwatch and even a horse brass. And there's more, much more, including Ian's framed ticket from the big day, a World Cup ice bucket and a packet of Typhoo tea (unopened) signed by Alan Ball. There's also a badge proclaiming 'England for the Cup', sponsored by the long-forgotten *Daily Sketch*.

Most poignant, perhaps, is the three-lions badge once worn by George Cohen, the first but by no means the last of the '66 side to sell his winners' medal to help make ends meet. A reminder there that the England team that won the World Cup for the one and only time had nothing like the financial security guaranteed for those who flew back from Brazil at the end of the group stage, 2014, without a win to their name.

* * *

Geoff Elliott was never a collector of football memorabilia but, like almost everybody who was there, he has retained his programme from the '66 Final. Indeed he has two, to be on the safe side perhaps, and he has just reacquainted himself with one of them nearly 50 years on at his home in Southsea. The first thing that strikes him is the cover, resplendent in the Union Jack and bearing in red the old Wembley's proper name, the Empire Stadium. 'That tells you much about the age,' he muses. 'As does the full-page picture of the Queen before anything else is said inside. There are the names and pictures of Lord This and Sir That yet curiously no mention of Ramsey or any other manager. Two-page ads for Cadet and Embassy cigarettes are an indication of how many were smoking in the crowd. For two shillings and sixpence you got 64 pages in black and white. That was just over 12 pence in the 'new money' that would test people's arithmetic 5 years later: a huge amount for the money compared with today's souvenir prices.'

On the other hand, Geoff and his old mate Tony had each shelled out what would have seemed at the time a large sum to watch a single football match: 'We had, I think, paid £24 for a package of tickets that allowed us to watch a series of games during the tournament. But we were too busy chasing girls and drinking beer to bother much. It was getting to see the Final at Wembley we paid for, even though, of course, it might have been between Hungary and Uruguay or two other teams we couldn't have cared less about. So that meant it was a big gamble on Alf Ramsey's men. Everybody thought we were mad. Until we won and then we were sort-of heroes. We'd shared a piece of history that still inspires people to say: "You were there? You mean you were actually there?!"'

At the time Geoff was 21 and working as a reporter on the *Coventry Evening Telegraph*, a paper that he would later edit with distinction before moving to the *News* in Portsmouth, becoming president of the Guild of Editors, founding president of the Society of Editors and being made a CBE, no less. He remembers travelling down the 'nearly-new' M1 in his Vauxhall Victor – 'the one with a red bench seat up front, American column-change and foot-dip switch,' he adds with a Coventrian's seemingly inbuilt consciousness of cars.

And Tony? Apparently he 'made spectacles' in '66, but didn't wear them. For the big match he wore a Beatle jacket, which must have given him a sort of retro-chic among the gabardine macs and flat caps that Geoff recalls being much in evidence at the end where Hurst completed his hat-trick and put the icing on what you might call England's Cup-cake. 'He [Hurst] aimed straight at us. Only the net saved one of us from a bruised face.'

Geoff had been born two days after VE Day and had grown up in an English city with more bomb craters than most, the centre of Coventry having been almost destroyed by the Luftwaffe. Perhaps that made him more conscious than most of anti-German feeling in the crowd on July 30, 1966. He recalls seeing some 'straight-arm salutes and index fingers across upper lips'. But songs other than the national anthem were notable by their absence, as indeed were 'chants of questionable content'. The one about 'two world wars and one world cup' would be belted out many years later by youths and young men who, unlike their granddads, had never seen a shot fired in a mass conflict, let alone witnessed the devastating consequences.

Incidentally, the 24 quid that Geoff and Tony each shelled out to see the World Cup Final would now buy you a seat to watch Coventry City play third-flight football in a two-thirds empty Ricoh Arena, owned by a Premiership rugby club with its roots in London. It wouldn't quite run to a programme as well, however.

* * *

Here's your starter for ten: who was the first Englishman to touch the ball after the kick-off in the 1966 World Cup Final? Was it Alan Ball? No. Bobby Moore? No. Gordon Banks? The answer's still no and, before we go through the entire team, let me tell you the correct answer. It was Neil Rioch.

Who?

Brother of Bruce Rioch, as it happens. They both played for Villa in the 1970s. Scotland, too, in Bruce's case. In fact, he became the Scottish captain although he was born in England, as indeed was Neil. No, of course he didn't play for England. Let's just remember at this point who's asking the questions here. If you want a fuller answer to the last one, let me hand you over to the man himself:

'Uwe Seeler kicked off for Germany and Wolfgang Overath played a pass out to the right wing but it went out of play. I was the ball boy positioned right in front of the royal box. I reckon I had a better view of the game than Alf Ramsey. I was playing for

Bedfordshire Schoolboys at the time and we'd been selected by the FA to be just behind the line for the France versus Mexico group game at the White City and for the Final. We didn't know it was going to be England at the time. That just made it all the better.'

As a budding footballer, he might have been tempted to show off in front of such a huge crowd. Trap the ball with one foot and flick it back with the other, perhaps, straight into the arms of whoever was coming over to take the throw-in.

Perish the thought! 'We were under strict instructions not to kick the ball under any circumstances. So I ran to it, picked it up and threw it to Marin Peters.'

Neil and one of his fellow ball boys weren't quite so obedient when it came to the FA's edict about not running on the pitch at any time. 'We were 15 and thought "When are we going to get the chance again"? So we ran on at half time only to see the massed ranks of the military bands marching towards us. It was time for a sharp exit, stage left.'

Many years later, Neil was in the overseas property business and staying at the Hendon Hall Hotel overnight. Yes, *that* hotel – the one the England players stayed at on the eve of the Final. Nobby Stiles must have had fond memories of the place because here he was again, just across the dining room. 'When he'd finished his meal, my wife Lynne went over and told him that I'd been a ball boy at the Final. Nobby and I got chatting and sat up, talking about football, until well into the early hours. The following day Nobby was signing copies of his book in Brent Cross and Lynne bought a copy. As soon as he saw her, he told everyone in earshot: "This is the woman who kept me up half the night." But he still signed the book "To the ball boy".'

* * *

As I mentioned in the Preface, English football's Premier League is dominated by four or five prosperous clubs; six at a push. And the England team is largely made up of players from those clubs, even though most of them can't guarantee much more than a place on the bench at Old Trafford, Stamford Bridge, the Etihad or the Emirates because the teams they represent are stuffed with vastly expensive imports from Europe, South America or Africa.

There was no Premier League in 1966. The triumphant national side of '66 included players from the likes of Leicester City, Fulham and Blackpool. Admittedly there were two from Manchester United and one from Liverpool. But nobody from Manchester City, Chelsea, Arsenal or Tottenham – not in the 11 that won the Final, anyway. There were, however, no fewer than three representatives of West Ham United.

Club versus country has always been an issue in England, and passionate Spurs supporters such as Allister Craddock were indignant about the exclusion from the final 11 of their prodigious goal-poacher Jimmy Greaves. 'It was mortifying,' he growls nearly 50 years on before moving his tongue from one cheek to another and adding: 'Who was this Geoff Hurst?'

'The one who scored a hat-trick,' I remind him.

'Okay so he scored three and, admittedly, that last goal was just wonderful. And okay we were jumping up and down going berserk. But I still reckon Greaves would have taken the ball round the German goalie before putting the ball in the net.'

Allister smiles and takes another swig of his pint, unable to keep up this Pythonesque what-have-West-Ham-players-ever-done-for-us line for much longer. He even concedes that Alan Ball, who would eventually go on to play for Arsenal, was his man-of-the-match. 'When you're there rather than watching on TV,' he says, 'you get a picture of the whole game and what's going on off the ball. I was very aware of Ball's immense contribution. He must have covered every square inch of the pitch and played like two men. So did Nobby Stiles for that matter. One of my abiding memories is of him jigging round the pitch at the end like an assassin with his fangs showing.

The other things I'll never forget are the sheer volume of the noise – someone could have dropped a bomb on the stadium when Bobby Moore picked up the Cup and nobody would have heard it – and the extraordinary theatrical experience of Wembley Way before the game. It felt like a fiesta. Although there was a very real tension, there was already a sense of celebration that we'd made it to the final after the slow burn of the build-up.'

At the time he was living in a hostel in central London owned by the BBC in whose news information department he was working. Many years later he would become a television producer in current affairs and politics in the Midlands. But for now he's sitting in a pub near his home in Nottingham revelling in memories of being 18 and up for the Cup.

Every few minutes he had kept checking in his pocket to reassure himself that the ticket was still there. 'I had a family friend called Tony in St Alban's to thank for it. Through some evidently good contacts he got me one for the Quarter Final, two for the Semi and one for the Final. My older brother Malcolm came to the Semi-Final against Portugal and neither of us will ever forget that second Bobby Charlton goal. It was right in front of us – a typical thunderbolt with a real swerve on the ball. Bobby was all power and grace.'

'Grace' was a term rarely applied to his brother Jack. He was, nevertheless, a key defender for England in that tournament and one of the other images of the final that has remained with Allister to this day is of the tall and gangly Jack slumping to his knees when the Germans equalised just before the referee was about to blow his whistle for full time. 'He was absolutely distraught and it just summed up how we were all feeling. I remember my mate telling me to calm down and he was quite right. My language needed moderating.'

The same 'mate' was with him throughout that emotional rollercoaster of an afternoon. 'He had a ticket for another turnstile, but we were young and cheeky and had managed to talk our way past the gatemen to get to the same spot behind one of the goals.' And sure enough they went out on the town together that night. After the first few pints, Allister's sharp memories become a little more blurred, although he does recall being in Trafalgar Square after the pubs shut. 'I wasn't in the fountain. There wasn't room. But I do remember getting wet anyway. There was so much water flying about.'

By that time his indignation at the omission of Jimmy Greaves had simply been washed away.

* * *

Reflecting on his exclusion by Ramsey some years later, Greaves himself said: 'I'd danced around the pitch with everyone else but even in this moment of triumph and great happiness, deep down I felt my sadness. Throughout my years as a professional footballer I had dreamed of playing in a World Cup final. I had missed out on the match of a lifetime and it hurt.'

Rob Boddie was not so much hurt as disappointed, having made a last-minute decision to go to the Final on the Saturday morning. 'You could do that sort of thing in those days without a wallet bulging with £50 notes,' he says. Mind you, it helped if you lived just down the road in Ealing and could just jump on the 83 bus.

Rob was 20 at the time and working in a local government office for little reward. But his Dad, who had been in military intelligence during the War, was evidently not short of a few bob.

'He gave me a fiver and told me to go and enjoy myself.' Only after investing half of that money on a ticket from one of many touts outside – 'I still had change for a programme and a hot dog' – did he glance at the *Evening Standard* special souvenir edition and read that an apparently fit Greaves had still not been restored to his place in the England side. 'I don't think I'd have gone if I'd known that beforehand,' Rob maintains. 'But once I got inside, I was just carried away by the atmosphere. I was standing right by the German fans on the East Stand Terrace when their right-back, Horst-Dieter Hottges, came over and shook hands with those closest to the pitch. As for the England fans, the flags being waved were Union Jacks rather than the cross of St George.'

The United Kingdom felt more … well, united at the time. Rampant Scottish nationalism was still some way in the future, even if news of England's victory plunged the pubs of Glasgow into mourning that evening (see Chapter Nine).

Rob leapt up 'more in hope than expectation' when the Hurst header hit the underside of the crossbar and he joined the full-throated roar of relief when the Hammer completed his hat-trick at the end of extra time. So why does he still feel ag-Greaved, as it were, nearly 50 years on? It wasn't as though he was a Tottenham supporter. In fact, he was a season-ticket holder at Brentford. Still is.

'It's just that the Spurs double-winning side was easily the finest football team that I'd ever seen at that stage of my life,' he asserts. (That goes for me too, Rob, even if I was nearly crushed to death when they came to Villa Park for a fifth-round Cup-tie.) But hang on a minute: Spurs added the FA Cup to the League Championship in May, 1961, while Greaves didn't arrive at White Hart Lane until December of that year, disillusioned with Italian football and Italian food. He wanted a bash at the bangers and mash his mother used to make and Peter Sellers used to sing about.

Rob, now curator of the Cricket World Museum at Sussex County Cricket Club, is a stickler for dates and well aware of the disparity. 'All I'm saying is that Greavesie's goals came close to winning the double for them again after a poor start.'

He's right about that. In the second half of that 1961–2 season, Greaves scored 21 times in 22 matches to ensure that Tottenham not only won the Cup again but finished just four points behind the champions, Ipswich Town, a comparatively small club with a manager who was adept at turning sows' ears into silk purses. Went by the name of Ramsey.

'You have to hand it to him,' Rob concedes. 'Alf won the World Cup with just four top-quality players: Gordon Banks, Ray Wilson and the two Bobbys, Charlton and Moore. There would have been a fifth, of course, if Greavesie had been picked.'

Once again I find myself pointing out that Geoff Hurst came good on the day. 'Yes,' chuckles Rob. 'But my argument is that we wouldn't have needed to go through the tension of extra time if Greaves had been up front.'

There's no answer to that. All we know for sure is that the England manager chose to stick with the team that had triumphed over Argentina and Portugal against the odds, despite the availability after injury of one of the finest goal-scorers that England has ever produced. So perhaps there was another reason why Greaves was not brought into the final side, at the expense of Roger Hunt if not Hurst. Greavesie liked a drink, as indeed did his fellow East Ender Johnny Byrne. Their sniggering at Ramsey from the back of the England team coach may have been louder than either of them was aware. Three years before the Final, Ken Jones of the *Mirror* overheard the manager hiss under his breath: 'If needs be, I'll win the World Cup without either of those two.'

And he did.

It's worth recording at this point that Bobby Moore, too, liked a drink. Nor was he averse to taking the mick out of Alf. But some players are simply indispensible and, for all the mistakes that haunted his personal life in later years, the ultra-cool England captain was destined to be remembered as one of football's enduring icons. Unlike the great Greaves, he didn't miss out on 'the match of a lifetime'.

* * *

Greaves had been by no means the only British footballer to try his luck in Italian football in the early 1960s. Nor was he the only one to decide that it wasn't for him. Denis Law and Joe Baker both came back after just one season. The only one to stick it out and adapt to the Italian lifestyle was my boyhood hero Gerry Hitchens.

Well, he did he score 42 goals in a season for Aston Villa, a post-war record that seems unlikely to be broken. (As the 2014–15 season progresses, the whole team seems unlikely to muster that many.) Crucially, he scored two for England against Italy in Rome in the summer of '61. Italian scouts were looking on. Cue exit for Milan, then Turin, Bergamo and Cagliari. He was away for the best part of a decade.

Now, Gerry may not have had quite as much natural talent as Greaves and Law. What he had was strength and determination in abundance, and that made him difficult to dispossess once he'd latched on to a ball. He came from mining stock in the Shropshire village of Highley and knew what it was like to work at the coalface in seams no higher than 3ft6. Professional football seemed like a permanent holiday by comparison. He also knew what it was like to play against Clee Hill quarrymen wearing pit boots. 'Italian defenders were a doddle after that,' someone confided when I visited Highley in 2012 while researching a book on Britain's lost mines.

The Hitchens family used to come back to Gerry's roots every summer to visit friends and family. They also travelled west, across Offa's Dyke, to see his wife Meriel's family in Pontypridd. On July 30, 1966 however, Gerry was in the crowd at Wembley with many a former England player. And Meriel was alongside him, dressed up to the nines, like many an England player's wife, past and present. She had expected to travel to the ground by taxi from the West London home of their host Brian Glanville, who was covering the match for the *Sunday Times*. Perhaps his expenses were not as high as those of the tabloids because, according to Hitchens' biographer Simon Goodyear, 'they headed to the nearest underground station' on his insistence.

Back in Pontypridd that day, three of the five Hitchens children were gathered around the television with their grandparents. 'They had their own business and were quite affluent,' the oldest child, Marcus, recalls. 'They lived in a large Victorian house with Mrs Edwards, their lovely housekeeper. Marcus was seven at the time and has the impression that 'everyone was elated by England's victory, even in Wales'.

Well, maybe in that big Victorian house and its immediate environs. Somehow I suspect that the elation was rather more muted elsewhere in the Rhondda and up in North Wales. Within a few months of the Final, as it turned out, the entire nation would be plunged into grief by the disaster at Aberfan. The death of 116 children and 28 adults under a collapsing colliery spoil tip 'put football in perspective', as Marcus reminds me.

There have, of course, been plenty of great Welsh footballers, including John Charles who survived in Italy for five years before the arrival of Greaves, Law, Baker and Hitchens. But what the Welsh really enjoy is beating England at rugby. And why not? It's their national game and, in the days when it was for amateurs only, Wales wasn't plagued by the class distinctions that prevailed across the border. Former miners and steel workers could relish knocking six bells out of the chaps from 'Twickers'. In England, of course, former miners or steelworkers played football or rugby league in the winter months.

Gerry Hitchens, alas, had his life cut cruelly short when he collapsed with a heart attack while playing in a charity match in 1983. He was 48. But he'll live forever in the memories of those of us who looked on in awe from a Holte End smelling of smoke, damp macs and beery breath while he soared above centre halves or stuck his head down and homed in on goal.

He was picked only seven times for England but still managed to come up with five international goals, the last being against Brazil in the Quarter Finals of the World Cup in Chile, 1962. They never picked him again. As Greaves himself wrote in the introduction to Simon Goodyear's book: 'Like the great John Charles, he spent so long playing in Italy that he is overlooked when people start talking about the outstanding British players of the 1960s.' And like Greaves himself, Hitchens had to look on from the sidelines in '66. I suspect that he would have given up his entire wardrobe of beautifully tailored Italian suits to have been out there on the Wembley turf hounding the German defence.

CHAPTER FOUR

Those for whom the most colourful occasion in English football history will be forever remembered in fifty shades of grey

Dawn on July 30, 1966 was a little on the chilly side for high summer. Or at least it was in the field in the hills above Bath when I awoke to discover that I had put my foot through the bottom of my cheap sleeping bag. A cow's shiny nose was about a foot from mine, its wide and uncomprehending eyes peering at this prone intruder as he groped around the dewy grass in search of a jacket to cover his freezing toes. Don't ask me what kind of cow it was. I came from Birmingham. So did my pal, Paul, who was still asleep nearby. We had no tent.

Sleeping under the stars had seemed like a romantic notion when we'd set off a few days previously, hitting the open road with thumbs outstretched. We were 17 and I was still at school, albeit in the 6th Form and full of pretentious notions fed by Bob Dylan and Jack Kerouac. The only thing that we carried, apart from sleeping bags stuffed with some spare clothing and a toilet bag, was an acoustic guitar which Paul could play. He had already left school, fondly imagining that he was going to find fame and fortune as bass guitarist with his 'group', as rock bands were known in those days. For the life of me, I can't remember what they called themselves.

Anyway, we both fondly imagined that the guitar gave us a freewheelin' Dylanesque demeanour that would make us irresistible to girls. Apart from a brief dalliance with two strapping daughters of Devizes, it had failed to weave much magic so far. There now arose the even more pressing issue of finding somewhere to watch The Match. Later – much later – we lugged our sleeping bags and the guitar up the crunchy gravel drive of a bungalow in deepest rural Wiltshire.

Here lived my 'Auntie', who was really my Mum's cousin, and her female companion. They could well have been younger than I am now but, at the time, they seemed incredibly ancient. The journey to their home had not been easy. It had taken some time to find an un-vandalised phone box to ring ahead and warn them that we were on the way; even longer to flag down a passing lorry willing to give us a lift as far as Stonehenge where we were sitting on a grass verge tucking into bacon rolls purchased from a van in the car park when two cars collided on the main road. One swerved within about two feet of us before regaining control. I remember looking down a few minutes later and noticing that my roll was sprinkled with shards of broken glass. It was evidently going to be our lucky day.

And so it proved on a distant field in North West London. Neither my 'Auntie' nor her friend was remotely interested in football. But they did have a television that was sizeable by the standards of the time and they looked on with amusement as we went through intense reactions to that rollercoaster of a match. When it really was all over and a seemingly toothless Nobby Stiles had danced around the touchline wielding the Jules Rimet trophy, we were provided with a hot bath and a hot meal.

All England drank, danced and sang that night, from the miners' clubs of Ashington to the 'boozers' of the old East End and beyond. But here in Wiltshire, the appeal of clean sheets and a soft mattress proved irresistible after several nights when sleep had been difficult to come by. We should have been out celebrating. Instead we stayed in and slept, for 10 hours at least. Sunday morning was well advanced by the time that we set off. Birmingham beckoned. It was many hours before it materialised, but at least we were warmed by a July sun and the knowledge that the World Cup was ours, for four years at least.

* * *

Patrick Collins spent the afternoon of July 30, 1966 sitting on the sofa with a sister or two, as the Beatles might have put it. Like 32 million or so of their fellow citizens, the Collins family were watching television coverage of the World Cup Final. Unlike most of them, however, Patrick's eyes should really have been focused elsewhere. He was down on the diary to cover a County Championship cricket match between Surrey and Essex for a long-forgotten newspaper called the *Sunday Citizen*.

'We lived in South London and it had rained in the morning and early afternoon, so I assumed there'd be no play,' he recalls. 'But as the match at Wembley wore on, the sun came out.'

Any guilt at that point?

'No, to hell with that. I wasn't going to miss the Final.'

An understandable reaction, you may feel. He was 22 and already had his own column. What's more, he had covered the group match against France and the Semi-Final against Portugal. Come the Final, however, the *Citizen*'s sports editor had pulled rank. He would go to Wembley. Young Collins would be despatched to the Oval. 'I could have rushed along there after the Final had it been necessary. It wasn't, and I didn't.'

For the record, Surrey eventually beat Essex by seven wickets in a low-scoring game after some improbable declarations. Patrick arrived in the office on the Tuesday, the beginning of the working week on a Sunday paper, expecting some kind of interrogation as to the lack of copy in the July 31 edition from that rain-interrupted first day at the Oval. But questions came there none. 'Nobody even mentioned the cricket,' he says.

Certainly his absence from Kennington and Wembley that day did him no harm in the long run. He went on to become an esteemed columnist on the *Mail on Sunday* and has been named Sportswriter of the Year on no fewer than five occasions.

His first taste of champagne, however, came later on July 30 when he was invited to a celebratory evening at the Knightsbridge Sporting Club. 'Eusebio was there, having won some sort of award for being the tournament's top scorer,' he confides. 'Lots of hacks were present as well and it must have gone on quite a long time because I remember being served bacon and eggs at one point.'

A champagne breakfast was at least some compensation for being denied a grandstand view of the biggest day in England's football history.

* * *

The World Cup Final not only intruded on the middle of the cricket season, it also scheduled itself in the early stages of the school holidays. They were heady days for John Timewell, 12 at the time, living in Liverpool and passionate about supporting the sides managed by Bill Shankly at Anfield and Alf Ramsey at Wembley. 'I'd watched every World Cup game at home on our 12-inch black and white Bush television,' he recounts proudly.

Then something terrible happened. His parents told him that they were going on holiday to the seaside on July 30. What's more, he was coming with them.

Never had the leaving of Liverpool seemed so grievous to a lad on the threshold of adolescence with a strong sense of injustice. 'While the rest of the country was settling down to watch the Final on TV, I was heading south in the back of my father's car. We didn't have a car radio, so I took a cheap transistor with me. The reception was woeful.'

Stuck in a traffic jam with the sound of constant whingeing overlaid by static that made Radio Luxembourg sound crystal clear by comparison, his father made an executive decision. He would, reluctantly, come off the main road, drive to the nearest centre of population and allow the back-seat bleater to watch the rest of the game in a TV rental shop window.

'Don't ask me where it was, but it seemed to me like a prosperous market town,' John tells me from his current home in Ashton-in-Makerfield, near Wigan, where he works as a carpet-fitter. 'There were quite a few people outside the shop looking in, so I got down on my hands and knees, crawled through a forest of legs and watched with my nose pressed up against the window.'

His Dad, meanwhile, stood at the back, peering over shoulders every now and then while glancing anxiously at his watch. Extra time was not what he needed. 'He was never an avid fan like me,' says John. 'You must have been happy, though', I suggest. 'And the telly must have been bigger than the 12-inch at home?'

'Yeah, but you couldn't hear any commentary outside the shop. I missed the roar of the crowd that might have given the occasion some atmosphere. After the final whistle and the presentation of the trophy to Bobby Moore, everybody around me silently drifted away. I wanted to jump up and down and have a party. Although I was elated that England were world champions, the lack of a celebration afterwards remains one of the biggest let-downs of my life.'

All he had to look forward to was a couple of weeks of purgatory at the seaside before the pearly gates of Anfield heralded the promise of a new season. Earth had not anything to show more fair to a young Scouser in 1966 than Shankly's Liverpool and Ramsey's England.

* * *

Tommy Charlton had a ticket for Wembley. Big brother Jack had made sure of that, as one of quite a few miners from the North East who had escaped from a working life underground into the sunlit uplands of professional football. What neither he nor Bobby had thought to send him, alas, was the train fare.

Tommy was the baby of the Charlton family, the youngest of four brothers, and in 1966 he was an apprentice at Ellington, one of five collieries in and around his native Ashington. Apprentices didn't earn much. 'I didn't go to the game because I didn't have the money to get down there and I didn't know where I'd stay if I did,' he tells me from his current home in Rotherham.

Couldn't either Bobby or Jack sort that out?

'They had far too much on their plates to worry about me. I didn't want to put them under any more strain. I've spent all my life trying not to be trouble.'

That ticket, of course, was worth a fair bit of money. 'I was offered a tenner for it,' he says, 'and that seemed like a lot to me at the time. But I'd already promised it to the foreman in the repair shop at Lynemouth pit, a nice old feller called Norman Conn. He rode all the way to London on his bike, stopping at youth hostels on the way.'

'That's a round trip of 600 miles. It must have taken foreman Norman a hell of a long time', I suggest to his nephew Ron Conn. 'Cycling was his hobby and he'd think nothing of covering 50 miles a day on a sturdy old-fashioned bike with two saddlebags either side of the back wheel,' Ron confirms. Even then it would have taken him the best part of a week to get back home.

The youngest Charlton brother, meanwhile, had watched the match on television at his then girlfriend's house. 'Neither she nor her Mam and Dad knew much about football but, like everybody else, they were up in the air at the end.'

So what did you do then, Tommy? Hit the pubs and clubs of Ashington? As a Charlton, surely you wouldn't have had to put your hand in your pocket all night. 'Nah. The last thing you did in Ashington was to brag about anything, let alone your family connections. There was no messing about. I was brought up that way.'

He went on to become a member of the mines' rescue service. The man who didn't want to be any trouble spent much of his life getting other men out of trouble, no doubt putting his life on the line on more than one occasion.

Did he tell me that?

As if he would!

* * *

Down south in Newcastle (it's not often you can say that in England) John Hudson felt hemmed in. The family's small front room seemed decidedly overcrowded as the match got underway. Apart from John and his Mum and Dad, there were visitors from Ireland: his Uncle Eddie and Auntie Mary, plus two female cousins, one 17 and the other 16, the same age as John. His older sisters had already left home. Just as well, perhaps, on this occasion.

John liked his cousins, his auntie too. 'But they didn't understand football and I had to keep explaining what was happening. I wanted to concentrate on the match, invest in the occasion and let rip when England scored. Uncle Eddie understood the game well enough. He used to go to St James's Park with my Dad when Jackie Milburn was in his prime and Newcastle won the FA Cup three times. What he didn't want was to look as though he was supporting England. He was generally sarcastic about it.'

Come the break between full time and the beginning of extra time, John found himself pacing around the back yard in sheer frustration. 'I kept asking myself why the women didn't just go out shopping and take Uncle Eddie with them.'

All that tension evaporated with Hurst's two goals in extra time. 'At last I felt able to enjoy myself and ignore the visitors,' he says with the feeling of a Geordie so passionate about football at the time that he would go to see Newcastle one week and Sunderland the next.

A few days after England's greatest triumph, however, John was corralled into joining his parents and their Irish visitors on a trip to the cinema to see *The Sound of Music*. It was one of those movies that women in particular would drool over time and time again. You'd hear them banging on about it on the last bus home. 'Wasn't Julie Andrews wonderful? Wasn't *he* good ('he' being Christopher Plummer as Captain Von Trapp)? And weren't the children lovely?' It was just what you didn't want to hear or see as a male teenager with aspirations to appear hip, or 'cool' as they'd say today.

For John, though, there was an unexpected silver lining during that trip to the flicks. 'The Pathe News showed the highlights from the World Cup Final. In colour! It was an unexpected pleasure that made sitting through *The Sound of Music* just about bearable.'

Years later he became head of English at an inner-city comprehensive, learned to play the guitar and regaled many a social occasion with his songs: Irish folk music a speciality. Uncle

Eddie would have enjoyed hearing them a lot more than he enjoyed watching England lift the World Cup.

* * *

John Rubidge had the less than enviable task of sifting through the potential pigswill deposited from the scraped plates of diners at Butlin's holiday camp in Minehead. 'As kitchen porters we were expected to delve into the dustbins to fish out the knives and forks that had dropped in accidentally during the somewhat frenzied scraping process.' By 'we' he means himself and two students, one from Sheffield, the other from Austria. John had come to Minehead from nearby Bath in the summer of '66, having recently completed his A-levels. He was bound, eventually, for teachers' training college in Coventry, but first came the task of earning some much-needed cash during the holidays.

'We quickly worked out that pigs wouldn't eat knives and forks,' he goes on. 'So we decided to club together a small portion of our earnings and give the farmer a tip. He used to take the swill away and bring back the bins in the morning with nothing more than the knives and forks inside them. It meant that we weren't wasting an hour, maybe two, after each meal sitting.'

Saving time became a particularly pressing issue after lunch on Saturday, July 30. 'Everybody on the staff was aware that the big match was coming up and worked out ways of avoiding having to do anything from 3 o'clock onwards,' he explains. 'Apart from the cooks, that is. They would have missed the match because, although the campers would have spent the afternoon glued to the telly in one of the big public rooms, they'd still expect their tea to be ready almost immediately afterwards. Everything was done with military precision.' After all, Butlin's was based in a former army camp, surrounded by barbed wire.

There was a substantial contingent of German students among those gathered in that crowded staff canteen full of fetid, food-encrusted overalls. They were all craning forward to focus, like almost everybody else, on a tiny television perched on two tables, one on top of the other.

So how did the Germans react, John, when Geoff Hurst's shot hit the bar, landed on the line and was eventually judged to be a goal?

'There was a bit of moaning and groaning but no arguments. Although we English jumped about a bit and cheered at the end, it was all remarkably civilised compared to what it would be like today. There wasn't that intensity of emotion. Some Swedish and Danish students were there as well. They were supporting England, but in a rather detached sort of way, like an academic exercise. The waitresses weren't really interested at all, but that may have been because they all seemed to come from Glasgow.'

Surprise, surprise, they weren't really interested in the kitchen porters either. Not while they were in those fetid overalls at least. 'We used to get spruced up at night and try to get work in the Hawaiian Bar,' John assures me.

Not surprisingly, it was quite lively in there and in other Butlin's bars and cabaret rooms on the night of July 30. 'There was a big sing-song between the variety acts with a bit of anti-German stuff,' the kitchen-porter-turned-barman recalls. "We've done you again," was the gist of it. But it was all a bit half-hearted.'

Many of those campers would have lived through the war and knew about its brutal realities. Perhaps most of them didn't feel inclined to pretend that a football match was in any way comparable.

* * *

What was it like to be an England supporter in a German bar on the day of the 1966 World Cup Final? The regulars, clad in lederhosen to a man, would be slapping their thighs and bawling their all for Deutschland. Huge foaming tankards would be ferried around by buxom frauleins in low-cut costumes. English visitors would be left in no doubt that the better team had been robbed and that 'Russian' linesman would be cursed to kingdom come.

Well, it might have been like that in Munich or West Berlin. But it certainly wasn't like that when Patrick Freestone and his friend John went for a walk in the Black Forest and found a village bar with a television that Saturday afternoon.

Bear in mind that, apart from the occasional afternoon drinking club (mainly sited in Soho), such a facility would not have been available in the UK. Pubs shut sharpish at any time between 2 and 3pm, depending in which part of the country you lived. It would have been three in the Mile End Road, Stepney, where Pat had a flat next door to the old Charrington's Brewery. Kick-off time, in other words.

In this German enclave they not only served beer considerably stronger than Charrington's, it came in litres rather than pints. What's more they had a television. Only a comparatively small black and white one, needless to say, but a telly nonetheless. Few English pubs offered that sort of facility back in '66. Matches beamed into bars on big screens would have been considered vulgarly intrusive.

Patrick would eventually go to Lancaster University, train as a teacher and finish up as principal of a central London college of further education. But at the time he was 18 and he and John were attending a youth work camp somewhere in the forest.

'That Saturday we sat at a little formica-topped table, got merrily pissed on three litres and enjoyed the match,' Pat recalls. 'Elsewhere in the bar there seemed to be an overwhelming lack of excitement. There were very few people and nothing like the intensity that such an occasion would arouse today. Even John and I weren't really engaged with the World Cup as a total phenomenon. We'd been away throughout the build-up to the Final, but we left the bar feeling very happy.' No disputes, apparently, no thigh-slapping in lederhosen and no buxom frauleins in low-cut costumes.

So much for stereotypes.

* * *

Michael Jeanes was in ready-mix concrete. Readymix was the name of the firm he worked for in the days when companies encouraged their workforce to get involved with sport, particularly football and cricket. Michael loved both, being a keen supporter of Aston Villa and Warwickshire. He was also wicketkeeper for the technical department cricket team who were playing the transport section on a summer's evening in 1966.

Venue: Ward End Unity's ground in Birmingham. Time: 5pm sharp. Date: Tuesday July 26th. And every man playing was acutely aware that England were due to kick off against Portugal, Eusebio and all, in the Semi-Final at 7.30. Michael had become used to clock-watching that summer. The family had 'raced' home from holiday on the Norfolk Broads to catch the Quarter-Final against Argentina, as far as one could ever race through the by-ways of East Anglia in the days before the dual-carriageway A14. He and his wife Sue had gone back to their home near Bromsgrove, his sister Betty, parents Maude and Fred, and various uncles and aunts to their home in Brewery Street, Handsworth.

At least it meant that they could watch the match without having to slot a shilling in the meter, as they'd had to do during the earlier rounds of the World Cup. For younger readers, a shilling was worth five pence, and it was what millions of us had to put into meters at regular intervals to keep the gas supply going –

electricity, too, it would seem, in rented holiday cottages.

'Dad always seemed to have a shilling to watch the football, but never had any change when Mom and I wanted to see *Coronation Street*,' Betty confides. (The ever-green soap opera was six years old and in its grainy black and white prime at the time, with Ena Sharples, Elsie Tanner, Len Fairclough and a youthful Ken Barlow proving that working-class characters could sustain a show in their own right, rather than be treated as comic walk-ons to be patronised or ordered about.)

Now let's get back to that cricket match. What happened, Michael?

'We managed to bowl them out for not much more than 50. Then our captain said to me: "Don't bother taking your pads off. To save time, you're opening." Our number 11 was sent in at the other end because he hadn't been called upon to bowl.' While he kept up one end, young Jeanes proceeded to set about the transport department's bowlers with some gusto, hitting two sixes on his way to the only half century of his cricketing career. And, no, he didn't expect to be chaired shoulder-high from the field. He simply ran hell-for-leather towards the pavilion with the other batsman, the umpires and the fielding side. The rest of his own side were already getting the beers in and settling down to watch the match.

'We had a few drinks, saw the whole game and then had a few more drinks,' he recalls happily. The Final was still to come and he could watch it at home with Sue without having to feed any shillings in the meter.

* * *

On the morning of the World Cup Final, Brian Mills received an unexpected call from the captain of Coventry and North Warwickshire Cricket Club. Would he, by any chance, be available to play for the first team? One or two senior members had suddenly developed unexpected injuries that would require them to do nothing more strenuous than sit at home watching the telly instead of taking the field for an away match at Olton and West Warwickshire.

Brian was 16 at the time but wasn't entirely wet behind the ears. 'I soon grasped what was going on,' he recalls. And while he too would have liked nothing more than to watch events at Wembley unfold in the family living room, he couldn't turn down the chance of premature elevation to the senior ranks.

Luckily, there was a television in the Olton pavilion and, just as luckily, the away team won the toss and elected to bat first. Brian settled down to watch the match with the rest of the 'lads' only to feel his stomach lurch as a loud appeal signalled the early dismissal of one of the openers. Every subsequent appeal brought a similar wave of anxiety to the teenage debutant who was already padded up and ready to take the field. Fortunately for him and the rest of the team, none of those appeals was successful. So you never had to leave the telly and walk to the middle, Brian? 'That's right. Alan Gordon, who later played for the full county side, and Mike Cheslin batted on and on.' And on. Both scored undefeated centuries and arrived back at the pavilion for an extended tea break that just happened to coincide with extra time at Wembley. Both had earned the undying gratitude of their team-mates, including young Millsy. Nearly 50 years on, he can't remember which team won the cricket match. All he *can* recall are fragments of a very long Saturday night celebrating England's victory in the bars of both clubs. He may have been under-age but, having made his debut with the big boys, he wasn't going to be left outside with a packet of crisps and a bottle of Vimto.

The popular BBC series of the time, 'Til Death Us Do Part', featured avid Hammers supporter Alf Garnett, played by Warren Mitchell (see chapter 8).

BBC TV (L–R) Eric Robinson, Reg Varney, Leslie Crowther, June Whitfield, Roy Hudd, Charlie Drake, the other Jack Warner (not Fifa's), Pat Coombs, Ian Carmichael, Peter Byrne, Alan Melville and Dennis Price.

(L–R) Norman Hunter, Martin Peters, Bobby Charlton, Ron Springet, Jack Charlton, Geoff Hurst and George Eastham playing cards.

With the inevitable entourage of autograph seekers, Bobby Charlton (right) and Ray Wilson return to their Hendon, London, hotel after a shopping expedition a few hours before the World Cup Final.

Martin Peters (l) and Geoff Hurst (r) sign autographs for young fans outside the Hendon Hall Hotel on the morning after the team's victory over Portugal earned them a place in the World Cup Final.

England fans watch the team's victory over Germany in the 1966 World Cup.

Actors Rex Harrison and Samantha Eggar, with chimpanzee Chee-Chee, sit down to watch the Football World Cup Final during filming 'Doctor Doolittle' at Castle Coombe, Dorset.

(L–R) England squad members watch the match from the sidelines: Peter Bonetti, Norman Hunter (top), Ron Springett, George Eastham (on floor), John Connelly, Terry Paine.

The Queen shakes hands with Bobby Charlton following England's 4-2 victory over West Germany. Skipper Bobby Moore holds aloft the Jules Rimet Trophy. He is followed by Geoff Hurst.

Bobby Moore (c) shows the Jules Rimet trophy to manager Alf Ramsey (l) as Nobby Stiles (r) tries to extricate himself from the boss's grasp. Looking on are Peter Bonetti (l) and Ron Flowers (r).

England fans celebrate winning the World Cup in the fountains at Trafalgar Square, London.

Cissie Charlton showing Gordon a film of the match when he finally came home from sea in September, 1966. (Reproduced with kind permission by Vince Gledhill)

The victorious England world cup team stand on the balcony of the Royal Garden Hotel in Kensington, London and acknowledge the cheers of the crowds.

Bobby Charlton Snr raises his glass in a toast with the girlfriends and wives of the England team at the Royal Garden Hotel. The players had their own celebratory banquet in another wing of the hotel.

Bobby Charlton reads a newspaper at the Royal Garden Hotel, the day after he helped England to win the 1966 World Cup Final.

England World Cup hero brothers Bobby (l) and Jack Charlton set off on a triumphal tour of their home-town of Ashington in an open yellow Rolls Royce to head to council offices for a civic reception.

CHAPTER FIVE

Those who were on holiday, on duty, getting married, getting lost, playing cricket or fast asleep

Quite why the Frenchman put down his drink, picked up his knife, lurched and lunged towards a party of English teenagers glued to the television in a Boulogne café must remain a mystery. Okay, England had beaten France 2-0 in the group stage of the World Cup finals. And, okay, the 6th-formers had just knocked over a table in sheer excitement after Bobby Charlton, an old boy of their grammar school in Bedlington, Northumberland, had just scored a characteristically spectacular goal against Portugal in the Semi-Final. None of that was reason for the brooding solitary drinker to resort to the threat of violence.

'Luckily, the woman who ran the café was built like Two Ton Tessie,' says Ian Richardson, one of 'eight lads and three lasses' in that party, along with the Latin master and two school mistresses. Madame la patronne interposed her considerable frame between the knife-wielder and the English kids before, as Ian puts it, 'grabbing him by the scruff of the neck and pushing him out of the door'.

Teachers and 6th-formers then apologised profusely for the overturned table, explained that they were from the school where the goal-scorer had been a pupil, and offered to pay for the broken glasses. 'She was fine about it,' Ian tells me over the mobile phone he has taken to his allotment. He has now retired from his post as chief environmental health officer in Northumberland.

On the afternoon of July 30, 1966, he was 17 and stuck in a Dormobile with his schoolmates somewhere between Bordeaux and Biarritz while the World Cup Final itself was underway. 'The trip had been planned long before we knew that England were going to be playing in that Final,' he explains. 'We were booked in somewhere in Spain that night and there was no way the teachers were going to let us stop to watch the match in another café.'

Today, any coach-load of teenagers would be tuned into their smart phones and plugged into their ear-pieces. But back then such technology would have been in the realms of science fiction. 'The very faint radio signal disappeared completely the further south we travelled,' Ian recalls. 'We didn't know the score until the Dormobile drew up outside a boulangerie. Me and another lad were sent in to buy some bread for the evening ahead. The woman who ran the bakery soon worked out that we were English and passed on her congratulations. I remember coming out of that shop and doing a celebratory drop kick with one of the baguettes. Some passers-by were a bit surprised, but the lady in the bakery just laughed when I was sent back in to buy a replacement.'

The school trip went on for most of the summer holiday, through Spain, Italy and Switzerland. 'And because we were from the country that had just won the World Cup, everybody on the camp sites we stopped at wanted to play us at football,' Ian remembers. 'I lost count of the times I represented England against the rest of the world.'

* * *

Bob Barber was representing England against Australia in January, 1966, when he hit a sublime 185 on the opening day of the third Test match at Sydney. Those who saw it will never forget it. Six months later, the demon Barber had scored exactly 84 for Warwickshire against local rivals Worcestershire at Edgbaston when he looked up to check the time on the pavilion clock. It was five to three and I'm sure you've guessed the date. As Worcestershire's Bob Carter tells it: 'Up went his head and over the lot went.' In other words, he was clean bowled by Basil d'Oliveira 16 short of his century and he didn't seem at all distressed. On the contrary, he seemed relieved. 'Cheers chaps,' beamed one of the most swashbuckling batsmen of the 1960s before heading hurriedly for the pavilion where the television was on.

Carter elaborated on this story to the cricket writer Stephen Chalke for his book *Caught in the Memory*. 'As he came out after lunch,' Worcester's fast-medium bowler recalled, 'Bob had said to us: "I think I have more chance of watching this football match this afternoon than you lot."'

If the fielding team felt aggrieved about that, so did Dennis Amiss, the next man in for the home side. Like many professional cricketers, he was also a useful footballer who played in the Worcestershire Combination league and he had been keen to see the kick-off at Wembley and as much of the World Cup Final as possible. 'As it turned out, I don't remember seeing it until the replay later that night,' he tells me. 'That was Bob for you. A very fine player, for sure, but you never knew what to expect from him.'

Officially, the distinction between (amateur) Gentlemen and (professional) Players had been abolished four years previously. But Barber was still very much a cavalier gent, educated at public school and Cambridge, and able to please himself. He retired early in 1969 to concentrate on the family business producing those blue toilet-cistern cleansers. He now lives in Switzerland.

Amiss, on the other hand, still lives in Birmingham where he was born and joined the county ground staff at 15. He, too, would go on to become a distinguished batsman for England, making his Test debut later in the summer. But as a young professional, who depended on cricket for his income, he didn't have the luxury of being able to give his wicket away.

Incidentally, he was one short of his half-century in the second innings when another gent, Mike (MJK) Smith, declared and Worcestershire went on to win by three wickets. Whether the result would have been the same had Barber stayed at the wicket on the Saturday afternoon will have to remain a matter for conjecture.

* * *

Jim Cumbes was a man for all seasons. Professional football was his game in the winter months, professional cricket every summer. You could still do that in the '60s and '70s, just about, but it was becoming increasingly difficult. By the early to mid-'80s it was almost impossible as the football season expanded its already ample girth further over the belted flannels of county cricket.

Jim's heyday had been 10 years previously when he guarded Aston Villa's goal in the season that they won the League Cup and promotion back to the top flight shortly after his medium-fast bowling had helped Worcestershire to land the County Championship.

Back in '66 he was goalie at Tranmere Rovers while also on the books at Lancashire CCC in his native Manchester. But he was some way down a pecking order of bowlers that included Brian Statham and Ken Higgs. So, on the afternoon of the World Cup

Final, the 22 year-old found himself playing for Chorley in the ultra-competitive Lancashire league. 'We used to get paid a tenner,' he recalls. But it was the toss of an old-fashioned 'tanner' that decided which team would have the chance to watch at least some of the dramatic events at Wembley unfold via the tiny telly in the dressing room.

'We were praying that our captain would win that toss. Needless to say, he went out and lost it and we were in the field.' Jim shakes his head at the memory before taking another sip of his coffee in the Altrincham branch of Costa. 'Then our prayers *were* answered when it started to rain quite heavily.'

On the west side of the Pennines? Surely not.

'We kept protesting to the umpire that the pitch wasn't fit to play on, but he wouldn't have it. Perhaps he was conscious of the old boys sitting on benches around the boundary, arms folded defiantly, as if to say "cricket's our game and we've paid good money to see it". I was fielding at third man, closest to the pavilion, so somebody kept updating me on the Wembley score, which I'd pass on to the rest of the lads as best I could.'

And when did you finally see England's greatest ever triumph, Jim?

'I think I saw the goals on the Pathe News about a week later.'

Still, when he signed for West Bromwich Albion three years later, he saw the likes of Bobby Charlton and Geoff Hurst in close-up. Rather too close up for comfort. They were running towards the goal that he was defending with the ball at their feet. Not a reassuring sight for any goalkeeper.

* * *

The wedding invitation arrived in February. Time and date were duly noted in the diary. You've guessed it: 3pm on July 30.

Venue: the chapel at Worcester College, Oxford, where the groom was a fellow post-graduate student. For Roger Magraw it was something to look forward to. Until the date drew nearer and nearer and – aaaaaaargh! – it became apparent that there would be a clash with a somewhat more nationally significant event to be played just down the Bakerloo line from his home town of Watford.

Roger had been to a grammar school where rugby was compulsory. But his first love was the round-ball game, as an Arsenal supporter and a member of the Worcester College first 11. The groom was an ex-public schoolboy, an old Merchant Taylor, no less, who preferred rugby and didn't seem too dismayed to discover that he would be waiting for his bride around the same time as a huge crowd at Wembley would be waiting for the teams to run out. Many of his fellow former Merchant Taylors, a significant section of the congregation, felt much the same.

The football supporters were a minority, surreptitiously glancing at their watches as kick-off time came and went, as indeed did the first half. 'Eventually there was a general surge out of the wedding,' Roger told me shortly before his death in November, 2014, by which time he was Dr McGraw, emeritus reader in modern history at Warwick University, and an eminent author on French culture. 'Some of us just grabbed a glass of champagne and made for the kitchen where there was a small television high up in one corner. All the cooks and the rest of the staff were watching the match and didn't seem to mind us joining them. We managed to see some of the second half and all of extra time. My parents were also invited and brought with them a German exchange student who was staying with my younger brother, Stephen. He was about 16 and keen to see the game. I must say he took our victory with admirable stoicism.'

At least the buffet was still open when the football contingent finally returned to the throng. 'We'd missed the speeches,' Roger admitted. Nor had they raised a glass to toast the bride and groom. But at least they'd seen Bobby Moore raise the Jules Rimet trophy and point it to the heavens. The rugger-lovers among the guests would have to wait until 2003 to see an England captain do something similar, and even then it would be on the other side of the world.

* * *

Nearly 260 miles to the north of Oxford, in Newcastle-upon-Tyne, the wedding of Eunice and Peter Bell was done and dusted by 3pm. 'We'd had the ceremony at 12 and the reception afterwards at the Co-op Rooms in Longbenton,' Eunice, a retired nurse, recalls. 'Some of the guests were already listening to transistors while the photos were being taken.'

The speeches were somewhat hurried and a little on the short side, particularly from the best man. And the groom? 'Peter's not a well man now but, at the time, he was a big supporter of Newcastle and England,' his bride points out. 'After every preliminary round we were involved in, he kept coming to see me and saying rather nervously: "England have won." And I'd say: "That's good, isn't it?" He'd nod doubtfully and then say: "Yes, but what if we get all the way to the final? We could be hitting a problem."'

The couple had originally planned their nuptials for July 2, 1966. 'But his sister and her family lived in Spain and they couldn't make it,' Eunice explains. 'That's why we put it back to the 30th.'

Take it from me as the father of three daughters, weddings today cost about as much as the gross national product of a medium-sized Greek island and go on all day and all night with the bride and groom as full participants. But far fewer couples lived together before marriage 50 years ago. Once the 'wedding breakfast' was over, speeches given, toasts raised, the bride would disappear after a while and re-emerge in her 'going away' outfit. Then the happy couple would do just that: go away and travel to wherever they had booked their wedding night.

In the wedded Bells' case, their ultimate destination was a boarding house in Dumfries. Scotland! On the day that England were to win the World Cup! The omens were not good for Peter. But a man's got to do what a man's got to do, especially when many of the 50-odd guests were bidding him farewell with undue hurriedness. It was a case of speed the parting hosts. 'As kick-off approached,' says Eunice, 'the general attitude seemed to be: "Aren't you going now?" We had a cursory wave and then most of them piled into my Mum and Dad's flat to grab a place on the floor so they could watch the telly.

'I remember us driving through deserted country lanes, looking for filling stations so that Peter could ask what the score was. They were all closed on our side of the border and few and far between on the other side. As time went on, he was reduced to pushing on pub doors. Either they weren't open or they wouldn't let him in. I think the people who ran the guest house told us the result in the end. Years later I bought him the video and the DVD of the World Cup Final, but my husband still swears to this day that he's never seen the match.'

* * *

Brian Rogerson was never that bothered about football. Neither was his bride Yvonne. Just as well. Yvonne was a friend of Eunice Bell (see above) who was married on the same day and also happened to be a trainee nurse at Newcastle General Hospital. 'You had to have matron's permission to get engaged at that time,' Yvonne explains. 'And you weren't allowed to get married at all until you'd finished your training. Otherwise you had to leave the course and forget about being a nurse.'

Both trainees knew that they would be qualified by July, had the nod from matron to carry on, and had planned their weddings accordingly. Only as time went on did the significance of the last Saturday of that month become apparent. 'It didn't bother Brian and me but it certainly bothered my brothers,' says Yvonne. 'They were both Newcastle United supporters who loved their football. On the big day itself they were so distracted that they decorated the wrong car. The reception was at the Townley Arms Hotel at Rowlands Gill and there was a Mini parked in the car park that they assumed was what we'd hired to drive off on our honeymoon. They duly covered it in ribbons and red lipstick before tying balloons and a pair of boots to the back bumper. We came out at around 4pm, climbed into a Ford Escort and drove off to Derwentwater in the Lake District.'

Around 120 wedding guests had sat down to lunch at 1.30, most of the men among them looking somewhat edgy and constantly glancing at their watches. 'By the time we came to the speeches, there was hardly a man left in the room, and quite a few women had joined them out in the car park listening to pre-match talk on radios,' Yvonne recalls. 'My father started panicking and we managed to round most of them up. But as soon as the speeches were over, they were back in the car park again and tuned in to the commentary from Wembley.'

Some of them absent-mindedly waved goodbye to the happy couple as Brian and his bride set off on honeymoon in their hired Ford Escort, idly wondering why that Mini was covered in lipstick and bedecked with ribbons, balloons and boots. 'It didn't belong to one of the guests,' Yvonne confirms, 'and I've often wondered what the owners of felt when they finally returned to the car park.'

* * *

Newspaper sales have dropped drastically since 1966. The provincial press in particular is now a shadow of its former self, employing far fewer staff. Evening papers that once boasted several editions, usually culminating in a Late Night Final with updated front pages plus a 'stop press' for last minute news and the most recent racing results, now share the morning news stands with the nationals. There are no updates, except on-line. As for regional morning papers, they've become an endangered species.

The growth of the World Wide Web and social media has taken its toll, but the decline in sales has been a lengthy process that preceded the digital revolution. Some regional morning papers closed in the days when newspaper offices still resounded to the clatter of hot metal presses and heavy typewriters. The *Nottingham Guardian Journal*, an august organ that briefly counted Peter Pan creator James Barrie and novelist Graham Greene among its former employees, shut up shop as long ago as 1973.

David Lowe had started work there as a cub reporter 10 years previously. He would go on to become a respected football correspondent and later feature writer on its sister paper, the *Nottingham Evening Post*. But on the last Saturday of July, 1966, he drew the short straw – duty reporter on the evening shift for the *Journal*. There was no paper on the Sunday, but somebody had to make those calls to police and the other emergency services in case something big broke on the Saturday night.

Of course, something really big had happened late on that Saturday afternoon. As a keen student of the game, David had been glued to the 12-inch set at his parents' home in the inner suburb of Basford. With full time approaching and England leading 2-1, he might just have time to see the presentation before legging it to the bus stop and boarding the 43 into town.

We all know what happened next. But nobody was talking about the German equaliser on the 43 as it sped along deserted roads towards an eerily empty city centre. 'There were about three people on the bus,' David recalls. 'All sensible people were glued to their TV sets.'

Buses had conductors in those days. They were known as 'clippies' because they clipped your ticket and handed it over with your change. On this occasion, money was exchanged but no conversation. 'I was too grumpy to talk to anyone, knowing that I was missing the climax of the match of the century,' David admits. The clippie evidently felt much the same. He, too, seemed oppressed by the heavy hand of duty.

Deputy news editor Harold Dewey was the only other person in the *Guardian Journal* office that evening. As the feed came through from the Press Association, he peered at a tele-printer that now seems as dated as pigeon post and strolled over to David's desk. 'We won, old man,' was all he said.

There would be big matches to come, at the City Ground, Nottingham, the Baseball Ground, Derby, even at Wembley. There would be FA Cup Finals and internationals, and David would have a grandstand view of all of them from his seat in the press box. But like most of his generation – my generation – he knows in his heart of hearts that England are unlikely to win the World Cup again in his lifetime.

And he'll always be aware that, unlike most of his generation, he missed the two goals that sealed it last time round.

* * *

Ken Lomas's mother-in-law Dorothy liked an afternoon nap. She was in her late sixties at the time of the World Cup Final and she wasn't going to let the small matter of well over 90,000 spectators roaring through her television divert her from her regular visit to the Land of Nod. There would have been plenty of noise from some of those assembled in her front room in Derby as well, not least from young Ken and his wife Pat as the emotions of that unforgettable afternoon ebbed and flowed. England goals brought cheers, German ones groans. Oblivious to it all, Dorothy slept on. 'Her sister didn't like football much either, so she pointedly read a book all the way through the match,' Ken recalls.

His mother-in-law finally came to with a start as the immortal words of Kenneth Wolstenholme winged their way from Wembley: 'Some people are on the pitch. They think it's all over.' Well, you know the rest. As the vast majority of the crowd roared their approval and Geoff Hurst turned away from the goal in which he'd just buried a belter with Alan Ball clinging to his neck and punching the air, Dorothy's first words were: 'Who's won?'

'She much preferred watching snooker on the telly,' says Ken. Now there *was* a 'sport' to sleep through. It didn't arrive on our screens until three years after England's World Cup triumph. By that time colour television had arrived in the UK, though the cost was prohibitive for many households. The commentator, 'Whispering' Ted Lowe, who spoke like a man trying hard not to wake up the more soporific viewer, had his own immortal line: 'For those of you watching in black and white, the pink is next to the green.'

Hitherto, snooker had been a game played in dingy rooms known as 'halls' and usually sited above Burton's the Tailors. Being good at it was said to be a sign of a misspent youth. But the halls also tended to attract professional footballers after training in the days when they didn't earn quite enough money to be wholeheartedly welcomed into the snootier golf clubs. Ken, an avid Derby County fan, remembers seeing some of his football heroes playing snooker in the years just after the '66 World Cup when Brian Clough was busy transforming the club from Second Division no-hopers into potential League Champions. In the 1970s they would entertain the likes of Benfica and Real Madrid at the Baseball Ground where the pitch was as different from the surface at Wembley as a peat bog from a snooker table.

Cloughie, rightly known as the greatest English manager never to manage England, would later travel down the A52 to Nottingham, walk over the Trent and transform Forest from Second Division no-hopers into League champions and then European Cup winners. Twice.

Television snooker, meanwhile, continued to rise in popularity. In May, 1980, the same month that Forest retained their position as champions of Europe, the BBC was inundated with complaints after it interrupted the Embassy World Championships to show dramatic live coverage of the SAS storming the Iranian Embassy in London to end a siege by gunmen.

By 1985, not yet 20 years since England's greatest triumph, football appeared to be at its lowest ebb (though Hillsborough was still to come). In May the tragic fire at Bradford City's stadium had been followed by the horrors of the Heysel disaster. Only the previous month a television audience of 18.5 million had tuned in to watch Dennis Taylor wrest the world snooker title from Steve Davis. Okay, it was still way below the 32 million who had watched England beat West Germany in '66, but those are the kind of figures that television executives would kill for in today's multi-channel world, and the audience was watching two admittedly highly skilled players do nothing more energetic than bend over a table and flex an arm.

Still, I'm sure Ken Lomas's mother-in-law enjoyed it, if she managed to stay awake. Ken would go on to become director of property services at Coventry City Council, but his heart has always remained at the Baseball Ground. And Dorothy? Well, she lived to be 102 which, if nothing else, suggests that taking a regular afternoon nap may have long-term benefits.

* * *

David Harding was ten in 1966 and it's fair to say that his love of football far exceeded his sense of direction. Luckily, he wasn't required to direct his parents from their home in Swanley, Kent, to West Wittering in Sussex where they had rented a bungalow for the annual family holiday. 'We set off a day or two after England had beaten Portugal in the Semi-Final,' he recalls. 'I was very excited, having been allowed to stay up and watch all the England evening matches on the Ferranti in the corner of the living room.'

Although it sounds rather racy, the Ferranti was really a rather sedate kind of television – the sort of set on which millions watched the Queen's coronation. A tiny screen was surrounded by what seemed like acres of walnut veneer. Some of the snootier middle classes liked to pretend that they didn't watch television at all, 'except for the natural history programmes', and had doors to cover the frontage for most of the time to make the telly look like just another cupboard.

I suspect there may have been quite a few sets with doors in West Wittering, even by 1966. But, alas, there was not a Ferranti or any other kind of television in the Hardings' holiday home. How were young David and his father going to see the big match? Despite coming from football pedigree (her father Reg John had played for Queen's Park Rangers and Charlton Athletic), his mother couldn't resist the lure of all those posh shops in nearby Chichester on a Saturday when there would have been very few customers.

'Off she went in the car with my grandmother in the passenger seat, leaving Dad and me to walk to my Auntie and Uncle's house in nearby Bracklesham Bay. They'd invited us to watch the match. Dad had never been there before and I'd only been driven there by Mum. But I was confident that I knew the way and I was fairly sure it was not much more than a mile.'

On and on they walked, along main roads and up side streets. Well populated as it was with retired colonels and other ex-army top brass, this neck of the woods was hardly a football hotbed. Yet the east side of West Wittering was as deserted as anywhere else on the afternoon of July 30. There was nobody about to ask the way. 'We didn't even have the address,' David admits. 'I just thought I knew where it was. But I evidently didn't. As a child, your sense of distance isn't quite right and I began to panic. In the end, Dad bought me a *Famous Five* book as some kind of compensation for missing the match and we went back to the bungalow.' He spent the rest of the afternoon sitting on an otherwise empty beach reading Enid Blyton rather than watching Bobby Charlton and co.

David finally got to see the famous four on the Pathe News, plus the two German goals as well. 'But I didn't get to see the whole game until 40 years later when I bought the DVD from HMV and watched it with my middle son Jamie.' That would have been at the Harding homestead in Greenwich, a long way from Hammersmith where David works as production editor of the *Tablet* newspaper. Somehow he finds his way from South East London to West London every working day. Not on foot, needless to say.

CHAPTER SIX

How they celebrated in London, Ashington, Essex and Shanghai

Jack Charlton had at least £100 burning a hole in his pocket. That would have been slightly more than the average weekly wage for a top-flight professional footballer in 1966. Players received an extra £60 for turning out for England. Those who won the World Cup were eventually granted a bonus of £22,000, to be shared between the whole squad of 22, not just the 11 on the day. You don't have to be a mathematician to work out that that amounted £1,000 a head. And you don't have to strain credulity too far to realise that some of today's Premier League stars wouldn't get out of bed unless they received at least 70 times that figure *every week*. More still in some cases. But football was still in touch with reality back then. As Alan Ball once told Simon Hattenstone of the *Guardian*, 'the boys of '66 didn't feel it necessary to hide behind electronic gates and blacked-out windows. We were still part of the people … You were welcome to walk the streets, you were patted on the back, you were touchable, reachable.'

Jack had done his bit, and not just on the field. He had waved to the crowds thronging the streets en route from Wembley to the Royal Garden Hotel in Kensington. Then, after meeting his parents in the lobby, he had taken them up on to the hotel balcony and waved to the crowds again with the rest the team. What's more, he had sat through the official banquet of smoked salmon, chicken and a heavily laden sweet trolley, and listened to seemingly endless speeches from FA officials and indeed the Prime Minister, Harold Wilson.

Unlike the other players, however, he didn't have a wife waiting upstairs in the burger bar to join him on a postprandial jaunt to Danny la Rue's nightclub where Ronnie Corbett was topping the bill. Jack's wife Pat was back in Leeds, waiting to give birth at any moment.

James Mossop's wife, meanwhile, was at home in Manchester while he had been covering the match, extra time and all, for the *Sunday Express*. Jim had eventually driven to the team hotel in his battered Mini. 'I'd had a bit of a crash on the way down to London, but it was still just about driveable,' he says. 'And the crowds outside had dispersed by then so it was easy to park. I just wanted to check on any post-match stories before heading home.'

Jack had other ideas. 'Come on, Jimmy,' he said. 'You and me are going out on the town.' An abridged version of what happened next appears in Jack Charlton's autobiography. The story below is distilled from Jim's more detailed take on what happened that night:

'I remember saying to him: "But Jack, I've only got a tenner." To which he replied: "We'll spend this 100 quid *and* your tenner as well." At this point Harold Wilson was leaving the hotel. We sneaked out, ducked behind the prime ministerial limo and jumped into a taxi that was parked nearby. Unfortunately, there was somebody already in it. "Sorry about this," I said. And Jack put in: "We'll pay for your cab and drop you wherever you're going."'

The passenger failed to recognise the lanky England centre-back. It seemed to dawn on him, though, that something momentous had happened that might explain the presence in his taxi of two men with accents that owed more to the far North of England than South West London. 'Has there been some sort of footie match this afternoon?' he enquired in a tone that evoked images of highly polished cut glass.

On being told that England had won the World Cup, he appeared somewhat underwhelmed. 'I'm a classical organist,' he said, as if to explain his indifference. 'Could you drop me somewhere near the Wigmore Hall?'

They did. The cab driver then took them on to the Astor Club in Berkeley Square. The Astor had gained some notoriety the previous Christmas after a confrontation between the Krays and the Richardsons that would lead, eventually, to Ronnie Kray shooting Charlie Richardson's henchman George Cornell in the Blind Beggar in Whitechapel. The 'summer of peace and love' was still a year away and, like 'Swinging London', it proved to be a somewhat elusive concept in that turbulent decade.

Messrs Mossop and Charlton no doubt had other matters on their minds as they strolled into the club. At least Jack was recognised there. 'As soon as he was spotted, the band stopped playing and everybody applauded,' Jim recalls. 'We sat down at a table and a bottle of champagne appeared, as if by magic. Then two girls came and joined us. What was going on?'

He knew full well what was going on. 'And we weren't really happy about it,' he stresses. 'But somehow we got talking to three respectable women on the adjoining table. They were with a bloke called Lenny who turned out to be the husband of one of them. She asked if Jack's wife had had the baby yet. He didn't have a clue. She then said: "We're going back to Walthamstow for a party. Why don't you join us?" So we nipped off to the gents, gave the hostesses the slip and climbed in the back of what turned out to be quite a large car. There were six of us in there with Lenny driving.

'It wasn't much of a party as it turned out, but there was plenty of booze there. Eventually we crashed out in the lounge, Jack on one settee and me on the other. In the morning, Lenny's missus knocked on the door to say there was some tea and toast available. Meanwhile, the Sunday paper had arrived with the full match report.' Not the *Express*? 'No, it was the *News of the World*. I remember us sitting out in the garden, eating and reading in the morning sunshine, when – and this is really hard to believe – a woman poked her head over the garden fence and said in a broad Geordie accent: "Eeeee, it's Jackie Charlton. What are you doing here?"'

England's centre-back naturally asked the same question of a woman he recognised from his home town of Ashington. 'I was in your mother's house only last week,' she told him before going on to explain that she was just visiting relatives.

'That's funny. I'm just visiting some friends of Jimmy's,' said Jack. 'We're going back to the hotel now.'

And so they did, with Lenny at the wheel. 'Apart from the taxi fares, we'd hardly spent a penny of that 100 quid, and I hadn't touched my tenner,' Jim grins. 'One of the reporters outside the hotel asked if there was any news of the baby. "No, no, nothing yet," said Jack. He still hadn't a clue what was happening at home in Leeds.'

But he did have a bit of a surprise when he loped into the Royal Garden lobby at around midday. There to greet him was his mother, the formidable Cissie Charlton, demanding to know why his bed hadn't been slept in.

In the best traditions of British journalism, James Mossop made his excuses and left. He had a long journey ahead of him in a battered Mini with a thumping hangover and the prospect of a disgruntled wife waiting for him in Manchester. Again, in the best traditions of sports journalism at the time, he didn't write or breathe a word in public about the previous evening's escapades until many years later.

* * *

Those lining the route from Wembley to Kensington in the early evening before the celebratory banquet had eyes only for the England team and manager. They wouldn't have noticed the car in the immediate wake of the open-topped coach as it made its stately progress – although the man driving it had a face that would soon become as familiar to sports fans as that of Bobby Moore. Another two years would pass before Frank Bough made his name as a regular host on the BBC's flagship Saturday-afternoon programme *Grandstand*.

For now he was known mainly to viewers in the North East where he had hosted regional news programmes and commentated on some of the World Cup group matches, including the sensational 1-0 victory by North Korea over Italy at Ayresome Park, Middlesbrough. 'On the day of the Final itself my commitments to the BBC had finished,' he says. 'The attitude of my boss was "Well done, my good and faithful servant. Now go and enjoy the match".'

Frank did as he was bid, with the benefit of a ticket to one of the best seats in the house, offering a fine view of the afternoon's dramatic events. 'My car was in the car park and I wanted to wait until the traffic had died down a bit before heading home [to Bray in Hertfordshire]. So I walked to the place where the BBC had set up its temporary headquarters – a hotel as I seem to recall – and enjoyed a glass or two of bubbly to mark the occasion.'

By the time he returned to the car park, the traffic had indeed thinned out. There was just one large vehicle edging its way out of the gates, the England team coach, and Frank knew immediately that he wouldn't be going home just yet. Journalistic instinct kicked in and he decided to 'stick with it' and give . . . well, not exactly chase but crawl.

'People were already lining the kerbs and hanging out of the window,' he tells me from his current home in Kent. 'As we neared central London, the crowds became thicker. And the nearer we got to Kensington, the more animated people became. They were hanging off balustrades and out of office-block windows. I remember thinking at the time: "This is very un-English".'

He stayed with the coach until it pulled up outside the Royal Garden Hotel. Young Bough knew that he had little chance of following the players and their families past the uniformed jobsworths on the hotel door. After his lengthy diversion at a stately pace, it was time to set off through the London traffic on the last leg of his journey from Wembley to Bray.

* * *

Just over two weeks after the post-match banquet in Kensington, there was another celebratory reception in a very different part of England, a long way from London. Ashington was not only known as 'the biggest mining village in the world' in 1966, it was also renowned as a breeding ground for professional footballers. The Charlton brothers had grown up in Beatrice Street and their mother, Cissie, had four brothers who had turned pro. What's more, her cousin was none other than Jackie Milburn whose escape route to St James's Park, Newcastle, was the X22 bus. He would go on to become a celebrated England international and there's now a statue of him in Ashington High Street, bringing the ball under control outside Burton's and looking as though he might smash it through the window of H Samuel. But 'Wor Jackie' never earned much more than 12 quid a week in the old First Division. That was the maximum wage during a top-flight playing career that had effectively ended in 1957.

The Charltons were earning considerably more, albeit a fraction of what a player of Bobby's talents could command today. For their Ashington homecoming in '66, they swept into town in an open-topped 1927 yellow Rolls Royce, its progress slowed to walking pace by crowds of well-wishers surging around them. The reception had been scheduled for early evening, but children had started gathering outside the Charlton family home from 10am. Cissie recalled in her autobiography: 'Our only toilet stood at the bottom of the yard and anyone using it had to do so with several well-wishers clumping around on the roof over their head.'

Not long after 6pm, Bobby and Jack were ushered into Ashington's town hall. The council chamber was packed with councillors and aldermen in all their finery. One of the guests lucky enough to be invited in as well was Bill Ogilvie, senior welfare officer for collieries in Northumberland and what was then Cumberland. 'I remember the Council chairman making a speech and telling them how proud we all were. Then he invited the Charltons to say a few words. Bobby looked distinctly awkward. He didn't want to say anything at all. But Jack stood up and spoke for about 20 minutes, without notes. He was terrific. There were lots of reminiscences about when they were kids. Bobby sat nodding and smiling every now and then, but I'm sure he was thinking: "I'm glad you're doing this."'

The meeting then adjourned until councillors, aldermen, officials and committee members of Ashington's many miners' welfares reconvened for dinner. A procession of cars set off from the town hall, one of them driven by Vince Gledhill, Ashington correspondent of the *Newcastle Chronicle and Journal*, who would later ghost Cissie's autobiography. 'I wasn't invited to the dinner,' he recalls, 'but I offered a lift to anyone who needed one.' Eschewing the open-topped Roller, Jack Charlton crammed himself into the passenger seat of Vince's ancient Triumph Herald. 'He didn't say much but, as soon as he spotted a mate of his in the crowd, he asked me to stop. Everybody behind me had to stop too. Roy Nuttall, the town clerk, was furious.'

As Vince would later write in Cissie's words: 'Jack had taken it into his head to pop in for a pint and see some old mates regardless of the fact that a banquet organised in his honour would have to be held up until he arrived. Red-faced Roy jumped from his car and ran to the club doorway, barring Jack's path. It says something for his powers of persuasion that he talked Jack back into the car. Jack has never been one to change his mind after deciding to do something.'

The venue for the official dinner was the Hirst Welfare, a club adjoining one of many pitches where Bill Ogilvie, no mean footballer himself in his day, had first cast a judicious eye over the precocious talents of a youthful Bobby Charlton. 'He was younger and smaller than anyone else, but he stood out. Unbelievable ball control and so far advanced in technique. As for his shot, it was so powerful …' Bill's voice trails away in a reverie of reminiscence.

Now in his mid-80s, he doesn't have such a memory for food and drink. Can't for the life of him remember what they had to eat at that celebratory meal or whether they washed it down with wine or beer. We can only fantasise that it may have involved the local *pièce de resistance*, pease puddin', and pork from Jack's favourite Ashington butcher, Anderson's, based just off Milburn Road. It also seems likely that Newcastle Brown Ale would have been more prevalent than any of the fine wines plucked from the dustier recesses of the cellars of the Royal Garden Hotel, Kensington, just over a fortnight previously.

* * *

Vince Gledhill, once the assiduous Ashington correspondent of the *Newcastle Chronicle and Journal* (see page 87), is one of the few residents of that football-mad town to have no interest in the game whatsoever. On the afternoon of July 30, 1966 he was despatched to Newbiggin-on-Sea to cover Lifeboat Day and interview a 96 year-old former life-boatman called John Grant who had received a long service award from the Royal National Lifeboat Institution. But for the paper that came out on the Monday after the final, Vince filed a story under the headline 'World Cup Eileen Soccer Casualty'.

Eileen Sweeney had celebrated England's victory, it seems, like many another child at a time when there were far fewer concerns about children 'playing out' unmonitored by vigilant adults. She had rushed onto the street to play football, fondly imagining perhaps that she was Geoff Hurst or, more likely for a kid from her neck-of-the woods, Bobby Charlton. Skipping ropes and dolls had been abandoned. Eileen's mother Jean Sweeney told Vince on her way back from the outpatients department at Ashington Hospital: 'All the local kids, even the girls, seem to be playing football just now. There was only one boy playing in the game and Eileen had just scored when she fell over and broke her arm.'

Photographed with the ball tucked under a left arm encased in plaster-of-Paris, Eileen announced that she still intended to be at the official homecoming reception for the Charlton brothers. 'I don't want to miss them,' she proclaimed, 'and my broken arm won't stop me playing football.'

* * *

Shanghai in 1966 was nothing like the bustling economic powerhouse that it has become in the 21st Century. Chairman Mao's 'Cultural Revolution' had begun in May of that year and its brutal, stifling effects were taking their toll here, as they were all over on China. By 1968 some of the student 'revolutionaries' at

UK universities would be chanting Mao's name as an inspirational figure, unaware perhaps that he was just getting into his stride as a mass murderer. Merchant seamen such as Gordon Charlton had far more idea what the Chinese were going through and, of all the gin joints in all the towns in all the world, he wouldn't have chosen a bar in Shanghai to celebrate an England victory in which two of his brothers had played a part.

'Most of the bars were closed down and, anyway, it wasn't the kind of place you'd want to hang around at night,' he says. 'Everyone wore overalls and most of the Chinese had never seen people who looked like us before.' They might have landed from outer space rather than walked down a gangplank, it seems. 'One of the lads, who had a ginger beard, was followed around by a lengthy trail of children. But every port had the equivalent of a seamen's mission and that's where we went when we docked on that Sunday lunchtime [July 31] for a meal and a few Tsingtao beers.'

Gordon had endured a fraught Saturday night. He was on board *MV Glengyle*, some 30 miles off shore. More to the point, he was on shift in the engine room around 11pm local time when one of his shipmates who had been tuned into the BBC World Service burst in and spat out: 'That bastard brother of yours has given a goal away!'

Fifteen seconds before full time, Jack Charlton had held on to Siegfried Held while heading the ball away and the Germans had equalised in the scramble that followed the resulting free kick. Most English hearts sank at that moment, but Gordon felt as though his had sunk to the bottom of the East China Sea.

He still didn't know the final result as his shift ended and he climbed towards the upper deck. The outcome became evident, however, as he approached the purser's room and saw his usually stern and remote captain performing a somewhat ungainly jig.

The warm sea air off Shanghai resounded that night to the sound of British ships hooting their horns as the sailors toasted 'that bastard brother' of Gordon's and every other member of the victorious England team.

* * *

Around the time that Jack Charlton and James Mossop were leaving the Astor Club and heading east (see page 83), John Holmes was being violently sick in a pub car park in rural Essex. Serve him right, you might say, for having drunk not just seven pints but seven barley-wine chasers. Formidably strong stuff, barley wine; not to be treated lightly even by experienced drinkers.

John would later become not only a Radio 4 producer and a Radio Nottingham presenter but also something of a real ale buff. These days he goes for quality rather than quantity. Back then he was in his late teens, home from university and out to celebrate England's victory with the headstrong abandon of youth.

'We'd watched the match at a friend's parents' house and the tension had been so great that we just wanted to let rip,' he recalls. 'Quite how we finished up at the Punchbowl at Paglesham I don't know. It's miles from where we lived and we'd already been to a pub much closer to home in Leigh-on-Sea.'

It looks as though you drove, John.

'I did,' he admits, 'with my then girlfriend Fran in the passenger seat. She was still with me at two in the morning while I was still being sick. I remember there'd been a great party atmosphere and probably a bit of a lock-in. Pubs normally shut at 11pm sharp in those days.'

It was 10.30 in many other parts of the country. The very possibility that licensed premises might one day be able to stay open all day and all night would have seemed preposterous. That sort of thing was all very well for those referred to as 'continentals'. But we English drank in pubs, not bars. And since the First World War at least, licensing laws decreed that licensees should flash the lights and call, 'Time, gentlemen, please' shortly before tea towels went over the pumps. Sometimes he or she might include 'ladies' as well.

Of course, the Punchbowl would hardly be the only pub on the night of July 30, 1966, where the doors were locked and the curtains drawn after 11pm to keep the police out, if they weren't inside already. But there would be nothing like the mayhem that might have followed had England been remotely good enough to get beyond the group stage, let alone win the final in 2014 – particularly in towns and cities where many more pubs, bars and clubs would have been open all night. Streets would have been strewn with broken glass, crumpled cans, vomit and a few prone bodies. Accident and Emergency departments would have been overwhelmed. Police cells would have been full and supermarket shelves emptied.

On the other hand, few people would have risked driving home after a 'skin-full'. In 1966, as we've already noted, the introduction of the breathalyser was still a year away and drink-driving was far more socially acceptable, as UK road deaths statistics reflected. There were 7,985 deaths in '66, the highest rate ever in peace-time. By 2012 there were over 6,000 fewer, and 2014 was the safest yet on Britain's roads.

Now let's return to the car park outside the Punchbowl in Paglesham. 'At some point the landlord must have noticed that we were still there,' John vaguely remembers. 'He came out with a wet towel and told Fran to slap it on my forehead as a cold compress. "That'll sort him out," he said.'

And did it?

'Well, I drove home eventually as Fran didn't have a licence.'

Luckily, he didn't lose his licence on the journey and, more importantly, no more lives were lost to add to the staggering statistics of carnage on UK roads.

CHAPTER SEVEN

How 'West Ham Won the Cup': the views of two Jews who have 'kept the faith' for 50 years

The writer David Rosenberg is sporting a claret-and-blue West Ham scarf of such venerable vintage that it could have been knitted by his grandmother around the time that he watched the 1966 World Cup Final at her basement flat in Dalston. 'She was always more interested in wrestling than football,' he confides to me in a coffee bar near his current home in Tufnell Park. 'Not sure where Granddad was. Probably in the betting shop.' David's mother, meanwhile, was round the corner from the flat, having her hair done.

Jewish families were still prevalent in the East End at the time, the exodus further east into the promised land of Essex and north to Golders Green and Finchley only just beginning to gather pace. Having been brought up in Hackney, David had made a brief foray out to Palmers Green in 1966 with his parents and older brother – but only because his father worked in a chemist's shop and there was a flat available upstairs on a short-term lease. Soon after the Final, they were back living over another shop much closer to Upton Park.

That famous ground would become something of a spiritual home for the youngest Rosenberg. 'Having three West Ham players in the England side that won the World Cup really excited me,' he recalls. 'I was eight at the time and I was already keen on football. Strangely enough, I started going to watch it in November, 1966, because of the synagogue. The father of one of my friends there was a West Ham regular who also ran a pub. He used to take us.'

On the Sabbath?

'Well, I don't suppose the rabbi would have approved, but our family was not exactly orthodox.'

Both his parents were of Polish-Ukrainian extraction, his father having been brought up in Toronto and his mother in Stepney. Like many an England fan, David's allegiances veer more towards club than country. 'Obviously I didn't grow up surrounded by flags of St George and displays of English nationalism,' he says. 'But I really wanted England to win.'

And not just because of the presence of Messrs Moore, Hurst and Peters in the national side. 'Whoever we had been playing, I'd still have wanted an England victory,' he re-emphasises. 'Still, there was an *extra* pride in beating Germany. Okay, I'm probably being unfair to many German people at the time, but I came from a family that wouldn't buy anything made in Germany.'

As we've touched on elsewhere in this book, the war had ended only just over 20 years previously and with it had come full exposure of the horrors of Auschwitz, Belsen, Treblinka and other outposts of Nazi atrocities. The Rosenbergs were members of a race that a German government and bureaucracy had systematically tried to erase from the face of the earth. Of course, members of the West German football team of 1966 would have been far too young to have had anything to do with the Holocaust. The great Franz Beckenbauer, for instance, wasn't born until four months after the end of the War. All the same, it's easy to understand why an eight year-old Jewish boy might feel even more aggrieved than most of us when Wolfgang Weber equalised on 90 minutes. Even that was nothing to his sense of injustice at what happened next.

Having returned from the hairdresser's at the end of full time, his mother announced that they had to go back to Palmers Green. Now. 'What about extra time?' chorused the Rosenberg brothers. To no avail, it would seem. 'We made it plain that we weren't happy,' David shrugs, 'but Mum was adamant. There was something she just *had* to get back for.' Perhaps her husband expected his tea on the table after a long afternoon waiting for somebody – anybody – to come into the chemist's shop in need of a prescription or a packet of Tunes.

A few years later the family had saved enough money for a down payment on a house in Ilford. 'Dad was still working all hours, so Mum tended to go to look at properties on her own,' their younger son explains. 'One day she came back to say that she'd been shown round a big terraced property in Glenwood Gardens, owned by a nice couple who were moving out to Chigwell. She'd only been to look at Bobby Moore's house! Then she said it was a bit out of our price range,' he adds wistfully before going on to point out that Moore was a glamorous national hero yet still living close to the people who paid to watch him play. 'Most players were approachable in those days. Every summer West Ham played cricket against Ilford CC in Valentine's Park and, as they sat outside the pavilion, waiting to go into bat, the likes of Moore, Hurst and Peters would happily sign autographs. They had time for you.'

That immortal trio, however, could not compete with the Englishman, the Irishman and the Scotsman who were propelling Manchester United towards the League title by the end of the 1966–7 season. Bobby Charlton, George Best and Denis Law were at their peak when they arrived at Upton Park towards the end of that season. 'United won 6-1, but their fans also caused mayhem at our end.' David shudders at the boyhood memory of shrinking away while youths and young men wielding bottles as weapons invaded a terrace packed with Hammers fans and started indiscriminately lashing out.

Only nine months previously England had played their one-time wartime enemies in front of un-segregated supporters. Now the police and the football authorities were faced with keeping fans from different parts of same country (and sometimes the same city) apart as the violence and hooliganism that would plague the game for another 25 years or so began to take hold. Those of us who complain bitterly about the pollution of the game by big money should perhaps recall that the coming of the Premier League in 1992 helped to fund facilities that reduced the threat of being caught up in turbulence and mayhem. New grounds are often soulless arenas, more corporate than communal, but at least they offer comparative safety and comfort – give or take the occasional pitch invasion.

Overt racism has also reduced, despite the best efforts of the more cretinous contributors to social media sites and some travelling Chelsea fans to keep it alive. Pioneering black players such as Clyde Best must occasionally shake their heads in amazement at the transformation. Best joined Moore, Hurst and Peters in the West Ham side of the late '60s and took terrible abuse from the terraces at home as well as away, as David recalls sadly. In an article for the *New Statesman*, published in November, 2012, he wrote: 'Apart from highly publicised individual incidents involving Premier League stars, most commentators would say it [racism] has receded over the last 25 years. Nowadays, fans prefer to cheer rather than jeer the performances of black players. But anti-Jewish feeling continues to flourish. I can't actually recall a West Ham game against Spurs where I have *not* heard some anti-Semitic abuse ...'

Back in the early '80s, constantly distracted by jibes and chants behind him, he turned round to see a young man openly sporting a swastika badge. Thirty years later he emerged from Upton Park after a game against Stoke to hear one 'bonehead' leaping around, shouting: 'Who we got next then?' When his mates replied 'Spurs', he screamed: 'The Yids! Gas 'em all! Gas 'em all!'

Spurs, of course, are known to have a significant number of Jewish supporters. Some of their fans proudly, if controversially, proclaim themselves to be a 'Yid Army'. But the truth is that there are plenty of Jewish followers of other London clubs, including West Ham. And the miracle is that those, like David, who started going from the synagogue to the terraces in the wake of England's triumph in the golden summer of '66, have continued to support the Hammers despite the occasional outbursts of anti-Semitism they've had to stand and sit through in the intervening 50 years.

* * *

Rabbi Dr Tony Bayfield, CBE, doesn't believe that West Ham supporters are more anti-Semitic than any others. 'In fact, never an anti-Semitic word was uttered when [Eyal] Berkovik and [Yossi] Benayoun were playing for us,' he says. 'But on reflection that could be because they're Israeli and most of the crowd may not have realised they were Jewish!'

The rabbi has always 'kept the faith', as he puts it. Well, what else would you expect from one of such influence in the synagogue and, indeed, the Movement for Reform Judaism where he was elected president in 2011? But he's not talking about religion in this context; he's talking about football. More specifically, he's talking about being a long-term Hammers supporter.

---

*David Rosenberg is the author of *Battle for the East End: Jewish responses to fascism in the 1930s* (2011, Five Leaves Publication)

Somehow he has managed to square being a season-ticket holder at Upton Park with other demands on a rabbi's time on the Sabbath. Even today, when satellite television so often dictates kick-off times, the majority of matches are still staged on a Saturday afternoon. And that was the norm in the mid-'60s, which Rabbi Tony looks back on as a golden age for West Ham. 'In 1964 we won the FA Cup, in 1965 the European Cup Winners' Cup in front of 98,000 Hammers fans and 2,000 Germans at Wembley, and in 1966 we won the World Cup,' he says, pausing for dramatic effect before adding: 'It's been downhill ever since.'

Hang on, Rabbi. Let's just re-wind a moment. 'We' won the World Cup? West Ham?

Once again he's talking tongue in cheek, it seems, and only repeating what was claimed in the pubs and perhaps the synagogues of Plaistow and Poplar, Ilford and Romford at the time. After all, the club had not only supplied the international side with its captain but also two players that shared all four England goals between them. 'I was over the moon when I heard about Hurst's hat-trick,' the Rabbi recalls.

Forget the lapse into 'football-speak' and note that word 'heard'. He didn't *see* the '66 World Cup Final live, either at Wembley or on television. And what he could hear was hardly crystal clear. It was being beamed over the Channel via the BBC World Service and transmitted through those few transistor radios that could be found on a beach in Brittany. Not that the French were listening in great numbers. Having been knocked out by England in the group stage, most of the locals mustered a collective shrug of Gallic indifference on being asked 'Quel est le score?'

There were a few English holidaymakers on the beach, however, and young Tony managed to hear a few snatches of the match commentary before being moved on by his girlfriend Linda's sister and brother-in-law – or 'our chaperones', as he rather gloomily recalls them.

It's fair to say that he was having a frustrating time and the details may surprise those who fondly imagine that the so-called 'Swinging '60s' were all freewheelin' and 'free love'. He had met Linda in 1962 when he was 16 and she was 14. By the summer of 1966 Tony had just completed the first year of a law degree at Magdalene College, Cambridge, the call to the rabbinate being still six years in the future.

'Linda used to come up to Cambridge to visit me regularly, but she was not allowed to stay overnight,' he confides. 'We wanted to go on holiday together, but her parents would only allow it if we went with her married sister and her husband. So there we were, together but aware that we were being watched like hawks. We had to fit in with what our chaperones wanted to do. They were thwarting our desire to be alone and, on that Saturday afternoon, to watch the match.'

Did Linda like football?

'It comes as a package with me. She even converted for my sake.'

To Judaism?

'No, to West Ham. Her Dad was a Spurs fan.'

His name was Hymie and he was all too typically 'an over protective middle-class Jewish parent', according to his future son-in-law. 'I was actually in the house when Kenneth Tynan said the F-word on television for the first time [in 1965]. Hymie switched off the television and slammed out of the room. He wouldn't tell Linda's mother what had been said and she couldn't guess.' (Heaven knows what Hymie would make of the average Channel 4 drama 50 years on. Come to think of it, he'd be slamming the door almost immediately after the opening credits.)

Anyway, Tony and Linda married in 1969 and were together until her death in 2004. 'My eldest daughter married an Arsenal fan,' the Rabbi sighs, and I can almost hear him shaking his head over the phone-line from his current home in Hampstead Garden Suburb. One of his few moments of unadulterated West Ham glory since the heady days of the mid-'60s was beating Arsenal 1-0 in the 1980 FA Cup Final.

All the same, he has been a season-ticket holder at Upton Park for the past 20 years or so. 'I go to the synagogue in the morning and I've come to the conclusion that it's a pretty good way for a Jewish family to celebrate the Shabbat – especially as, on Friday night, we've also been to synagogue and had a family meal together.'

The 'we' includes his son Daniel – 'At least he's kept the faith' – and his two older grandsons, aged six and four, their faith no doubt sustained by occasional stories of the day that West Ham won the World Cup.

CHAPTER EIGHT

'White; that's England's colours': the other 'Alf' at Wembley that day

The quote above comes from Alf Garnett, another one who would have enjoyed West Ham's prominent role in the England side that day had he not been a fictional character. Mind you, the views that he expressed were all too common in the real-life England of 1966. His creator Johnny Speight was well aware of that – as, indeed, was Warren Mitchell, the Jewish socialist who played him. Speight hoped to hold up a mirror, or perhaps an echo chamber, to the millions who tuned in to watch the hugely popular series shown on the BBC between 1965-75. Yes, he wanted to make the audience laugh, but he also wanted them to hear the poisonous prejudices that this sour old bigot was spouting and recognise them for the nonsense that they were.

Unfortunately, it didn't quite work out like that. The satirical aspect of the show was largely lost on a significant number of viewers for whom 'good old Alf' became something of a national treasure. The scene where he goes to the World Cup Final with his 'Scouse git' of a son-in-law, Mike, was part of a feature film 'in glorious Eastman colour'. Otherwise we viewers of black and white tellies would never have known that Alf was sporting a scarf and rosette in the claret and blue of the Hammers while Mike was decked out in the red and white of Liverpool FC.

Through the extract posted on YouTube we can also remind ourselves that England were playing in red shirts that day. Hence the Garnett whinge about white being England's colours – although, being Alf, he was probably not *just* referring to the shirts. We can also see that the man at his left shoulder on those thronged and jostling terraces looked understandably startled for a moment when the old boy who had been shouting abuse at the Germans threw his arms around him at the final whistle and gave him a kiss, knocking off his England hat in the process. Alf looked a bit surprised, too, when he realised that he'd just planted a smacker on the cheek of a black man.

Nearly 50 years on, there's nothing unusual about black faces in the crowd at Wembley or, indeed, on the pitch in the white shirts of England. (No Asian faces in England shirts, mind you, but that's a story for another day.) There were six black players in the squad that set off from Heathrow to Brazil in 2014. In 1966, of course, there were none. And although Arthur Wharton from Ghana was playing in goal for Darlington as long ago as 1886 and the mixed-race comedian Charlie Williams had established himself as a regular centre-half for Doncaster Rovers 70 years later, black players were still thin on the turf in English League football 10 years after that. Admittedly, John Charles (no, not that one) played alongside Bobby Moore in the West Ham defence of the mid-'60s and, as mentioned in the previous chapter, the Hammers would bring in Clyde Best later in the decade and Ade Coker in the early 1970s.

As the '70s progressed, however, the focus switched from West Ham to West Brom. Albion fielded three black players, Cyrille Regis, Laurie Cunningham and Brendon Batson, under the management of Ron Atkinson who christened them the Three Degrees after the black American (female) soul singers of the same name. It's also the title of a book by Paul Rees describing in some detail the horrendous racism that those players endured, particularly during away matches. National Front members would greet them in the car park with insults and gobs of spit. Bananas would be hurled onto the pitch and boos would echo around the terraces every time they touched the ball.

Unfortunately, the boos usually drowned out the 'oohs'. And there were plenty of those for a triple act that could be electrifying. Cunningham, sadly, is no longer with us, but he was good enough to become the first British player to attract the attention of Real Madrid. The Spanish giants paid £950,000 for him in 1979.

Batson, remarkably, had never seen a game or kicked a ball when he arrived in Tilbury from Grenada in 1962. He was nine. Just nine years after that, he was on the books at Arsenal. 'I was already playing Sunday league football by 1966,' he tells me. 'The lads I fell in with were football mad and we all wanted England to win the World Cup. I distinctly remember Bobby Charlton's goals in the build-up to the Final, particularly the one against Portugal in the Semi-Final. But Eusebio made an even bigger impact on me, particularly when he scored those four goals against North Korea.'

Batson has been a major figure in the campaign to Kick It Out, as the movement to push racism out of the British game was christened when it was set up in 1993. 'We didn't have much help from the authorities up to that point,' he says. 'The general attitude was "That's football".'

Such complacency now seems shameful when you consider what happened after Ron Greenwood finally picked Regis to play for England against Northern Ireland in 1982. Regis opened one of many envelopes sent to him at the Albion's training ground. Inside was a message painstakingly pasted onto grubby paper from letters cut out of newspaper headlines. 'If you put your foot on our Wembley turf,' it read, 'you'll get one of these through your knees.' The accompanying bullet was carefully wrapped in cotton wool.

Regis had arrived in this country, aged five, three years before the '66 World Cup Final. In his autobiography, *My Story*, he recalls seeing 'the hurt in the eyes of my parents' as they trudged from one boarding house to another to be confronted by those signs on which was scrawled: 'No blacks, no dogs, no Irish'. Having grown up with racism, he had long ago sworn that he was never going to be intimidated by racists. So he binned the letter and kept the bullet as what he later called 'a reminder of the force and anger and evil some people had inside them back then'. It only made him more determined to run onto the Wembley turf in the 65th minute as a substitute for Trevor Francis. He would play five times more for England but never, sadly, for the full 90 minutes.

Five years after his international debut, however, Regis was one of three black players in the Coventry City side that won the FA Cup in 1987. I remember coming out of the Semi-Final at Hillsborough and hearing a teenage girl in the colours of the defeated Leeds United screaming at Sky Blues fans: 'At least we don't have n*****s in our side.'

It shocked me then, but not half as much as it would shock me if I heard anything like it at a match today. Yes, there are plenty of trolls lurking in the murkier depths of social media, yes, some Chelsea fans disgraced themselves and their club on the Paris Metro as recently as February, 2015, and yes, black managers are proportionately far less prevalent than black players in English football; but blatant racism in grounds is largely a phenomenon of the past – in this country at least. It's one of many aspects of life here that have improved markedly in 50 years.

Few people are more aware of that than Sam King, MBE, former Mayor of Southwark and co-founder of the Notting Hill Carnival.

Born in Jamaica in 1926, he was sitting with his family in front of his television in South London 40 years later, rooting for England in the World Cup Final. 'Of *course* I wanted England to win,' he booms in a voice still rich and resonant for a man not far off his 90th birthday. Of course? When you hear what had happened to him and many like him since arriving on these shores, you wouldn't have thought that there would be any 'of course' about it. Except, we were playing one half of Germany and Sam had come here in the first place to fight for the 'mother country' of the British Empire against a power that he regarded as far more sinister.

'I've always been grateful to the British for teaching us cricket,' he smiles. 'If the Germans had learnt the game, I don't think there would have been a Second World War.'

The idea of the Luftwaffe hurling down bouncers instead of bombs is an intriguing one, but it needn't detain us here. Sam's wry comment is just another reminder of how close the war seemed to those who lived through it when they think about the 1966 final. He had done his 'bit' as one who had volunteered to join the RAF in 1944 when he was just 18. Like many another volunteer from 'the colonies', he was sent home to the West Indies in 1947, only to return on the Empire Windrush the following year with 491 fellow passengers. By then the bomb-ravaged mother country had decided that it was short of labour, particularly on building sites and in the newly nationalised industries. 'We wanted a better life for our children and grandchildren,' Sam reflects. But it took a while to find it amid the pinched and rationed wreckage of post-war Britain.

Sam remembers being shown genuine kindness and generosity by some white English people, notably the parents of two former RAF colleagues who 'treated me like one of the family'. But he also encountered the usual 'very hurtful' prejudices – the 'no blacks, no dogs, no Irish' signs that were not made illegal until the Race Relations Act of 1968; being refused a mortgage by building societies despite having raised the money for the deposit; being turned down by the Metropolitan Police despite passing the entrance test.

He got around the mortgage problem by setting up a co-operative with his brother to raise the money to buy houses for themselves and other West Indian families. And the police?

'Many years later, when I was Mayor, I was approached by the Met commissioner about how to recruit more black police officers.' He smiles again at the irony before his brow furrows as he recalls that in the same year, 1983, he needed round-the-clock police protection for six months. The National Front had greeted news of his appointment as Southwark's first black mayor by publicly threatening to slit his throat and burn down his house.

Thankfully both are still standing. Indeed there's now a blue plaque on the house in Herne Hill where he lived for many years. But his footballing allegiances lie some way to the north. 'I've supported Manchester United ever since 1948 when I was stationed near Chester and went to see them play with a girl I knew at the time. Liverpool was closer but they were not so good in those days and, anyway, she was a United supporter.'

One of his fondest memories of the '66 Final is of United's Nobby Stiles, 'the dancer', prancing around Wembley with the cup. But, in truth, his fondest sporting memory of all is not of Wembley but of Lord's. 'I was there in 1950 when the West Indies beat England for the first time and I'll never forget it,' he beams before bursting into a rendition of that old calypso song about 'those little pals of mine, Ramadhin and Valentine'.

In those days at least, cricket was one game where you could guarantee that white was England's colours. It was also the West Indies' colours. And Australia's and India's and Pakistan's. South Africa's, too, in more ways than one. Sam may have been grateful for the British or, more specifically, the English for 'teaching us cricket'. But, as with the other national game, much of the rest of the world eventually became better at it than the ones who invented it. Mind you, England's cricketers occasionally make a comeback to reclaim the status of top dogs. Unfortunately, it seems rather a long time since we could say the same about England's footballers.

* * *

As for England's female footballers, they're getting far more coverage on the sports pages today than they did in 1966. Never more so than on Monday 24 November, 2014, the day after England's Lionesses played at the new Wembley for the first time. Their opponents just happened to be Germany. And, yes, the Germans won by three goals to nil, suggesting that the country that we like to imagine as our greatest rivals are now some way ahead in the women's game as well.

Still, let's look on the bright side from a feminist perspective. Football was not an option for most girls in 1966. Today more play it than netball. Indeed, it has become the UK's largest women's team sport. That may go some way to explain how a crowd of 46,000 turned out for that Wembley 'friendly', some 6,000 more than watched their male counterparts against Norway two months previously.

Impressive for sure, but not unprecedented. Just as there had been black players in England long before the 1960s and '70s, female footballers had proved a big draw in the early 20th Century. A crowd of some 53,000 converged on Goodison Park on Boxing Day, 1920, to catch sight of the all-conquering Dick, Kerr 'ladies' team, representing a factory of the same name from Preston. Another 5,000 were locked out of the ground.

The 'ladies' had not only flocked to the munitions factories during the First World War to keep production going while the men were fighting on the Western Front, they also filled the breach on the football field. Lily Parr, star of the Dick, Kerr side, was the most celebrated female footballer of the age. She could propel one of those heavy case balls faster and further than most men at the time. Aged just 14, she scored 43 goals in her first season, by which time the war was over and the FA was becoming increasingly agitated about the growing popularity of the women's game.

The final straw came in 1921 when many a team of 'ladies' played charity matches to raise money for the families of striking miners. FA-registered clubs were promptly banned from allowing women's football on their grounds.

Lily Parr was never going to return to housewifely duties full time, however. Despite a prodigious appetite for food and Woodbines, she carried on playing until 1951. By that time Dick, Kerr had long been known as Preston Ladies. They lasted until 1965. The FA's ban was finally repealed in 1971, thereby allowing the existence of a Preston North End WFC.

In 2002 Lily became the only woman inducted into the Hall of Fame at the National Football Museum. As female players begin to elbow their way onto the sports pages once more, it's a rum thought that nearly a century has passed since a celebrated daughter of Preston was once capable of attracting crowds as big as those who would later turn out to see Tom Finney.

* * *

A considerably smaller crowd was present when one Stephanie Roche scored the sort of goal that Geoff Hurst or even Bobby Charlton might have struggled to emulate. Nonchalantly trapping the ball in mid-air, a foot or so off the ground, she flicked it onto the other foot then back again before volleying into the top corner from the edge of the area. George Best would have been proud of that one. At the time, Stephanie was playing not too far from his Belfast birthplace, albeit south of the border down Peamont way.

Fewer than 100 were present to see her score that snorter for Peamont United against a team from Wexford. But it promptly 'went viral' on YouTube and Stephanie was duly signed by a top-flight French women's club. Her stunning strike, meanwhile, found itself shortlisted for the Fifa Puskas Goal award for the period from September 2013 to October 2014. She was up against somewhat more elevated company: Robin van Persie of Manchester United and Holland, and James Rodriguez, the real winner, of Real Madrid and Colombia, the eventual winner.

Fifa runs world football, of course, and Fifa it was that came up with a somewhat different but rather more significant award – the decision to allow Qatar to host the 2022 World Cup. For a start let's explain what the initials stand for. Fifa's full title is the Federation Internationale de Football Association, although I'm sure some of us could think of some rather more apt, if unprintable, use for the two 'Fs' in that acronym.

And Qatar? If that were an acronym it might as well stand for Quite As Terrible As Russia: only more so. Much more so as a World Cup venue. For one thing, its summer temperatures sometimes edge towards 50 degrees Celsius, which means that the tournament will have to be played in the winter months, disrupting domestic seasons and, in England's case, ensuring that football expands even further into what used to be cricket's domain. The World Cup Final, 2022, is now scheduled to be staged two days before Christmas. More importantly, Qatar may be the world's richest state per capita but the migrant workers imported to build its footballing infrastructure have been treated like slaves. The death toll at the last count was *one every two days.*

Michael Garcia's report into Fifa corruption was slickly sidestepped by president Sepp Blatter as not providing enough evidence to justify stripping either Russia or Qatar of the 2018 and 2022 World Cups respectively. Nonetheless, Mohammad Bin Hamman, Fifa's executive member for Qatar resigned in 2012 and was subsequently banned for life by the governing body's ethics committee. (Yes, there is such a thing.)

Blatter was re-elected as president in May, 2015, despite the arrest of nine senior Fifa officials in Switzerland on corruption charges two days previously. He resigned four days later, seemingly swept out of the door on a tidal wave of criticism. Blatter's former vice-president Jack Warner, who had been forced to resign in 2011, was vigorously denying new charges that he was heavily involved in soliciting a £10 million bribe from the South African government ahead of its successful bid for the 2010 World Cup finals. As this book was going to the printers, Warner was promising to blab about Blatter's part in various corruption scandals.

It seems a long time since Jack Warner was a name that rolled up with the credits on Dixon of Dock Green, a reassuringly old-fashioned copper who warmed our cockles on Saturday-evening telly in the 1950s and '60s. And it seems a very long time indeed since Fifa awarded the 1962 World Cup to Chile, not because it had 'loadsamoney' but because over 5,000 people had lost their lives in a devastating earthquake two years previously.

Yes, football, like life, has changed for the better and the worse since the '60s. The hooliganism that became rife soon after the '66 Final is far less evident – inside grounds at least. Overt racism has declined, too, since Alf Garnett's heyday. And, yes, the women's game is no longer patronised and excluded from coverage. On the other hand, football at the top level has become not just bloated but coated in allegations of sleaze and corruption. That may have begun to change by the time you read this. As things stand, the World Cup Final may as well be rechristened the World Cup 'Venal'.

CHAPTER NINE

'Och, nooooooo': the view from the other side of Hadrian's Wall

Jim Marshall was glad of one thing. Despite being a sports sub-editor on the *Daily Record* and *Sunday Mail* in Glasgow, he wasn't called upon to lay out the Press Association's report of England's victory over West Germany on the evening of July 30, 1966. Had that grim task fallen to him, his inclination as a journalist would have been to recognise a big story and give it the appropriate space. His inclination as a Scot would have been to give it a couple of paragraphs on the inside back page.

'To be honest, I can't remember how we covered the World Cup Final in the end,' he says. He can, though, recall that his colleagues felt just as 'gutted' as he did at the result. Never mind that some of the older ones might have been fighting shoulder to shoulder with the English only just over two decades previously. Never mind that others would have remembered all too vividly the bombs falling on Clyde-side and indeed nearby Clydebank. When it came to football, England were the Auld Enemy, a lot 'aulder' than Germany.

Wanting the Auld Enemy to lose was just about the only outcome that Rangers and Celtic fans could agree upon. 'My Dad always claimed that whenever Celtic or England were on the telly, he could never get a signal,' Jim grins. 'So on the afternoon of the match, he went out with my Mum. I was 22 at the time and I remember watching the game at their house on my own. When the Germans equalised on the stroke of full time, I leapt out of the chair and almost hit the ceiling.'

By the end of extra time, he was a lot closer to earth. Gloom descended on the pub where the sports desk tended to gather at opening time for a pint of heavy and/or a 'wee half' before starting on the night shift. In those days journalists tended to gravitate towards the nearest pub at fairly regular intervals, especially in Glasgow where the local licensing laws meant that they had only until 10pm to get as much down their necks as possible while still being able to come up with a half-decent headline.

Pub hours were even more restricted on Sundays. Not that Jim was too bothered on Sunday July 31. He was off on holiday to Ibiza. Dance clubs and ecstasy were still some way in the future. Discos with ultra-violet lighting that made everyone's teeth seem unnaturally white were the height of sophistication. 'There was only one hotel in San Antonio with a swimming pool,' he recalls grimly. 'But I'd been looking forward to going until I realised that it would be full of English.'

He was right about that. It was also full of Germans. One lot was crowing, the other lot moaning. 'Every time a German started getting agitated about Geoff Hurst's second goal and insisting it wasn't over the line, I had to say: "Hang on a minute, pal, I'm Scottish. Nothing to do with me."'

Jim's telling me this hundreds of miles south of the Scottish border in a pub once run by Jim Holton, Scotland's formidable centre-back in 1974 when Scots worldwide were ecstatic that their side qualified for the World Cup finals and – even better –

England didn't. Better still, the same thing happened four years later. The Scots were eliminated by the end of the group stages on both occasions. But they've always been able to argue that they only went out, undefeated, on goal difference in '74 while in '78 they had that victory against Holland and Archie Gemmill's stunning goal to confirm their status as valiant underdogs.

Sadly, Jim Holton died in 1993, aged just 42, after suffering a heart attack. That's about the last year that I visited his former pub and it's fair to say that the ambience and the beer are nowhere near as good as they were in the days of 'Big Jim'. But this is where Jim Marshall comes once a week to play cards with two of his many English friends, former colleagues from the nearby *Coventry Telegraph*.

He has mellowed a bit since 1966. Indeed, he's checking his smart-phone at regular intervals to keep us abreast of the Warwickshire cricket score. 'I don't mind too much if England win these days,' he concedes without adding 'as long as they're not playing Scotland'. That goes without saying. But he does say: 'Coventry has been good to me.'

Never more so than in 1992 when his record of tipping winners in the local paper earned him the title of *Sporting Life*'s Tipster of the Year and the celebrations on the sports desk were characteristically lengthy and boisterous. Don't expect Jimmy Marshall to back England to win the World Cup in 2018, however. Or Scotland for that matter. He's far too sensible for that.

* * *

Alan Taylor should have felt at home. Having been born in Bethnal Green at a time when London traffic noise hadn't quite drowned out the sound of Bow Bells, he had lived in the West Lothian shale-mining village of Winchburgh from the age of two until seven. His mum was Scottish, his dad an East Ender (London, not Glasgow), and they had met during the War. Alan would eventually follow in his father's footsteps and become an optician, but back in the summer of '66 he was 16 and hitchhiking back to Scotland with a mate during the school holidays.

Although their ultimate destination was the Highlands, for the afternoon of July 30 they felt glad to have reached Winchburgh in one piece. 'I remember having to grab the wheel off one driver who'd drunk far too much and was nodding off,' says Alan.

Ah, yes, the heady days of the open road. Sticking out your thumb in the vague direction of pastures new was a popular pursuit among those of us who were teenagers – although, as I've mentioned elsewhere in this book, it was infinitely more dangerous than it would be today. Compulsory seat belts for drivers and front-seat passengers weren't introduced in the UK until 1983, and cars had none of the safety measures that we now take for granted.

Still, young Taylor was safely in the bosom of his family to watch the match. Admittedly his parents were back home 'down South', but his uncle was glad to welcome him back to Scotland. 'He was an anglophile, but he was very much in the minority in that packed front room,' Alan recalls. 'Most of his friends had never been to England yet they were passionately anti-English when it came to football. Even those who had fought in the War were shouting for West Germany with a vengeance. We were a bit bemused by it, to be honest. I've always felt that loyalty should radiate outwards. If Scotland had been in the World Cup Final, I'd have been shouting for them.'

As it was, the shouts for England were drowned out in that small and noisy room as grey and blurry pictures were beamed in from a Wembley that might have been on the dark side of the moon. When Wolfgang Weber stabbed that 90th-minute equaliser over the line, the roar could have been heard ten miles away in Edinburgh. And what happened at the end of the match, Alan?

'The room just emptied in comparative silence. We were going to go out and celebrate that night but decided against it.'

Next day the English teenagers thumbed their way safely to the Highlands where the Scottish hospitality was as warm as ever. But nobody mentioned football.

* * *

Denis Law famously played golf on the afternoon of the 1966 World Cup Final, despite the presence of two of his Manchester United teammates in the England side. On hearing the result, his alleged response was short and to the point: 'Bastards.'

The bastards would remain undefeated by any team until April the following year when Scotland beat them 3–2 at Wembley, with Law scoring one of the goals. Cue claims from north of the border that the Scots were now world champions. Not quite. But Celtic did become the first British club to be crowned champions of Europe the following year with a side in which every man was born within ten miles of their home ground. And then there were the Home Internationals ....

For those of us who lived in London in the 1970s it was a case of batten down the hatches and hope for the best. The invasion started long before the Saturday afternoon kick-off. You'd be waiting for the tube on the Friday morning when someone would lurch towards you and thrust forward a whisky bottle while growling: 'Ha'e a drink, Jimmy.' Diplomatically declining, you'd point out that it was a bit early and, anyway, you were on your way to work. The response was either a shrug followed by a long swig or a volley of incomprehensible abuse.

Skirting Trafalgar Square en route to the sanctity of the office, you'd notice that the side of the fountain, the base of Nelson's Column and the steps of the National Gallery were bedecked with Scottish flags, while Scottish fans were either in the fountain or strewn across the slabs in some numbers, dancing, chanting, singing, swigging or sleeping off hangovers. At such times the glorious afternoon of July 30, 1966, seemed a very long time ago.

Never more so than in 1977 when the match ended in victory for Scotland followed by a pitch invasion and the pulling down of a cross-bar, as if to permanently exorcise the ghost of Geoff Hurst's controversial headed goal 11 years previously.

Plenty of Scots were appalled by that scene and, God knows, England had more than its fair share of home-grown hooligans; but the desecration of the cross-bar remains one of the lowest points in international football's oldest fixture. Still, at least it speeded the end of the Home Internationals.

For Scottish football followers there remained the pleasure of supporting 'anyone but England'. Glaswegian Bill Walker found himself in his London 'local', the Three Crowns in Stoke Newington, for England's Quarter-Final with Cameroon during Italia '90. 'Everybody in the bar was either Scottish or African, and we were all cheering for Cameroon. There was a pause at one point and a Cockney voice chimed up: "Farcking hell, lads, give us a break".'

Bill chuckles at the memory. He is a social worker who has lived in England since 1971 when he moved initially to Cornwall – about as far away from the Scottish border as it's possible to be in this sceptred isle. 'Wanderlust is part of the national character,' he insists. An amiable man, he has plenty of English friends, yet England's victory in 1966 has somehow been wiped from his memory. 'Well, I was 15 at the time so I was probably trying to get off with girls. I usually was at that age. I know I wasn't bothered about the match. It just didn't matter to us. My family were all members of the Communist Party. I remember my Dad asking why we should support a country that let itself be ruled by Germans and Greeks.'

Eh?

Apparently he was referring to the Queen's German ancestors and Prince Philip's Greek heritage. 'All that nationalistic fervour, national anthem and all, didn't suit my Dad,' says Bill.

What about 1974 and '78 when Scotland were followed to West Germany and Argentina by a passionate Tartan Army? Was that not nationalistic?

'Oh, that was something else. Nationalism takes many forms and the whole concepts of English and Scottish nationalism are very different things.'

I'm not sure where that leaves those of us who are by no means English nationalists but have nobody else to support at international level. Despite the closeness of the referendum result on Scottish independence, however, and despite the poisonous atmosphere created by both sets of fans at what was laughably called a 'friendly' at Celtic Park in November, 2014, some of us still find it difficult to say 'anyone but Scotland'.

CHAPTER TEN

Hello, 'ello, 'ello: how the police kept an eye on England during a notably law-abiding Saturday afternoon

Alan Ball and Nobby Stiles wanted a beer, and who could blame them? They had both given their all for their country's cause for over 100 minutes on Wembley's energy-sapping turf in the heat of July. One had run his socks off and the other appeared to have lost his front teeth. Or so it seemed to the millions peering at black and white televisions with screens that were lacking in size and clarity by today's standards. In fact, Bally's socks were round his ankles and Nobby's gnashers were quite possibly languishing in Steradent.

In their quest for the nearest bar, they did what most would have done in similar circumstances: they asked a policeman. He just happened to be standing on the edge of the pitch that they had just run around with the Jules Rimet trophy. 'All I could offer them at the time was a cup of tea because I could see that they were going to be shepherded away to do interviews with the media,' says the bobby in question, one PC Ken German.

'I was born towards the end of the War and suffered for my surname as a kid right enough,' he confides. 'But it didn't really matter for the World Cup Final.' Certainly it hadn't mattered to the sergeant at Albany Road Police Station, near Regent's Park, when he had stepped forward with his 'good mate' Norman as one of the few volunteering to watch the crowd rather than the match that afternoon. 'I wasn't much of a football fan,' Ken shrugs. 'Although I played rugby, I was more of a petrol-head, into motorcycling and motor racing. But I was a young man of 23 at the time and I did get rather caught up with the party atmosphere at the end of the game. It was England, after all, and we'd beaten the Germans again.'

Hang on a minute, former PC German; weren't you supposed to be watching the crowd?

'Well, we did before the kick off, ready to counter any rowdy behaviour. But there wasn't any. So we stayed on the touchline and watched the match.'

Every time there was a goal, it seems, he and Norman took a cursory glance behind them. Still no rowdy behaviour. But they did manage to clock five 'young ladies' sitting in the crowd and make eye contact with two of them. 'At the end of the match they passed their autograph books through the barriers because we were guarding the players' tunnel,' Ken goes on. 'I managed to get quite a few for them, including Bobby Moore and Geoff Hurst. Moore asked if he could have a police whistle, which I sent him later. Stiles wanted a helmet. I declined, but I understand someone did get one for him.'

But what about those 'young ladies' in the crowd, Ken? They must have been grateful when you handed back their autograph books.

'They were. In fact, they invited us to a party in West Hampstead which went on for 36 hours. We were there all night, went on shift and then went back again. My football skills were very questionable, but not my stamina in those days.'

* * *

John Steel was in Trafalgar Square after the match, along with a Scottish pal of his called Jimmy who 'joined in the spirit of the celebrations' despite having supported the Germans all afternoon. 'He was in raptures when they equalised just before the ref blew for full time,' John recalls. 'The German fans were right next to us and he was jumping up and down with them.'

John and Jimmy played football for the City Road Police Station side at the time but, on the build up to the final, John was working as an aide to the Met's so-called World Cup Willie Squad. Their task was to stop the many fans in London for the tournament being ripped off in the 'clip joints' of Soho. 'Along with other members of the CID, we used to pose as foreign visitors, although my French accent wasn't very good,' he says. 'Think I settled on something akin to Swedish in the end. Working girls would come over and persuade you to buy them drinks. If the prices they charged turned out to be exorbitant, we had the power to threaten the club with closure.'

Soho had a reputation for raciness, of course, but it was also exceedingly seedy. Apart from the sex shops and strip joints, there were afternoon drinking clubs, usually run by matriarchs with names such as Muriel, to accommodate those who couldn't face the bleak couple of hours or so when West End pubs shut their doors. 'Soho's cleaner and smarter now and there's a buzz that wasn't there in the '60s,' John reminds me. Not that he's in London much these days. Soon after the World Cup he moved to Bournemouth, a place with a reputation about as different from Soho's as it's possible to imagine. 'There were only three nightclubs in those days and by one o'clock the place was dead.'

On the day of the Final, John and Jimmy arrived at Wembley 15 minutes before the kick-off. Neither had a ticket. Jimmy lived nearby so they could nip back to watch the game on television if necessary. It wasn't.

The biggest game in England's football history was not a sell-out. There was a vast acreage of terracing at the 'old' Wembley, which meant that the ground at the time could accommodate at least 100,000. But the crowd on the day was either just under 94,000 or just over 96,000, depending on whom you believe. How could that be?

Well, some of those who fully expected their teams to be represented in the Final – particularly the Portuguese, who had lost to England in that memorable semi – had gone home in sorrow or disgust. Surprise, surprise, their tickets found their way into the hands of touts who no doubt expected to make a killing. But there were so many tickets that supply exceeded demand. 'As kick-off approached, we were able to buy two at their face value,' says John who, had he been on duty, might have been called upon to arrest or at least move on the tout that he ended up doing business with. Lest we forget, however, this was the World Cup Final and he was a man who loved his football. So did Jimmy, even if he didn't love England.

The crowd may have been below capacity but such was the volume they generated that when John eventually emerged from the stadium, he couldn't hear a thing. 'There was just a ringing in the ears for a long time afterwards,' he says. It began to clear after he'd swallowed hard on a few pints in the pubs around Trafalgar Square. Then it was back to Wembley for a bite to eat at Jimmy's place before John set off to pick up 'the missus' from her parents' house in Southampton. And, yes, he was behind the wheel of his car. 'You didn't think too much about drink-driving in those days,' admits the former policeman who is now the safety officer at Bournemouth FC.

Incidentally, it wasn't just the breathalyser that was introduced, by Barbara Castle, Minister of Transport, in the year after the World Cup. Home Secretary Roy Jenkins managed to get onto the statute book a Bill legalising homosexuality between consenting adults over the age of 21. One bi-product, nearly 50 years on, is that Soho is more openly gay in the contemporary as well as the old-fashioned sense of the word.

* * *

Another police officer with the good fortune to be off-duty on World Cup Final day was Bryan Murphy, a constable in what was then the Buckinghamshire Constabulary. He had no ticket. Neither did his travelling companions, a former Wycombe Wanderers player who ran the aptly named Happy Wanderer pub in High Wycombe, and two colleagues, also off-duty, one of whom went under the splendid name of PC Sheldon Bressington.

Sheldon, too, was a useful footballer. Good enough to turn out for the British Police X1, where he had forged a friendship with a sergeant at Wembley Police Station. The 'sarge' *was* on duty that day, overseeing a gate that provided entrance to the stadium for officials and those who could afford seats on and either side of the half way line. 'It had all been pre-arranged that the sergeant would let us in,' Bryan remembers. 'Sheldon was quietly confident about it but, as time went on, we were really giving him some stick. There was no plan B. It would have been too late to get the train back and watch it on the telly.'

Kick-off time was only a few minutes away when – hallelujah! – a gatekeeper with three stripes on his uniform and jangling keys in his pocket materialised. 'The sarge took a look around, ushered us in and, as he shut the gate behind us, I remember him saying: "You're on your own now".'

Apart from a stand full of seated spectators, that is. 'Many of them were German,' Bryan recalls, 'and we ended up having some really good banter with them as we stood with our backs to the wall behind them. A steward came up and asked what we were doing there. He was becoming quite officious until one of our number, a big bloke called Len, told him to "go away", only not quite so politely. The view was fantastic. We were right opposite the Royal box and the Queen was dressed in bright yellow.'

Stood out like a daffodil on a dung heap, it seems, surrounded as she was by the great and the good, booted and suited in sombre shades. 'Banksy was wearing a yellow jersey in the England goal,' Bryan goes on, 'but it wasn't anywhere near as vivid.'

The evening of July 30, 1966 turned out to be quite a night in the public bar of the Happy Wanderer. 'It was very raucous and a bit rowdy, with lots of singing, including some rugby songs,' as Bryan vaguely remembers.

Any ladies present?

'A few, but they were in the lounge.'

Closing time came and went with little fear of the local constabulary arriving to break up the party. At least three of them had been inside since arriving back from Wembley and they wouldn't be leaving any time soon. 'To top it all,' Bryan chuckles happily, 'two of the bar staff were Scottish. They just had to grin and bear it.'

The Scots would have their revenge nine months later. Final score: England 2, Scotland 3, and 'Slim' Jim Baxter strolled around Wembley's wide open turf as though he owned the place.

* * *

Newport Pagnell is a historic town of some 15,000 souls separated from Milton Keynes by the M1. But to most of us it is far better known as a motorway service station, second only in age to Watford Gap. It was unusually quiet on the afternoon of July 30, 1966, for obvious reasons. Malcolm Penny, a traffic cop with what was then the Buckinghamshire constabulary, remembers driving up and down the Bucks stretch of the motorway looking for something – anything – to relieve the tedium. 'There were no trucks and very few cars, compared to a normal Saturday.'

Well, you had volunteered to work that 10am to 6pm shift, Malcolm. 'We'd had a bit of a straw poll the day before,' he goes on. 'Me and my crew-mate had told the sergeant that we couldn't care less about England being in the Final. I wasn't much interested in football and he was Scottish. But we did have a small portable radio – the "tranny" of yore – which we secured to the passenger sun visor.'

No, they didn't tune it into the Home Service, precursor of Radio 4, or Radio 3's equivalent, the *Third Programme*. Nor did they try to pick up one of those pirate stations, such as Radio Caroline or Radio London, that were beaming illicit pop music from ships docked off shore in the year before 'Auntie' BBC reluctantly yielded to the demands of the huge 'yoof' market by gifting us Radio 1.

No, the police pair stuck with the commentary from Wembley. Almost two years had passed since Raymond Glendenning had detached his handlebar moustache from the radio mic and retired, so coverage of the Final was provided by Brian Moore and Alan Clarke, supplemented by summaries from Maurice Eddleston. 'As the goals were scored, we announced them on the car's PA,' says Malcolm. 'We felt that we were providing a public service as well as enjoying the reactions of passers-by.'

Not that there were too many of them that day on the expansive, almost deserted car park of Newport Pagnell Services.

* * *

While Malcolm Penny and his Scottish mate in the panda car couldn't care less about the big match, some police officers who were also supposed to be on duty went to extraordinary lengths to ensure that they didn't miss it. One of the more ingenious was Michael Burdis, then a detective constable in Doncaster. During the early stages of the tournament, he and some colleagues had managed to rig up a makeshift TV in the CID office, wiring the aerial lead to the steel window-frame. 'It was an old set that one of the lads had scrounged from a friend,' he confides, 'and it didn't have a case so you could see all the valves and innards. But it worked reasonably well until the deputy chief made a rare visit. End of TV for the CID.'

Not for long, however. For the Final itself, Michael came up with Plan B. 'I'd recently dealt with a hire-purchase fraud committed by a local villain against the newly opened Comet shop and had managed to recover five or six of the missing televisions – much to the relief of the manager. So he was quite amenable when I asked if we could borrow a portable telly to watch the game in the office.

'Portables were very rare in those days. He only had one for display and the one I'd recovered. It was a 12-inch Ferguson, black and white of course, but with a brown, plastic, all-in-one case. I seem to remember that it cost about £50, more than five times my living wage at the time.

'On the day of the Final, I called in to collect it and gave the manager full assurance that we would look after it and return it, a bit like Cinderella, before closing time at 5.30pm. Luckily, it was a quiet afternoon for crime, the entire population of Doncaster being glued to their own televisions. The detective sergeant had to "pop out" and the uniformed inspector didn't trouble us. But extra time did. With the game only finishing at 5.25, we were beginning to panic. But that was nothing compared with what was to come '

As Michael hurriedly reached down to unplug the portable, he saw to his horror that the sun beating down on the west-facing window of the office had melted the back of the set. 'It looked like one of those chocolate fountains with oodles of creamy chocolate dripping down from the centre.'

But somehow he managed to get it back in the box and back to Comet where the manager was about to lock up. 'Just put it down there,' he said. 'Hope you enjoyed the match.' Michael confirmed that they had and then, in his own words, 'took the coward's way out by doing as I'd been told and disappearing sharp-ish'.

It was not a recipe for a restful Sunday revelling in an England victory. 'I'd lost interest in the football by 5.30 that Saturday afternoon,' he admits. Back on day shift on the Monday morning, he felt it was time to re-visit the shop and confess, or 'cough' as they used to say in the CID. By then the case of 'melted chocolate' had congealed around the valves. On having his attention drawn to this disgusting apparition, the manager appeared remarkably unconcerned. 'Well, you'd think they'd use more resilient plastic, wouldn't you?' he said before adding: 'I'll send it back as defective. Don't you worry. Better you spot the fault than a paying customer.'

Michael would rise through the ranks to become detective chief superintendent before retiring in 2002. He now maintains: 'I enjoyed every minute of my 40 years with the force.'

Well, apart from the five minutes between 5.25 and 5.30 on the afternoon of July 30, 1966.

POSTSCRIPT

Those who missed the 1966 World Cup Final had a chance to catch the highlights on the Saturday evening between 10.20–11.20pm. That was on the BBC, which also devoted 35 minutes of Sunday afternoon to re-showing the best bits of the Final. ITV was split into regions at the time and most showed *The Way to the Cup* between 2.30–3.35pm.

It would have made a pleasant change from the sheer purgatory of the '60s Sunday in most parts of the country. The only thing to be said for it was that it was marginally better than the '50s Sunday, largely because of *Round the Horne*, a slightly more risqué version of *Beyond Our Ken* on the old BBC *Light Programme*. Kenneth Horne and Kenneth Williams got away with the sort of *double entendres* that would have given the censors an attack of the vapours a decade previously – a small sign that Auntie was beginning to loosen her corsets just a little.

But we still had to endure *Two-Way Family Favourites* and, even worse, *The Billy Cotton Band Show*. They were the kind of programmes that your mother listened to while preparing Sunday lunch, a lengthy process in our house but worth waiting for in the case of my Mum's roast beef and Yorkshire pudding. (I was rather less keen on what Cassandra called in one of his *Mirror* columns 'boiled cabbage *à l'Anglaise*'.)

Everything was closed on Sundays. Except for the churches, of course. Oh yes, and the pubs. But they only opened between 7–10pm in the evenings and 12–2pm at lunchtimes when they were almost entirely populated by men. Or so I discovered when I was old enough to drink and became acutely conscious of my collar-length hair and faded jeans among the suits and military blazers that most factory workers liked to don at weekends. Many of them would come home late for lunch, complain that the meat was overcooked and then fall asleep in their armchairs, snoring loudly through the rest of the afternoon.

Around the time of the World Cup I was 17 and, as I've recounted in Chapter Four, I was hitchhiking home on the day after the Final. On other Sundays I would escape into town as early as possible and spend a lot of time hanging around in a coffee bar that broke all the rules by being open on this most restrictive of days. What passed for Bohemia in Birmingham gathered there to drink weak and frothy coffee – in those days we'd have assumed that a *barista* was a Brummie lawyer – and listen to a jukebox playing the kind of music never found on the *Light Programme*.

By then I'd given up playing football in the park on Sundays and my beloved Aston Villa were in the doldrums. But England's unlikely triumph in the World Cup had re-kindled my interest in the game, and I was far from alone in that respect. The country where football had been invented had reclaimed its position as top-dog and suddenly new possibilities were arising. Even Harold Wilson's promise of a more equal society 'forged in the white heat' of technological change seemed believable.

More importantly to teenagers such as myself, there was great music about, even though little of it could be heard on the BBC. Okay, Sundays were still purgatory and there were still too many crooners in the charts but, at last, the times did seem to be a-changing on this side of the Atlantic.

Fifty years on and the notion of greater economic equality has proved to be as illusory as England's top-dog status in the world of football. But the social changes that began in the second half of the 1960s planted the roots of the more open and liberal society that we enjoy or endure, depending on your point of view, in a very different England today.

BIBLIOGRAPHY

Charlton, J (1996) *Jack Charlton: The Autobiography*, London: Partridge Press

de Lisle, T (2010), *How Did Sport get so Big?* Intelligent Life Magazine, *Summer Issue*

Kelner, M (2012) *Sit Down and Cheer: A History of Sport on TV*, London: Wisden Sports Writing

Charlton, C and Gledhill, V (1988) *Cissie: Football's most famous mother Cissie Charlton tells her story*, Bridge Studios

Briggs, S (2009) *Don't mention the Score: a masochist's history of the England football team*, London: Quercus

Greaves, J (2004) *Greavesie: the autobiography*, London: Time Warner Paperbacks

Rees, P (2014) *The Three Degrees: the men who changed British football forever*, London: Constable

Regis, C (2010) *My Story by Cyrille Regis: the autobiography of the first black icon of British Football*, London: Andre Deutsch

Chalke, S (1999) *Caught in the Memory: county cricket in the 1960s*, Bath: Fairfield

Goodyear, S (2010) *From Mines to Milan: the Gerry Hitchens story*, Derby: Breedon Books